THE
ABSINTHE
FORGER

ALSO BY EVAN RAIL

A Full-Scale Model of the Universe
Good Beer Guide: Prague & the Czech Republic
In Praise of Hangovers
The Brewery in the Bohemian Forest
The Meanings of Craft Beer
Triplebock: Three Beer Stories
Tsunami
Why Beer Matters and Other Essays
Why We Fly: The Meaning of Travel in a Hyperconnected Age

THE ABSINTHE FORGER

A TRUE STORY OF DECEPTION, BETRAYAL, AND THE WORLD'S MOST DANGEROUS SPIRIT

EVAN RAIL

MELVILLE HOUSE
BROOKLYN • LONDON

The Absinthe Forger

First published in 2024 by Melville House
Copyright © 2024 by Evan Rail
All rights reserved

"Absinthe Robette" by Henri Privat-Livemont (1890), and "Absinthe Mugnier" by Lucien Lefèvre (1898), courtesy New York Public Library

"Absinthe Parisienne" by P. Gélis-Didot and Louis Malteste (1890–1900), courtesy Bibliothèque nationale de France

The Absinthe Drinker by Albert Emmanuel Bertrand (1890), courtesy Art Institute of Chicago

Monsieur Boileau at the Café by Henri de Toulouse-Lautrec (1890), courtesy Cleveland Museum of Art

All other photos courtesy of the author

First Melville House Printing: August 2024

Melville House Publishing
46 John Street
Brooklyn, NY 11201
and
Melville House UK
Suite 2000
16/18 Woodford Road
London E7 0HA

mhpbooks.com
@melvillehouse

ISBN: 978-1-68589-154-1
ISBN: 978-1-68589-155-8 (eBook)

Library of Congress Control Number: 2024938849

Designed by Beste M. Doğan

Printed in the United States of America

1 3 5 7 9 10 8 6 4 2

A catalog record for this book is available from the Library of Congress

For my father, DeWayne Rail

It stands alone: it is like nothing else:
it shimmers like southern twilight
in opalescent colouring: it has about it the
seduction of strange sins. It is stronger
than any other spirit and brings out the
subconscious self in man.

—OSCAR WILDE

CONTENTS

THE
ABSINTHE
FORGER

CHAPTER 1

LE FORGEUR

What is there in absinthe that makes it a separate cult? The effects of its abuse are totally distinct from those of other stimulants. Even in ruin and in degradation it remains a thing apart; its victims wear a ghastly aureole all their own, and in their peculiar hell yet gloat with a sinister perversion of pride that they are not as other men.

—ALEISTER CROWLEY

He was a clever man, charismatic and handsome, a lone figure passing through life like a shadow through cold water. Things were going exceptionally well. His career was sailing forward. Along the way, it was fine to have a little fun, to mess with those who thought they knew more than you did. And all he was doing, really, was putting new spirits into old bottles.

To do that, you had to have a keen visual understanding of how a vintage absinthe bottle is supposed to appear, honed by years of collecting and studying the rich history and culture of the drink. Even more important was the ability to identify hundreds or even thousands of distinct aromas that intermingled and overlapped within the bouquet of a hundred-year-old absinthe. And then, you needed the ability to taste: to read and interpret a liquid just like some people read books, feeling and understanding the viscosity and relative acidity of the spirit in much the same way that a careful reader senses the texture and thickness of paper, while also interpreting, identifying, and internalizing its flavors and aromas, just as the eye follows curls and spots of ink that swerve into letters before becoming words, which turn into sentences, and thus convey sense and meaning.

He had those skills, and many more. What was important, however, was that the others didn't. They didn't know. They couldn't taste. Their sense of smell was blunted, as if they'd never gotten over a bad cold, as if they'd never even fully been born, staying forever embryonic—piles of unrealized potential, all of them. They didn't understand how the world worked. They didn't understand how things were supposed to look, or even know the most basic history of a subject they claimed to love.

They were, in a word, dumb. And he was not.

⋮

The first version was just to see if he could do it, if he really had those skills. He had been part of the absinthe world long enough to have tasted dozens of samples from the golden era of absinthe, before it was banned in most countries in the lead-up to World War I. (In most countries, but not all: an important distinction.) He'd watched his friends share updates of stumbling across an unopened bottle of C. F. Berger at an estate sale, or an old Pernod Fils in the back of a dusty antique store, and he'd tasted many of the finds they'd shared. There were new makers, too, some of whom were quite good, turning out spirits that had much of the character of the drink that had attracted so many of his literary and artistic heroes: Rimbaud, Van Gogh, Degas, Manet, Picasso, Hemingway, and others. He enjoyed the new versions, especially considering their affordability and availability—even with all the money in the world, it's not easy to find century-old bottles of the absinthe favored by Toulouse-Lautrec, for example. And while the better new producers from Switzerland and France were hardly stocked in every corner store in his part of London, you could at least order them without too much trouble.

And yet there was something different about historic absinthe, beyond its age, beyond the fact that you were aware, while drinking it, that *this very spirit* might have been drunk by Charles Baudelaire or Oscar Wilde, that *this very bottle* might have been held to the frilly breast of a can-can girl at the Moulin Rouge or touched by the hand of Gauguin. Beyond the frisson of their time-shifting possibilities, the old absinthes simply tasted different—oxidized a bit, of course, hinting of old cardboard or a hot, stuffy room, but shifted along the flavor spectrum in other ways, too. Even the best new absinthes seemed to be missing something at the center, an obvious hole where their hearts should be. Žufánek's Ancienne and Rossoni's Italienne were good, even delicious, and yet somehow both fell short of what they aspired to be. Each spirit set up expectations that it didn't fulfill, as if a consumer products company had started out by publishing its brand book, and then launched its first products in the wrong colors.

How could you make the modern Italienne taste more like a vintage Pernod Fils? What was it missing? Less fennel, more anise, or the other way around? More presence, or more austerity? What did Ancienne have that l'Italienne didn't? What about a Swiss bleue, or a Spanish Pernod from the 1950s? How could you combine them, and in what ratio, to get a drink that tasted like history?

⋮

It was history, in part, that had originally attracted him to the spirit, well over a decade earlier, though that had come at a moment when absolutely everything seemed new and quick, a period of a hot few years that in his memories still seemed like a constant dawn. At the time he was a university student in a sleepy, second-tier city in England. Someone came back from a trip with a bottle of Czech absinthe—semi-contraband at the time, although the drink had technically never been banned in the United Kingdom. There was a swirl of rumor and innuendo around it, he knew, a cloud of romance, thanks to its association with writers and painters. In the university's fine arts program, it seemed like you were supposed to be familiar with those artists—with all artists, really—and their dissolute lives before you'd even seen their work. It was expected, he sensed, that a student aiming for a fine arts degree should know about absinthe, and he'd never even tasted it. No one there had. Nor had anyone even seen a bottle for most of a century. And yet by the start of 1999 it was suddenly not just available, but almost ubiquitous—vivid, bright green bottles of Hill's Czech "Absinth," spelled without the final E, poured over sugar cubes and lit on fire, the sickly blue-green flames drowned like heretics under a spray of water.

It was something, sure, but it felt artificial and wrong, from the mangled spelling on the label to its sudden trendiness, to say nothing of its bright green color and method of serving. If absinthe was part of a seedy, underground culture, why was a mainstream newspaper like the *Times* running articles about its popularity in the shiniest bars in London? If it was truly a complex, mind-expanding drink which could inspire artistic reverie, why did it taste so simple and crass, so coarsely bitter and astringent, leaving such a strong burning sensation on the tongue? Where was the liquid inspiration that had fueled the imaginations of Toulouse-Lautrec and Picasso?

There was a hint of it, a trace of the perfume of a disappeared friend, in the bright-green, no-E "absinth" he'd tasted, but the real thing was clearly hiding somewhere else.

⋮

It was later, shortly after he moved to London and started making real money, when he found it, or at least got a whiff of its trail: the sense of authenticity he liked to think of as the thing in itself. After graduating, he had taken his first job at the London branch of a big media agency. By that time the British importers of Hill's had founded their own absinthe distillery in France, the first makers to produce a spirit made with the main herbal ingredient, grand wormwood, in that country for over eighty-five years.

He followed their story with interest, admiring their ability to slip through century-old loopholes and use the law to their own ends: these were good skills to have. To introduce Hill's, they made a convincing legal argument that the reciprocity of the law inside the European Union meant that absinthe was legal in the U.K., since it was a member of the EU at the time. According to the regulations of the common market, anything that could be legally sold in one EU country was legal to sell in any other EU country, unless another country had specifically asked for an exception in its

entry treaty to the political union. Absinthe was perfectly legal in
the post-communist Czech Republic, then readying itself to become
a full EU member, which arguably meant that the drink had to
be legal throughout the common market. The arrival of legal but
certainly not very good Czech absinthe resulted in a whirlwind of
popularity for the spirit throughout Britain at the end of the 1990s.

And then, the next step. After launching the U.K. absinthe craze,
the importers of Hill's realized that the terms of France's "interdic-
tion" of absinthe from 1915 had only banned the *sale* of absinthe
in France, not its production, which led them to launch a new,
French-made product they called La Fée, or "The Fairy," from *la
Fée Verte*—"the Green Fairy"—the drink's longstanding nickname.
Initially the French government only allowed the company to make
La Fée for export, but a clever trick with language allowed the com-
pany to launch domestic sales in France in 2003. By that time, La
Fée had been joined by other French producers, including Pernod
Ricard, the corporate descendant of Pernod Fils, the greatest ab-
sinthe brand in history.

Technically, the drink had to be labeled as "spiritueux aux
plantes d'absinthe," or "spirit with absinthe plants," and not just
"absinthe"—a subtle switch that knocked out a law that had stood
for some eighty-eight years.

He adored linguistic sleight-of-hand and legal tricks. That was
among the best he'd ever seen.

La Fée was closer to the truth, he thought, but still not there,
missing a sense of itself, somehow. By that time he had joined several online forums for absinthe connoisseurs and had even contri-
buted reviews, though he had received enough of a spanking for
errors in his first few that he resolved merely to read the evaluations

of others until he knew more. These he studied regularly. Most of the tasting evaluations were for the new absinthes that started to appear after 2005, brands like Kübler and Pernod, both of which had been famous names in the absinthe world nine decades earlier. And then, every so often, someone would announce that they had encountered a "pre-ban" absinthe that had been produced during the spirit's golden era, before the interdictions and prohibitions had killed off absinthe production at the end of the Belle Époque, right at the start of World War I. Reviews for the pre-ban absinthes were invariably glowing, highlighting layers of complex aromas, and calling out the unexpected color—usually described as *feuilles mortes*, meaning "dead leaves"—as well as the drink's ability to "louche," or turn from clear to cloudy, when diluted with chilled water.

Eventually, he managed to buy a single shot—a sample bottle of just fifty milliliters, or about an ounce and a half—from another collector who had found a full bottle of pre-ban Pernod Fils and was willing to share.

It arrived a week or so later, a pamphlet-size brown manila envelope that reached him at his home a few stops short of the end of one of London's Underground lines, handed over by the postman along with the bills. On the outside, his name and address were written in the blue ink of a rather stylish hand, apparently using a fountain pen. Inside, he found a collegial note from the sender wishing him "Santé!" on a small piece of thick, watermarked paper, with the small bottle ensconced in a swirl of bubble wrap and tape that made it look like a coiled up cobra sitting in a woven basket.

He'd expected something like one of the mini bottles of gin or whiskey that you saw on airplanes, but this one looked like something from an old medical laboratory: thick dark glass, stumpy, with a broad cap of red plastic sealed up with packing tape. On the outside, a label of yellow paper said "Pernod Fils" in blue ink.

He set it on the table and watched it, as if it might start to move or even launch an attack, but the squat bottle just sat there. He removed the tape and wrap, checked the glass and cap for residue, and carefully twisted it open.

Less aroma filled the room than he'd hoped for, but the drink opened up when he poured half of it into a reproduction absinthe glass, filling the twenty-five-milliliter reservoir at the vessel's bottom to its limit. It was not so much a green fairy as it was yellow, almost mustard in hue, he estimated, though clear, which contrasted with its verdant aromas: some celery-like note (probably angelica), the grassy bite of wormwood, a fresh and cool whiff of fennel. He added fresh water to clean ice cubes in a small pitcher, stirred it until it was cool, then dribbled the cold water into the spirit.

The first drops changed the drink's complexion, forming white ghosts that soon merged into a milky cloud, overwhelming the pale yellow sea. The glass looked as if it were filled with a opalescent hurricane.

If the aroma was heady and intoxicating, the first sip seemed to sober him up: bright like camphor, hinting of candy sugar, yet peppery and spicy, a self-contradicting, this-but-also-that combination that forced him to concentrate on the insistent *now* that he was experiencing, much like he felt after a shot of good coffee. And yet it didn't also bring nervousness and jangly fingers the way espresso did: instead, something seemed to relax him and remove any sense of stress while also pushing him to focus, very clearly, on whatever he wanted to consider. His career was in the right place. His parents' desire for grandchildren was not a problem. The emptiness that had been chasing him around for months went away. His life was on track, and there was no need to worry. After the first sip, all he really felt was clarity.

He sat, sipping occasionally from the reproduction glass, for almost an hour. Things were falling into place, though he noticed that the initial understanding and calm concerning his life and work and especially money began to fade as he finished the drink. When the last sip was gone, he walked to the kitchen, chasing the final ghost of the aroma around the room. One point stayed with him: he had found the thing in itself, the sense of the authentic and true, that he had been dreaming about for many years.

⋮

It was a few years later when Facebook's mostly private absinthe groups took off, by which point he had tasted more than a dozen pre-ban absinthes, as well as most of the modern versions that were coming out of Europe, mostly from the drink's two traditional producers, Switzerland and France, but also from Italy, Sweden, and Germany. Even the Czech Republic had gotten in on the good absinthe game with the new versions from Žufánek, after kicking off the global absinthe revival with exports of its mouthwash-like Hill's. He had bought most of them and drank them carefully, much as one would approach a poisonous animal. They *were* poisonous, he knew: ethanol was literally a poison. It was an admirable twist of language—a kind of marketing, if you thought about it—that made people think of a poison as something to which you should shout "to health!" when you raised your glass.

On top of that, most absinthes were relatively high octane when compared to the 40 percent alcohol of standard whiskey and gin, sometimes coming in at 72 percent, or 144 proof. But something happened when you mixed alcohol with herbs, especially the herbs in absinthe, with which he had now become quite familiar.

Among enthusiasts, the first three ingredients were sometimes called the Holy Trinity: grand wormwood (*Artemisia absinthium*), anise (*Pimpinella anisum*) and fennel (*Foeniculum vulgare*). Of those, high-quality grand wormwood was seen as the most important, though anise was most obvious to the taste; connoisseurs debated the proper amounts and the discernible presence of fennel. In addition to the three main herbs, distillers could add other plants: Roman wormwood (*Artemisia pontica*), hyssop (*Hyssopus officinalis*), coriander (*Coriandrum sativum*), lemon balm (*Melissa officinalis*), lemon verbena (*Aloysia citrodora*), star anise (*Illicium verum*), angelica (*Angelica archangelica*), peppermint (*Mentha × piperita*), licorice (*Glycyrrhiza glabra*), white genepì (another type of Alpine wormwood, *Artemisia umbelliformis*) and many more. Most had been used as herbal remedies across Europe for centuries, and, as forum users loved to point out, many had proven to have stimulatory or calmative effects on the human nervous system. Some *absintheurs*—connoisseurs of absinthe called themselves by the French word—preferred more or less anise in their drinks, or very little fennel, or no coriander at all, though almost everyone agreed that there was something to the general mix of herbs in absinthe that affected them differently than other spirits.

The alcohol could be different, too. In some countries, producers might distill their own base alcohol, while producers in Switzerland generally used a neutral spirit, purchased from the government, derived from either grain or potatoes, no one was really sure. But in the Belle Époque, the best absinthes had been distilled from grape alcohol—young brandy, effectively.

Perhaps it was the mix of herbs they'd used. Perhaps it was the use of the grape distillate. Perhaps it was the century or more of time, not so much an added ingredient as it was an additional technique, unimagined by the original makers, that made the pre-ban absinthes stand out. Perhaps adding a hundred years to a modern bottle would make it different and more real, in the same way that all the pre-ban absinthes he'd tried differed wildly from the modern equivalents he was sampling and studying. Even when claimed to be made according to an original or historic recipe, modern absinthes were missing an element of the spirit where its heart should be. They mostly seemed real to him, but never as authentic and meaningful as any of the bottles that dated from before the Great War.

It wasn't just the drink that attracted him. As the years went by, he acquired scores of absinthe-related antiques, as well. At first, a historic absinthe spoon, a slotted silver utensil that could hold a cube of sugar over the glass as the drinker sent a rivulet of iced water into the spirit according to his or her taste. Then a beautiful, Art Nouveau fountain for the chilled water. Then an advertising poster, and then another. Then unused labels from old Edouard Pernod and Pernod Fils absinthes. Then empty absinthe bottles from before the ban. Then the metal capsules to seal them with.

Those all joined his books on absinthe, a mini library that occupied most of a full shelf in his study. In it, he placed his own book of handwritten tasting notes, studies of both the pre-ban absinthes he'd sampled and their growing modern equivalents. He had his own opinions of how absinthe should taste, but most of all, he wanted to find in the glass a sense of the authentic and real.

⋮

He spent a few days going over his notes, crossing out earlier descriptors and rewriting them with new terms: there was no sense in writing "licorice" in one place and "anise" in another, if what he was homing in on was the same flavor. He tried to avoid reading product descriptions on websites or bottle labels, as he found them unreliable, but in some cases it was unavoidable, and even helpful, to have an idea of the intentions of the distiller, or at least those of the distillery's marketing department.

He had a handful of vintage absinthes to hand, but in the end he decided to aim for a less-common example: a small bottle of H. Bazinet Jeune, which had been shared among only a handful of absintheurs, unlike the nearly commonplace bottles of pre-ban Pernod Fils.

He wasn't quite sure how to get the color right—after more than a hundred years, the original had barely any green, looking more like pale gold in the glass. Perhaps food coloring would work. There was a nuttiness and aged character to the pre-ban that was hard to find in modern absinthes, but one contemporary Swiss absinthe offered a trace that was similar, which seemed to multiply in the right way when he cut it with spirit from another producer. There was a hint of old cardboard in the vintage spirit, a trace of oxidation that none of the modern versions would have, but that could be approximated with absinthe from the Spanish city of Tarragona, where the great Pernod company had relocated after the 1915 ban on absinthe in France, producing the spirit in ever-smaller volumes and at progressively lower quality until the end of the 1960s. He mixed blend after blend, chasing a light note of caramel in his target spirit, working to even out the expression of anise, until he felt like he had a decent equivalent. And yet there was that lingering worry, like a splinter in the back of his brain, that they weren't quite close enough. It had to be because he knew which one was which. There was the ancient pharmacy bottle—bearing the ornate "H. Bazinet Jeune" label—and there was his obvious admixture, sitting there in a large, clear glass vial. If he couldn't see which was which, it wouldn't affect his judgment, and then he would know for sure.

⋮

It worked, naturally. He served it to himself in a blind tasting—the real H. Bazinet Jeune versus his bespoke version—and he couldn't tell them apart. Well, of course he could, *he* could taste the difference, but it was very close. Thanks to the dash of the Spanish Pernod, his version had the oxidation of the historic sample, as well as a similar soul and presence. Thanks to the modern Swiss and French absinthes, it had the proper amounts of anise and fennel. Even the colors were within a shade of each other. His version, to use a European expression, was correct.

And yet he had doubts. Perhaps he was fooling himself. Perhaps his palate wasn't as refined as he believed. No, that was stupid. But anyone could miss a step on a ladder or forget a passport before leaving to catch a flight. What he needed was to test whether any of the so-called experts in his groups could spot a wooden decoy among a group of real ducks.

He would make a few more versions, just for himself, to make sure his skills were honed. Then he would have to roll the dice and find out.

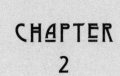

INVITATION
TO THE FRAUD

O r at least that's how I imagined it, once I started focusing on the story of the great absinthe forger from London, learning about his past and talking to his friends and victims, quite a few of whom ended up being both. Eventually, I spent a lot of time trying to figure out what he'd done and how he'd done it, and how he'd been caught by a small group of amateur absinthe detectives. I interviewed absinthe lovers across Europe and was even contacted by the absinthe forger himself. Figuring out the reasons behind his fraud became an obsession for me, consuming a few years of my life. But when Habu first reached out to tell me about the absinthe forger and the counterfeit bottles he'd sold, I blew him off.

I imagine there must be a list of the benefits of working as a freelance writer, with tons of entries under the "Pros" column in a cost-benefit analysis, but most of the time I find myself focusing on the long list of "Cons." There is, of course, a noticeable lack of stability in your work schedule and, more crucially, in your income. Another drag is that you are forced to come up with new story ideas constantly: some writers like to say that you're only as good as your last article, but I find that you're really only valued by editors in terms of your next. Another big downside is that you're often contacted by friends and strangers with suggestions for subjects they think you should write about. These are almost invariably subjects of personal interest for the people who contact you, a connection which would affect anyone's judgment, making a story idea that seems to me—the writer in question—like a total non-starter into a potential Pulitzer Prize winner in their eyes: their idea is something that must be covered, hopefully in the Newspaper of Record, preferably on A1, and of course above the fold.

That was pretty much where Habu was coming from. In this case, he wanted me to write about someone he knew. A former friend from the absinthe world had deceived him and a bunch of other collectors by selling them fakes—forged historic absinthes that were supposed to date from before the drink was banned and its production ended in France in 1915. The twist was that I knew him, too.

Habu's real name was Štefan Habulinec, not a very typical Czech first or last name, but most of the people in the absinthe world knew him as just Habu. We'd met a few years earlier at the Absinthiades, a big absinthe festival in Pontarlier, France, when I was researching a travel article about the modern absinthe trail for *The New York Times*. Although I don't have a Czech background, living in the country for a couple of decades and having a Czech wife has left me feeling like an adopted citizen, so I was happy to meet up with a few members of the so-called Czech Absinthe Mafia. I found Habu easy to get along with, bright-eyed and earnest, with what seemed like a hidden wild streak—yes, he might light a few fires, but he'd do so while laughing his head off. In the years since then, we'd stayed in contact on social media, where he reached out to me with a direct message in the middle of 2019.

He'd written an article on his Czech-language blog, he said, about the largest vintage absinthe fraud in history. I'd left a lot of social media behind and hadn't seen his post. No matter, he said. His gang of absinthe friends was starting to discover that the fraud was probably much larger than they'd first imagined.

"These fake bottles have been sent all across the globe," he said. "We're thinking about some kind of legal action."

I checked his blog and saw the full name of the man he'd accused of selling fake vintage absinthe.

"Christian?" I asked. "Oh man. That guy?"

Habu had plenty of details, which he shared in his typical rapid-fire way. Apparently, another member of the absinthe underground had sounded a warning about fake pre-ban absinthes circulating among collectors the previous year, though most collectors had paid that early caveat little attention. All of what they believed were forged bottles had been purchased directly or through eBay from Christian, a prolific collector—and presumed authority on absinthe—based in London.

The fraud potentially included a lot of money. A full absinthe bottle dating from before the 1915 ban usually retailed for around 3,000 euros, or about $4,000 at the time; so far, the group was estimating that Christian had made at least 50,000 euros by selling counterfeit absinthe, though the number could be much higher. After being accused a few months earlier, Christian had simply disappeared, and seemed to have stopped selling absinthe, but they thought he had recently started up again using a different eBay account, and the group wanted me to help get the word out.

"One of our ideas was to write an article about this incident which could attract a wider audience. I saw your article in *The New York Times*. Something like that might help."

It took about three seconds for me to think the whole thing through before telling Habu that this was almost certainly not a story for the Gray Lady, at least not without a court conviction, though I failed to mention that even if this idea were a shoo-in for the *NYT*, I'd have to be very lucky if I ended up being the one who wrote it, as a staff writer would probably pick it up, rather than a freelancer like me. He thanked me for considering it anyway, and other than likes on our Twitter posts and birthday greetings, our communication dropped for several months after that.

⋮

But the idea stayed with me, probably because Christian and I were acquainted. As I recalled, we'd met at an afternoon absinthe-drinking session in a vintage absinthe dealer's hotel room during the festival in Pontarlier, and then again at a soirée high up in the Alps on the final evening, sharing fondue and collectible drinks in a candlelit chalet with a handful of other absintheurs. My memories of Christian and the rest of the Absinthiades were shadowed in clouds, for what I imagine must be obvious reasons, but we'd been Facebook friends for several years, and I'd even reached out to him once before to ask about interviewing him for a possible article.

I remembered him as brightly conversational, and humorously sarcastic. He came off like something of a class clown, albeit one who might have a deep, not-at-all-forgotten injury hidden behind his goofy smile. He lived in London, I knew, because some of our mutual friends had visited him there. He'd been friends with the Czech distiller Martin Žufánek, who had made several very good absinthes of his own, and whom I'd met at the festival along with Habu. Before the news of the forgeries broke, Martin had told me that he'd purchased several bottles of vintage absinthe from Christian, sending over photographs of what he called his "beauties" as he acquired them, even inviting me to come for a tasting of historic pre-ban absinthes at his distillery, way out on the far eastern edge of the Czech Republic. When I started researching a possible article about vintage absinthe collectors in early 2018, Martin had told me I should definitely talk to Christian. He's a good guy, he said.

That must have been the first time Christian and I were in direct contact, when I messaged to ask about how collectors like him are able to find hundred-year-old bottles nowadays. He sent a quick and surprisingly fulsome response, though many of the things he said at the time read differently in hindsight. For the sake of the truth, I'll leave his spellings and punctuation as they appeared.

> Hi Evan. I don't really have any tips other than keeping your eyes and ears wide open at all times for bottles. They are now becoming SO scarce.. Add to this how popular it's become in recent years and the sheer number of people wanting old bottlings. I've been collecting them for 27 years now. Finding it harder and harder. I sell a few from time to time.

If he'd really been collecting for twenty-seven years, I reasoned, he must have started in his late teens, given that he seemed to be only a couple of years younger than me. That sounded strange when I thought of how I lived my life when I came of legal drinking age, but then again, what did I know?

When I asked where people could find vintage bottles today, he said things were very different where he lived.

> Auctions, estate sales, attics, cellars etc. These days in France there's hardly any left as they drank it all. Look to the rest of Europe. Especially the UK.

That seemed to make sense at the time, though when I look at it now, it also appears to justify claiming that he'd found a large number of vintage bottles from France while living in England, whereas other collectors seemed to come across hundred-year-old bottles of pre-ban absinthe very rarely.

Most strangely, he had claimed to find the stuff regularly in large amounts:

> I recently found 12 bottles in pristine condition of Pernod Fils.. Funnily enough Martin Zufanek just bought one from me.

In hindsight, with what I know now, these all look like obvious lies, but none of this sounded particularly suspicious at the time. The only thing that really caught my attention was when I asked if he would be willing to be interviewed for an article.

> I have over 100 bottles of Preban and because of that pre-
> fer the privacy.

It did not seem strange to me that some people don't want to go public with their stories—I certainly enjoy my privacy, whatever's left of it after spending more than half of my life online. What struck me was Christian's claim to have over 100 bottles of pre-ban absinthe in his possession, each of which could be worth $4,000 or more, which would value such a collection at $400,000. I knew other people had a lot more money than freelance writers, but that felt a bit ridiculous, as well as slightly cruel.

We'd said goodbye, and within a few days I'd forgotten about collectors of vintage absinthe. I cut back on Facebook substantially not long after that, so I initially missed many of the accusations that were made against Christian in the covert absinthe collecting groups I'd joined when I was researching my article half a decade earlier. Christian's name came up only when Habu contacted me in mid-2019, and I didn't think about him again after that until late 2021.

⋮

What happened then, of course, is that I eventually needed to find a new subject for an article, and I was running out of ideas. It had been a long, frustrating second year of the pandemic, and my work writing European travel articles for U.S. newspapers had disappeared, which I had mostly replaced with shorter and more topical articles about food and drink. It wasn't a great time, and I often found myself spinning in circles, unable to think my way out of my predicament.

In *Twilight of the Idols*, Nietzsche has a line about the value of footwork—"Only those thoughts that come by walking have any value"—which has stuck with me since my college days, though I've often misremembered it and have long misattributed it to André Gide. (I do this with virtually every quote I half-remember.) The point remains: I've often found the best way to come up with ideas is by hitting the cobblestones.

Prague is an easy city in which to do that, especially our somewhat isolated corner of the city center. Technically, our family lives in New Town, a formal part of the city since 1348 and the youngest of the five formerly independent towns that make up the historic center of Prague, though its origins as a neighborhood just outside of the former city walls—where tanners and other undesirables were allowed to live—are much older: one of the closest churches to us was founded in the eleventh century. Walking through our neighborhood and other nearby parts of Old Town is a near-hallucinatory experience, with your attention wobbling like a spinning top from the highest heights of Prague's architectural beauty to the dumbest of its modern eyesores and touristic claptrap. In one second, the eye takes in a broad, centuries-old, oak-and-steel gate flanked by two massive atlantes holding the world—or at least the heavy lintel of the building—on their shoulders. Before you can blink, you're looking at a nail salon or a grimy corner store with a garish sign that says ABSINTH SHOP.

The bottles are often on display in the window, as these were, enticing customers to come in and buy a souvenir skull-shaped bottle or one with some dusty-looking seeds inside, maybe even with a dubious claim to contain THC or cannabis. Some will even display the word "thujone" in big letters, and a claimed amount of the legal maximum content of that chemical compound. Connoisseurs, of course, know that thujone is not so important to absinthe; years ago, the American distiller Ted Breaux showed that many historic examples contained less thujone than we previously believed, often fitting under the modern legal limits. Thujone levels might qualify as relatively arcane, but even most non-connoisseurs should recognize that absinthe doesn't traditionally come in a glass skull, or in a container that contains hemp seeds. In this part of Prague, when your eye swings from the black spires of Týn Cathedral or the pastel facade of the Jerusalem Synagogue to a green bottle with a skull and a top hat that says HALLUCINATION, all you can think of is "fake."

Fake. Absinthe.

Though I didn't often drink absinthe, I'd tasted the real stuff, both modern masterpieces and one pre-ban, which made the fake versions sold in Prague's souvenir shops easy to dismiss or ignore. Most of the time I didn't even see them, the way I can admire the city's endless beauty without even noticing the stag parties and massage parlors. But one day on a walk through Old Town a windowful of fake absinthes stood out to me like a signpost, and when I came home I went back and looked up Habu's messages again, as well as his blog post accusing our mutual Facebook friend Christian of the greatest vintage absinthe fraud in history, complete with a photoshopped image of the smiling perpetrator behind bars.

⋮

I wrote up the story for the drinks website VinePair in its briefest form—guy in London sells fake bottles to collectors—but as I did, I realized there was a lot more to it that I didn't understand. There was a whole world of vintage absinthe collectors with legendary cellars that I'd only heard about and never seen in person. There was a possibly apocryphal tale about a palazzo in Italy where a bunch of bottles had been found, somewhere, if those bottles weren't also frauds. And when I talked with the absinthe collector who had identified an early forged bottle, I learned that there were others behind the discovery and proof of the counterfeiting: a group of amateur absinthe detectives who had somehow figured out the fraud. After that, the group's work had been confirmed by a young scientist in Germany, though I didn't understand how you could prove a supposedly vintage spirit was actually old or just a fake. But I didn't need to. What I got was enough for a brief article, though it left me confused and thirsty to find out more.

To be honest, so did Christian's behavior. We'd met in real life over a couple of evenings in France and chatted online about collecting in a friendly way after that, but as I was finishing up my article about the frauds, I decided to ask him if he'd talk to me. I'm a features writer; I have little experience—or interest, truth be told—in crime reporting. But I did at least one thing right: I googled him and read through his LinkedIn page, learning a bit about his career and background, before I wrote to ask if he'd talk about the forgeries.

I reintroduced myself, told him I was writing about the fraudulent bottles, and asked if I could get his side of the story. Would he be willing to tell me what happened?

There was no response, so a day later I wrote again. In hindsight, I probably could have been more diplomatic. Perhaps I should have told him I didn't think he'd done anything, though the public allegations naming him as a fraudster on Habu's blog and other websites looked pretty damning. Instead, I told him I would like to understand how it worked.

And with that, he simply blocked me. When I tuned in to see if he'd responded to my last message, I found the following:

"You can't message Christian. You can't message or call them in this chat, and you won't receive their messages or calls."

That wasn't such a surprise: I'd heard that he'd blocked almost all of his former absinthe friends, most of whom were much closer to him than I was.

What was surprising was what happened when I went back a day or so later to check his LinkedIn page. I couldn't find it. Even when I went to my own browser history, the links that I'd used to read his LinkedIn page no longer worked. It was as if Christian had wiped himself out of history.

⋮

It left me with a set of profoundly negative thoughts, a manifold sense of injustice and frustration. In my work, I'm usually writing about distillers, brewers, winemakers, or chefs: creative types who want to talk about their achievements and what they've created. This was the opposite: an arguably creative person who wanted to keep his work hidden from me. It was an unsettling feeling, like the kind you get after seeing something that is simply not supposed to happen. It was the opposite of the way things worked, as I understood them, a visit to the Upside Down, a notion that probably comes from me writing occasionally for publications like *The New York Times*. In my life, people don't just blow me off. It was a strange sensation, and I didn't like it.

The final bad feeling came with the personal awareness that I hadn't told the whole story. Freelance writing usually means that you move on to the next subject as soon as you hand a piece in, even before it gets published. With the absinthe forgeries, I'd seen only a glimpse of the truth, not the whole thing. I knew that there was much more to the absinthe fraud and the global absinthe underground than I had seen, far more than could fit into a single article. But this was, in fact, typical of my life at the time. The hamster wheel of freelancing had kept me from ever giving any subject the depth it deserved.

The pandemic was a years-long tempest of privation that had taken loved ones, jobs, and opportunities away from us, but it had also given me time to think about the changes I wanted to make in my life as I raced into middle age. Seeing a subject all the way through to the end was one of the most important. I had time to think about what I had been doing, as well as what I wasn't doing with my time, and I knew that I wanted to write a complete story, taking as long as I could to tell it. I wanted to get away from the constant rush of finding a new story before the old one had even been published. And I wanted to tell the truth, as much as I could, to measure my own abilities, even if crime reporting wasn't exactly my forte.

With family duties and an ongoing spate of freelance work, I certainly didn't have the time for it, and I didn't have the training I might need for parts of it. But I did have experience writing about spirits and producers, and enough knowledge of European languages and travel to make that work. I'd lived in France for a year during graduate school, and had also spent time in Switzerland, with a two-month summer job there as an undergraduate; in addition to being the land where absinthe was first invented, some of the forgeries even appeared to have been made with modern Swiss absinthes. It seemed to add up, despite all the challenges. And thus shortly after the end of my fifth decade on this planet, I resolved to figure out the story of the absinthe forger, what he'd done and why he'd done it, and write the truth of the tale.

The only problem was that I knew almost nothing about absinthe.

CHAPTER
3

A VERY
PARTICULAR
SPIRIT

That opaque, bitter, tongue-numbing, brain-warming,
stomach-warming, idea-changing liquid alchemy.
—ERNEST HEMINGWAY

It wasn't quite true that I knew zero about absinthe, of course:
I understood that it was an herbal spirit in the anisette family,
like ouzo or pastis, both of which had regularly been part of at
least a couple of my earlier lives. Pastis was the going-out beverage
for impoverished students when I was studying in Paris a couple of
years before the introduction of the euro, and I remembered that a
glass usually cost 10 francs—about $1.50 at the time—in the cafés
we used to haunt around the Sorbonne Nouvelle. Ouzo was another
familiar story for a kid with a lot of Greek relatives. And anyone
who's bounced around the Balkans would be able to recognize the

scent of anise and ethyl alcohol—in the form of rakija, raki, tsi-
pouro, and other variations—from the far side of a moonlit square.

Absinthe was similar to those drinks, but different: anise-
scented, but more complex and much more bitter from the use of
its namesake herb, *Artemisia absinthium*, commonly known as
grand wormwood. Once I committed to writing about the forgeries, I spent the next few days playing catch-up, trying to learn
everything I could about the spirit, or in some cases, re-learn a few
aspects I had forgotten.

I had mistakenly called absinthe a liqueur myself more than
once, but even before I started reading about it, I remembered that
it wasn't a true liqueur, as it generally wasn't sweetened before bottling. It certainly could give the impression of sweetness, thanks
to the anise that flavored it, as well as the addition of other sweet-
tasting herbs, like fennel. The most surprising thing was that there
didn't seem to be any EU legal documents that addressed absinthe:
in the regulations-loving Old World, you can't make a spirit called
"whiskey" or "whisky" that hasn't been made from grain and aged
for at least three years in a wooden vessel of less than 700 liters before being bottled with at least 40 percent alcohol. But something
called "absinthe" looked like a free ride, at least if you were going
by European law in the form of "Regulation (EU) 2019/787 of the
European Parliament and of the Council of 17 April 2019 on the
definition, description, presentation and labelling of spirit drinks."
I'd heard something similar during my trip to the absinthe festival in Pontarlier some ten years earlier. It was, unlike most food
and drink in Europe, a not terribly well-regulated product at the
EU level, shunted into the awkward catchall regulatory category of
"other spirits drinks."

But of course, I wasn't coming at it ex nihilo. There hadn't been any absinthe available in California when I'd gone to college a few years before Christian, but I'd found—and tasted—Hill's no-E Czech Absinth when I'd first come to Prague in 1998. At the time, it was served with a smirk, primarily to dumb tourists like me, in what came to be called the Bohemian Method: as a healthy shot in a wide tumbler or old-fashioned glass, with a sugar cube, a spoon, a box of matches and water, sometimes in a pitcher. The customer/victim was instructed to use the spoon to dip the sugar cube into the shot of absinthe just enough to moisten it, after which they should somehow strike a match—here it almost seems like a third hand is needed—and set the sugar-absinthe mixture in the spoon alight. After burning the sugar cube and absinthe into a syrup, the idea was that they should then stir the flaming mixture into the remaining volume of absinthe before drowning it with water. Obviously, this frequently meant that the remaining portion of absinthe caught on fire as well, and I'd seen enough absinthe flameouts in Prague's expat bars that I came to imagine that the Bohemian Method faded in popularity primarily because of the large number of insurance claims, employee injuries, and lawsuits. It was all hokum, but the world mostly didn't know that at the time, since we'd lost our collective memory and culture of absinthe in the eighty-plus years since it had been banned in France.

Even if the taste of Hill's was disgusting and the method of serving it was complete humbug, there was something special about the drink. For some reason, the world wanted it. *I* wanted it. Absinthe taught the drinking world something important. Absinthe showed us that one aspect of drinking is our intentional embrace of something very dangerous.

I didn't order it very often, but I did try it occasionally, continuing after I moved from Paris to Prague in the summer of the new millennium. To paraphrase Winston Churchill, I'm sure I got more out of absinthe than absinthe ever got out of me. To this day, I have a crystalline memory of drinking a few beers and a glass of Hill's one night in the company of some young women from my new job at the old English-language weekly newspaper in Prague, along with several of their friends—a band of eight or nine beautiful, capable young women, both Czech and international—on a night when I was just starting to realize that the relationship I'd moved from Paris to pursue was not going to work out.

That night my friends showed me support and helped me get happily stupid until a ridiculous hour, and as I walked across the city at dawn the chorus of birdsong seemed to echo into infinity: a shrieking, terrifying loudness that kept bouncing around my head as I attempted to find sleep in my nearly barren studio apartment, at which point I was certain I had glimpsed the jagged surface of my subconscious, or perhaps even my own brain. It wasn't entirely unpleasant, but for whatever reason, that was the last time I drank absinthe for many years.

After the bans on absinthe were struck down in Switzerland in 2005, followed by absinthe's re-legalization in France in 2011, I tried the spirit again. This time it was much better, though also a slightly spacey experience. By then I had met and married my wife, Nina, and had long since left my job at the English-language weekly, earning my living at that point by writing European travel articles for newspapers and magazines back home. (This sounds much cooler than it was. In many ways, it sucked.) An American friend in Prague had found an occasional gig leading tastings of the newly legal, much-higher-quality absinthe from across Europe at a bar on the other side of Old Town, and when I stopped by to see what they were all about, I found myself falling into a deep, absinthe-based reverie. In Paris I'd once had a near-psychedelic experience after sharing a pot of verbena tea with a fellow student, Atef, who was writing her thesis on Oscar Wilde. Verbena is supposed to be a calmative, but we both got extremely nervy, presumably from the tea, during which we had one of those conversations that you can only have in your youth: a talk about trust and friendship that somehow turns so earnest and edge-of-tears intense that every single word feels like an immense, almost unutterable truth. I couldn't sleep for hours afterward, nor could Atef, she recounted to me the next day, and though we never again broached the subjects we'd discussed that night, I did tell her I thought she should throw out that box of herbal tea.

The tasting with my American pal in Prague was enough to pique my interest in absinthe, and I set about learning more, eventually pitching and then writing a travel article about the newly emerging absinthe trail in western France and across the border in Switzerland's Val-de-Travers, a small valley near Neuchâtel where the drink had supposedly been invented some 230 years earlier, give or take a few decades. After Christian blocked me on Facebook, I reread my absinthe travel article from the *Times*, as well as my notebooks and journal entries from the trip, trying to remember what Christian had been like, as well as what I'd enjoyed about that trip. I didn't seem to have any notes about Christian, unfortunately, but I did have plenty of descriptive entries and tasting evaluations, including some lines about the only pre-ban I'd yet tasted. It was almost certainly authentic, an absinthe that the Distillerie Guy in Pontarlier had made before the ban, served to me and another visitor by the head of the distillery himself: a slightly oxidized, bitter sip with strong notes of anise and just a hint of licorice, so thick and complex in aromas and flavors that I started to understand why people would track down bottles that dated from years before their grandparents were born.

While on that trip, I'd learned a few things about modern absinthe, including the development of a new take on the spirit in Switzerland. Called *la bleue*, or blue (and sometimes called *absinthe blanche*, or white), it was in fact perfectly clear, like vodka or gin, a camouflage the Swiss distillers had used to keep making their favorite drink during the period of *l'interdiction*, their term for absinthe's prohibition. There were other changes that had come to the spirit during the ninety-five-year ban, including additional spices that didn't directly connect to the spirit that Henri de Toulouse-Lautrec used to drink while carousing at the Moulin Rouge. It was still an herbal drink based on the flavors of wormwood and anise, generally bottled at high proof. And in some ways, la bleue wasn't a completely new development: it turned out that there had been a few clear absinthes before the ban. However, in modern Switzerland the lack of color had become the default, unlike the dark green that was traditionally associated with the spirit. (It had been known in those days as *la Fée Verte*, after all, not *la Fée Bleue* or *la Fée Blanche*.)

As I started to get my head around the spirit and its growth over the decade since I'd last hit the French-Swiss absinthe trail, I learned of a recent addition to European law. There might not be any European regulations that defined absinthe as a spirit in general, but as of 2019 there was a Protected Geographical Indication, or PGI, on the books for the term "Absinthe de Pontarlier," meaning those words could only be used for an absinthe that met very specific criteria: it must be colored, meaning a *verte*, produced in specific locations around Pontarlier in France, and while it naturally had to contain grand wormwood and anise, it absolutely could not contain star anise, for some reason. The regulations said that an Absinthe de Pontarlier could be lightly sweetened, up to the level of thirty-five milligrams of sugar per liter, and while there was a legal maximum of thirty-five milligrams per liter on the amount of thujone any spirit or food could contain in the EU, anything called Absinthe de Pontarlier required a *minimum* of twenty milligrams of thujone per liter.

That struck me as bizarre. Thujone is one of the great bugbears in absinthe's history, a chemical compound and neurotoxin that is found in many plants and herbs, including sage and oregano, and especially in wormwood. When the French psychiatrist Valentin Magnan studied the effects of absinthe near the end of the nineteenth century, it was thought that thujone might be the component that made absinthe more dangerous than other forms of alcohol: in tests, pure wormwood oil had caused Magnan's laboratory animals to have seizures, giving justification to the international push to ban the drink, which fit nicely with Magnan's personal belief that absinthe—and what he called "absinthism"—was contributing to the decline of French culture. Even beyond absinthe, most countries have very strict regulations on thujone content in food and drink: although European regulations on thujone in food and drink had been relaxed in recent years, the compound has been effectively banned in foods in the United States since 1912, at the same time as absinthe, with a maximum allowed level of just ten milligrams per liter, which is effectively thujone-free. To say a drink was required to have at least twice as much to qualify for the use of a special marketing term sounded weird, but maybe there was something to it.

Thujone could have some positive physiological effects, according to several medical papers I found, and while it seemed to have carcinogenic properties, it also showed somewhat ironic promise as an anti-carcinogenic. It had once been thought to work on the same receptors in the brain as the THC in marijuana, but that theory has since been disproven. The modern consensus seemed to say that thujone itself wasn't responsible for the absinthe mania that had caused the drink to be banned at the height of its popularity: it was most likely the fact that absinthe simply contained high levels of alcohol, often bottled in its heyday at 144 proof, or 72 percent alcohol. It seemed that thujone could, just possibly, have some kind of mild psychological effect, especially when combined with other aromatic herbs, but the primary mood-changing agent in absinthe was probably just plain old booze.

⋮

Although I'd only known the made-up "Bohemian Method" when I'd first tasted the drink, my trip on the Swiss-French absinthe trail had introduced me to what was presented as a more traditional method of serving the drink. I was particularly impressed by the fountains: lamp-like, centerpiece tabletop vessels that were filled with cold water and sometimes ice, often with several spigots so that a number of drinkers seated around the table could dilute their drinks at the same time. If sugar was desired, you could use a perforated absinthe spoon to hold a sugar cube, through which you could aim the trickle of cold water from the fountain.

The first fountain I saw in real life was in the Val-de-Travers town of Couvet, with the distiller Claude-Alain Bugnon. Wearing a manual laborer's blue work jacket, Bugnon invited me to join a tasting with one of his clients, an absinthe seller from Germany. We sampled his exquisite absinthe, La Clandestine, without sugar, but with plenty of water, somewhere between three and four parts water to one part absinthe, which provides a drink that is roughly as strong as a glass of wine. Adding the water seemed to open up the aromas of the pure spirit, lifting up the minty, airy ribbons of aniseed, elongating the sweet mid-palate, and adding gravity to the heavy wormwood bitter notes in the finish. And even more important was its visual impact, I remembered: adding water to absinthe—or "troubling" the spirit—created the clouding effect known as the louche.

When I looked that up, I found that Wikipedia preferred to call it "the Ouzo Effect," though its article was illustrated with photographs of an absinthe verte going ghostly white as a stream of cold water was added to it. Back in the day, I remembered, one of the chief complaints against Hill's no-E Absinth from connoisseurs had been that "it doesn't louche." That had to do with some of its ingredients, or rather, the lack of them, I learned: most anise-based drinks, including ouzo, sambuca, and absinthe, turned cloudy white when water was added to them, thanks to the presence of the compound anethole, which comes from anise, though that effect could also be caused by other compounds from other essential oils. It was a form of emulsification, whereby the essential oils were able to mix with water and combine in an uncharacteristically stable combination. The louche was thought to be a sign of a quality absinthe, and because Hill's hadn't had it, it wasn't one.

In recent years, other ways of serving the drink have become more popular. After I finished my absinthe trail travel article for the *Times,* I mostly only drank absinthe as an ingredient in the occasional Sazerac, Corpse Reviver #2, or Improved Whiskey Cocktail.

But there had been a resurgence, I learned, in the popularity of the absinthe frappé, a onetime New Orleans classic. The cooking section of the *Times* had even published a recipe, albeit with the oddball additions of both heavy cream and lime juice, which had been called out in a comment from the cocktail writer Warren Bobrow. Despite the weird additions, that recipe made it seem like the formerly banned spirit had entered the mainstream.

Or perhaps that wasn't really the case, at least not compared to tequila or bourbon. Those two "brown spirits," followed by rum, had been the big stories in drinking for more than a decade, notching dizzying growth in volume of sales every single year. By comparison, absinthe was still underground. When I'd written my absinthe trail travel story at the end of 2013, it was only eight years after the end of the ban in Switzerland, and just two years after the French government voted to end *l'interdiction* in that country. Absinthe was available, but still relatively fresh and new, with only about twenty producers in the Val-de-Travers. Ten years later, I learned, the total was just over thirty. It had grown slightly, but it certainly wasn't doing anything like tequila's numbers. Part of that, I thought, had to do with its taste.

⋮

To refresh my memory of what absinthe really tasted like, I got out my bottle of Bugnon's La Capricieuse and tasted it unmixed for the first time in a decade. When I'd first tried the spirit with its maker, he'd been intrigued to hear me speak German with his guest from Berlin after talking to him in French. Of course, I made grammar mistakes and had my obvious American accent in both languages, but Bugnon hadn't seem to care. Nor did he believe me that I'd simply studied

French and German literature in college, or that I had worked in the dairy department of a Migros supermarket in German-speaking Switzerland before I'd attended graduate school in Paris.

"You're an American who speaks French and German?" he asked, playing at outrage. "You now live in Eastern Europe? No. You're NSA, monsieur!"

Ten years later, the memory of his joke still made me smile. Opening the bottle, however, quickly evoked other memories: the scent of the pastis I'd enjoyed regularly in Paris, and even a hint of ouzo from family get-togethers and Easter celebrations during my childhood. I didn't have real absinthe glasses to hand, so I measured out twenty-five milliliters, or a little less than an ounce, and poured that into one of our antique wine glasses, which Nina picks up on the cheap from bric-a-brac shops in Prague's Old Town. Naturally, we also didn't have an absinthe fountain, so I put a half-dozen ice cubes in a small pitcher and filled it up with cold tap water, stirring until it was quite cool. The moment the first drop of water hit the surface and "troubled" the spirit, a pale white cloud appeared, creating an ethereal, ghostly glow as I filled the glass.

If I were forced to describe its taste in one word, I'd probably reach for "minty," though of course the flavor of absinthe is anise, not mint; another drinker might use "licorice" instead. With dozens of herbs at the distiller's hand, there are thousands of potential flavor compounds in absinthe, and the "minty" or "licorice" taste is always quite complex, in my experience: in this glass, I was also finding notes of earthy black pepper and lemony-spicy coriander, as well as a strange herbal flavor and associated note of bitterness that lasted through the finish, starkly noticeable on my tongue long after I'd swallowed the sip. I could see why absinthe remained a staple in mixology: it had aromas for days. Even when only a few drops were used to rinse a glass, it could bring layers of complexity to drinks based on spirits like whiskey and rum that didn't normally offer bright, licorice-like aniseed notes.

It certainly could stand as a drink of its own, however. I hadn't added sugar—I'd always found that unnecessary, though of course I knew it had a historical role in how the drink was traditionally enjoyed in France—but the spirit already seemed sweet, almost too much so, without it. Tasting it again, I suddenly remembered oven-roasted fennel, the fennel notes in hanging cured sausages in delicatessens in Bologna, shaved-fennel salads with fresh lemon juice back in California, and the peppery bite of cinnamon-flavored toothpicks, a favorite among my more criminally minded classmates in elementary school. Without meaning to, I was daydreaming again, far off somewhere else, and the tension I'd been carrying in my shoulders and neck seemed to have disappeared around the same time. I wasn't halfway done with my drink, and I'd already gone on a vacation.

Delicious? Yes. A good absinthe really was delicious. It was bitter and sweet at once, lightly aromatic and slightly peppery. It was forged along that anise-licorice axis of ouzo and pastis, and while I truly enjoyed it, it wasn't the kind of thing I would reach for in midwinter: these were flavors for spring or summer, I thought, smelling like what you might imagine when shown a photograph of an alpine meadow in bloom. It was nothing like the no-E absinth I'd first encountered two decades earlier in Prague, not on any level, and while it tasted bright and optimistic, it also seemed to have a slightly darker side: some kind of mysterious herbal component imbued each sip, a weird taste that I simply couldn't identify. There was a psychological component to it, as well: something unique in its combination of herbs and alcohol had attracted me, and had clearly also captivated the absinthe forger.

.
.
.

And then there was the name.

In France, our professors had often pushed us to focus on language: etymologies of words, their meanings in other languages, their connotations, cognates, synonyms, and other aspects of philology. When I looked at the word "absinthe," I naturally thought of the word "absent" and the idea that something was somehow missing. As an allegedly psychoactive substance, perhaps it was that the drink had made people seem as if they were not fully there, "absent-minded" or simply not fully present in the moment.

In Degas's 1876 painting *Dans un café*, commonly known as "The Absinthe Drinker" or "L'Absinthe," the woman seated before the glass looks pretty vacant, as the Sex Pistols' third single put it, lost in her own memories and apparently unaware of the scene that is unfolding around her. A slightly different take on being "elsewhere" appears in the 1901 painting *The Absinthe Drinker* by the Czech artist Viktor Oliva, in which the drinker in question, deep in thought, seems to be oblivious to the ghostly green muse facing him at his table.

But as I learned, absinthe hadn't taken its name from French words like *absence* or *absent*, despite the seemingly poetic connection. It came from the ancient Greek word for wormwood, *apsinthion*, through the Latin term *absinthium*. Where that came from is unclear. What is known is that wormwood has long been associated with Artemis, the Greek goddess of the hunt, childbirth, childrearing, and chastity, as well as a patroness of healing, which led to the scientific Latin name for grand wormwood, *Artemisia absinthium*. Including the common kitchen herb tarragon, there are nearly 500 species of *Artemesia* in total, some of which are known as sagebrush, sagewort, or mugwort. Most are famous for their bitterness and interesting aromas, though grand wormwood is by far the most celebrated, an essential flavoring in both absinthe and vermouth, which takes its name from the German word for wormwood, *Wermut*.

Vermouth seems closest to how the ancient Greeks used *apsinthion*: infused, among other herbs, in wine, and employed as a balm or medicine. In Europe, wormwood was known as a digestive aid, and was believed to kill off worms and other parasites, among other treatments. "Wormwood . . . has been used in folk remedies in Europe as a gynecological agent for abortion and to induce menstruation," read one scientific paper I found. "Even now it is still used in Yemen to alleviate the pains associated with parturition."

But while herbal remedies of wormwood-infused wines were present in many European countries by the fifteenth century or so, it took centuries to distill it. That's not so strange when you think about it: although humans have enjoyed simple fermented beverages like beer and wine for most of our existence, distilled alcoholic beverages only appear to have been invented by scientists from the Arab world in the ninth and tenth centuries, taking another several hundred years before the very first versions of strong drinks reached continental Europe. An old-school spirit like brandy—distilled wine—might seem like it is "ancient," but it's only an "antique," dating back no further than the fifteenth century.

Eventually, knowledge of distillation marched across the Old

World, and by the end of the eighteenth century it reached a place where aromatic wormwood grew in abundance: the Val-de-Travers, a small valley in the Jura mountains.

Although it is currently part of Switzerland, the Val-de-Travers was not part of the Swiss Confederation at the time of absinthe's invention. In a bizarre twist of Continental politics following the Wars of Religion, when the first announcements for the sale of "extrait d'absinthe" began appearing in the area's French newspapers in 1769, the Val-de-Travers and its surrounding region were under the control of Frederick the Great, the King of Prussia, who ruled it from his home in Berlin, more than 500 miles away. A Protestant ethos and a far-off ruler who embodied the best aspects of the Enlightenment allowed the region a sense of independence and live-and-let-live that was hard to find elsewhere. When the philosopher Jean-Jacques Rousseau had to flee France after writing the scandalous *Emile, or On Education*—a book that was burned in public—he found succor in the Val-de-Travers, moving to the village of Môtiers after receiving Frederick's permission in 1762. In fact, there's every chance that Rousseau himself might have tasted early forms of absinthe in the Val-de-Travers. Just a few years later, the story goes, the first absinthe was invented as a patent medicine by a French doctor, the magically named Dr. Pierre Ordinaire, in the Val-de-Travers town of Couvet.

That story, I soon learned, is probably hogwash.

To start, Dr. Pierre Ordinaire was almost certainly not a real doctor. Instead, he was a former French soldier, originally from across the border in the region of Franche-Comté, who deserted from the French military garrison in Metz before hiding in the Val-de-Travers. Although some have claimed that Ordinaire was fleeing *la Terreur* that followed the French Revolution in 1789, he arrived in the Val-de-Travers much earlier, in 1767. In their series of books on the drink, the Swiss writers Jacques Kaeslin and Michel Kreis uncovered many of the unknown origins of the drink, as well as the lives of its "pioneers." In their writing, they lay out fairly definitive arguments, backed up by thousands of historical documents, that the first person to distill absinthe in the Val-de-Travers was not Pierre Ordinaire, but rather a woman, Marguerite Henriette Henriod, who had been largely written out of the drink's history. Kaeslin and Kreis not only tracked down evidence for Madame Henriod's distillation of absinthe, but the address of her home in the Bourgeau neighborhood on the north side of Couvet.

⋮

Complicated as its origins might have been, something simpler about this drink had drawn Christian in and inspired him. He hadn't forged whiskey or rum, and he hadn't made his own wine. He had been accused of making counterfeit historic absinthes by blending modern versions and other ingredients, connecting at least two historic eras in each faked-up bottle. For me, the main questions were why he'd done it, as well as how. Why would he betray people who thought they were his friends? Which modern spirits had he used? And how do you make a recent distillate taste like it's a hundred years old?

Within a few days, I had scheduled a return trip to the Val-de-Travers, the place where absinthe was born, to see what I could learn about the drink and the forgeries there. Before I left, I tried to remember everything I could about the culture of absinthe in the second half of the nineteenth century, how its popularity then had led to its demise, and why many people in the Belle Époque era believed that absinthe could drive a man insane.

CHAPTER 4

LES ANNÉES VERTES

Any tourist must have noticed at the tables outside the cafés the number of men, of all classes and professions, drinking a peculiar green liqueur. This is absinthe, the most pernicious and treacherously fascinating of all alcoholic stimulants. Those who begin to take it cannot give it up, notwithstanding its well-known disastrous effects on the brain, the spine, and the whole nervous system, even to the extent of causing epileptic attacks.

—*THE NEW YORK TIMES*, DECEMBER 22, 1889

Although we'd met at the festival in France, I didn't know much about Christian. I didn't know what had initially drawn him to absinthe. There was a whole world of spirits out there, but just one seemed to have spoken to him, and I found myself thinking that if I could see him, even just a picture of him, I might understand why.

Somewhere in my files I had a few rolls of medium-format film
I'd shot at the Absinthiades on an old Czechoslovak Flexaret mir-
ror camera from the late 1950s—a twin-lens reflex model, like the
more famous Rolleiflex camera. It was always a great icebreaker: it
looked cool, most people had never heard of a Flexaret IV or any
other camera brands from the former Czechoslovakia, and, most
importantly, as a photographer, you had to look down to compose
the shot. When you're taking pictures of people with a normal camera, shooting can be intimidating; when they meet each other, dogs
often look away or face down to avoid conflict and express submis-
sion. Similarly, using a twin-lens reflex often gets people to open up
and relax, showing their real faces and honest expressions, since
the photographer doesn't seem to be staring directly at them: the
subject gets to look at the photographer, but a bit like a submissive
dog, the photographer is looking down.

I'd taken pictures of Claude-Alain Bugnon at his distillery in
Couvet before I'd taken the train over the border to the festival in
France, I remembered, and I'd shot a bunch of people at the soirées there. I didn't think I'd even developed those shots, however,
and if I did have a photograph of Christian, it remained trapped
in one of those dark rolls of exposed but not-yet-developed film
a decade later, just like the static, shadowy memories held in my
mind.

The only picture I had to consider was the shot he'd used for
most of his social media, which I'd screen-grabbed before it disappeared. There was someone else it reminded me of, though that
man had been dead for over a century, and was usually shown with
much longer whiskers. Was I wrong in thinking that Christian
looked a bit like a certain troubled French poet?

That was probably where I should have been looking if I wanted to understand more about the absinthe forger: in the cultural world of late nineteenth-century France. That was what had attracted me to the spirit, after all. And to be honest, I was starting to get the impression that Christian and I might have a few things in common.

⋮

It had been over twenty years since I'd stopped reading and translating nineteenth-century French poetry for fun, after I'd left my program in French literature to pursue a career of service journalism that only really took off when I began telling readers how to get drunk in exciting new ways. I remembered that there were a bunch of poems that touched on absinthe, of course, though any specific titles escaped me. A fan of the drink, Charles Baudelaire had hinted at absinthe without ever using the word in his poem "Poison," hailing the sense of losing himself in a bitter gulf fed by the poison that flowed from his lover's green eyes. Other writers were only slightly more direct, sometimes playing on the homonym "absent," as when Rimbaud wrote that "real life is absent. We are not in the world." In one short story, the writer Guy de Maupassant tells how a small-town notary experiences the debauchery of "A Queer Night in Paris," starting with dinner in a Montmartre café called The Dead Rat, a famous artist and lesbian hangout, where the main character spots a group of lower-class, middle-aged women gossiping and drinking beer "like men," which caused the notary to move away, since "the hour for taking absinthe was at hand." Although many French poets, playwrights, and novelists were believed to have nearly lived on absinthe, the drink felt peripheral—an attendant part of the literature at the time, but almost never its main focus.

It had, however, shown up in an awful lot of paintings, perhaps because of its unusual color, a rather sickly pale-green hue—in part, the late nineteenth century was an era when what was widely seen as disgusting or even evil was almost automatically embraced in art and culture, meaning that somewhat sickly skin colors were kind of cool. In *Dans un café,* Degas echoed the color of the glass of absinthe in the zombie-like visage of the young woman behind it. There are similar green tones in the face of the title character in Toulouse-Lautrec's painting *Monsieur Boileau au Café,* as well as a green suit, green wall, green table, and a green collar, among other elements that repeat the color from his glass of absinthe. Van Gogh, a prodigious drinker of absinthe, left behind his *Still Life with Absinthe,* while Picasso made at least two early-period paintings that depicted the drink. Some of the best were by more obscure artists, like Albert Maignan's *La Muse Verte,* in which the ghost-like green muse appears to be tormenting a distraught young man—perhaps even leading him to commit some kind of fraud, I imagined.

Although a few nineteenth-century absinthe paintings depicted high-class drinkers, many seemed to hint at that darker side— poverty, madness, and crime. Something about it really turned on the artists of the time, rumors of which are still circulating today. When I told a friend of mine in Prague—an importer of artisanal wines—that I was writing a book about absinthe, he asked me what it was about the drink that had made painters like Van Gogh see such crazy things.

Despite Christian's art-degree background, I didn't see any parallels between him and the painters of that era. I didn't see anything that tied him to the writers I loved, either, and he had seemed to be pretty careless with his words and punctuation, which was never a good sign in my eyes. When it came to famous figures from the heyday of absinthe, I started to wonder if Christian was anything like the man with the darkest story concerning the drink, one of the most famous bits of absinthe lore ever: the murderer Jean Lanfray.

⋮

It sounds like a simple story: Jean Lanfray was a thirty-one-year-old Swiss laborer who drank some absinthe and subsequently murdered his family. The truth is much more complicated, involving wine cartels, nationalism, alcoholism, religious and ethnic bigotry, colonial misadventures in Africa, and an invasion of tiny insects.

Absinthe had grown spectacularly in popularity in French-speaking Europe in the previous four or five decades before Lanfray's crimes shocked the world in 1905, in part because of widespread damage to the European wine industry following the arrival, probably in 1858, of the North American aphid *Daktulosphaira vitifoliae*, a small insect commonly known as phylloxera, from the Greek words for "leaf" and "dry." While North America's native *Vitis* grapes were generally phylloxera-resistant, the traditional European *Vitis vinifera* grapevines succumbed en masse to the drying-leaf disease brought by phylloxera. Grape growers were so desperate that they sought out whatever remedies they could find, like burying a live toad under each vine to absorb the "poison."

When that approach surprisingly failed, French and other European grape farmers reluctantly began to try a new idea, starting around 1871: they could graft their traditional grape vines onto phylloxera-resistant North American rootstock. Vineyards grow

slowly, so it took a while for them to see if that would work better
than toads, but in 1888 and 1893 the French government awarded
prizes to Thomas Volney Munson of Texas and the Swiss-born
Missourian Hermann Jaeger, in recognition of two Americans who
had researched, developed and provided the blight-resistant plants
that ultimately saved French wine.

Four decades of reduced wine production at the end of the
nineteenth century had given absinthe plenty of time to find
its audience. (It was a neat fit in terms of timing: Manet's early
masterpiece *The Absinthe Drinker,* a painting depicting a rakish
drinker who would have been part of absinthe's relatively early
avant-garde, dates from 1859, just one year after phylloxera is believed to have made it to the Old World, shortly before European
vineyards began to suffer.) The drink hardly needed an introduction in France, since many former soldiers knew it from their time
serving in the country's nineteenth-century colonies, where absinthe and wormwood extracts had been issued as remedies for
disease—the Green Fairy had started out as a type of medicine,
after all, and even today, wormwood is still being studied for its
anti-bacterial, anti-fungal, antimalarial, and insecticidal properties. If winemakers were struggling, French men and women of
the 1870s and 1880s were quite happy drinking absinthe. (The situation also provided an important opportunity for growth, both
in Britain and on the Continent, for makers of Scotch whisky.)
Absinthe's role in society expanded, moving from what might
have been considered avant-garde in 1859 to an aspect of modern
life that was popular enough for its own time of day. By 1889, *The
English Illustrated Magazine* reported:

Parisian café life is most animated in the afternoon between five and seven, *l'heure verte*, the "green hour" when people are wont to drink absinthe, read the evening papers and gossip with their friends. Then every little table placed on the side walk in front of the cafés is occupied, the waiters clad in short black jackets, their legs swathed in a white apron that reaches down to their feet—the only waiter's costume that has character and *chic*—hurry to and fro bare-headed, carrying little trays laden with glasses, saucers, *carafes frappées*, and crying every minute *Versez absinthe! Versez curaçoa! Versez Turin Américain!* and a dozen other names of strange liquors which the butler or *verseur* proceeds to pour into the glasses and which when diluted with water look like infusions made with all the tints of a box of watercolours— green absinthe, opal gray orgeat, carmine red grenadine, dark crimson bitter and curaçoa, pale amber vermouth.

Yes, there were many other beverages on offer in the charming street cafés of Paris, but absinthe was front and center, with *l'heure verte* forming as much a part of modern life as the midafternoon *heure jaune* that was widely understood as the time for secret love affairs. Later, the entire era even came to be known among historians as *les années vertes*, or "the green years," thanks to the role of absinthe. And while wine had struggled temporarily, when the French wine industry, growing on American rootstocks, started producing in normal volumes again around the last decade of the nineteenth century, it wanted its drinkers back.

An important step: turning the Green Fairy into a demon.

:

With the rose-tinted lenses of a foreign tourist, that British magazine might have waxed rhapsodic about l'heure verte in Paris, but
other voices were already sounding less enthusiastic. In 1892, the
magazine *La Vie Parisienne* described l'heure verte as "a cue to
forget your activities, your worries, a perfidious toxin which ignites
ephemeral enthusiasms and edifies in an opaline vapor the visions
of fortune . . ." (That was all meant, if it's not clear, in the bad way.)
It got worse, especially when it came to medicine, which turned
against absinthe even earlier. That probably wasn't helped by the
drink's popularity among the writers and artists of the era.

At the time, many of them called themselves "Decadents" for
a reason: it would be hard to argue that the writers of nineteenth-
century France were not decadent and anti-establishment, even
what some might call degenerates. As beautiful as you might find
their works, you wouldn't trust Verlaine and Rimbaud to water
your houseplants while you were away, or let your kids read their
jointly written "Sonnet of the Asshole," a ruthless parody of a contemporary, Albert Mérat, who'd written poems praising the beauty
of his lover's body, part by part; the two dedicated their X-rated
response to one part of the body Mérat had skipped. Baudelaire is
almost more famous for the bizarre anecdotes from his life than for
his evocative, practically futuristic take on verse. (The best story I
heard in graduate school: in a park, Baudelaire asked a woman if the
newborn baby in the carriage she was pushing was hers. When the
young mother proudly answered yes, the poet replied that the child
was absolutely horrible.) Poets of the Decadent school got drunk,
fought, injured each other—in 1873, Rimbaud was shot through
the hand by an absinthe-sodden Verlaine, who was subsequently

imprisoned—and, in general, behaved badly by the standards of their own day, to say nothing of ours. Absinthe certainly didn't benefit from their association, especially once doctors like Valentin Magnan began to investigate the "degenerate" nature of the drink.

As the admitting doctor at the country's leading psychological asylum, l'hôpital Sainte-Anne, Magnan had plenty of experience with society's ills. In his eyes—and those of many others, to be fair—French civilization in the late nineteenth century was in decline, falling far from its lofty position at the start of the century, an example of so-called "social degeneration" that could possibly result in the end of the French nation. Such fears were widespread. Once a military powerhouse, France could not escape the memory of its grand, early-nineteenth-century empire under Napoleon, thoughts of which put its devastating 1870 defeat in the Franco-Prussian War—which brought about the end of the Second French Empire and the reign of Napoleon III—in stark relief. By the time the European economy collapsed in 1873, France was paying millions in reparations. The situation had been getting bad for years, and then it got worse.

Magnan believed that alcohol was causing the decline of French culture, but he saw absinthe as a special beast, and tried to present "absinthism" as its own disease, different from alcoholism. Other doctors supported the idea: "The spirit of absinth causes drunkenness, but also dizziness and a state of nausea which come from the wormwood and not the alcohol itself," one wrote. Another noted: "One must acknowledge that the frequent fatal accidents among drinkers of absinthe are due as much to this plant as to the alcohol." If absinthe was to blame for the degeneration of French culture, could the modern scientific mind not figure out why?

By 1869, Magnan began to research the plant in question, *Artemisia abstinthium,* and the effects of its chemical components, conducting tests in which laboratory animals were exposed to concentrations of the plant's essential oils in doses that were hundreds of times stronger than the amount in a full bottle of Pernod Fils. When I read Théodore Challand's 1871 report on Magnan's work, *Étude expérimentale et clinique sur l'absinthisme et l'alcoolisme* (or *Experimental and Clinical Study on Absinthism and Alcoholism*), I thought it sounded like straight-up animal cruelty: Magnan force-fed healthy dogs toxic levels of *Artemisia* essential oils, then injected more into their stomachs and hung them up by their front paws so they could not vomit it out. He forced smaller animals—cats, pigeons, chickens, rabbits, and guinea pigs—to inhale suffocating fumes. He injected 1 to 4 grams (that is, 1,000 to 4,000 milligrams) of pure *Artemesia* essential oils into animals' subcutaneous tissue, which he found very effective, though this caused the animals to have so many convulsions that it was hard distinguish one attack from the next. He used only slightly smaller amounts, 500 to 2,000 milligrams, when he injected the essential oil directly into dogs' main arteries. He also tried applying it to dogs' rectums, he noted, but it was difficult to keep there, despite having taken all possible precautions. This was, it bears repeating, in the name of researching degeneracy.

Regardless of how the essential oils of *Artemesia* were applied, the results were always the same: the dog would become very agitated, trembling at the slightest sound. Soon the dog would begin to twitch and have trouble breathing. Then the twitching would become more severe, especially in its hindquarters, as if the dog were receiving a series of electric shocks. Trembling, the dog would attempt to lie down or squat in a corner. If Magnan clapped his hands, hit the dog, or threw a rock at it, he noted, the dog's trembling would become much more severe.

It's not just that Magnan's research sounds cruel by our standards today. In 1874, a presentation by Magnan at the annual meeting of the British Medical Association in Norwich was broken up by protesters, who objected to his attempt to give a dog seizures by injecting it with *Artemesia* essential oils on stage. The Royal Society for the Prevention of Cruelty to Animals filed a criminal complaint against Magnan, and the Frenchman was forced to leave the country in haste. (Later, Magnan included excessive concern over animal welfare as a sign of social degeneracy and started diagnosing antivivisectionism as a hereditary mental illness.)

In a way, Magnan might have been right about absinthe being bad for French society. Lax regulations meant that even the cheapest rot-gut could be sold as "absinthe," though that had very little do with what the fancy types were drinking in sidewalk cafés during l'heure verte. And they certainly were throwing them back. The French nation consumed just under 500,000 gallons of pure alcohol in total in 1876, but that amount swelled to 6 million gallons by 1913, according to a 1915 article in the London *Times* cited by one scientific paper I came across.

After a start as a quirky patent medicine in a quiet Swiss valley, and then an avant-garde artist's and poet's drink, absinthe was one of the most popular beverages across French society: by 1913, the average absinthe consumption was fifteen times what it had been in 1875. Beginning with a single distillery founded by Henri-Louis Pernod in 1805, the city of Pontarlier swelled into the center of the French absinthe industry, with over a dozen new producers launching there between 1870 and 1890, eventually rising to a total of twenty-five. When Pernod began distilling in Pontarlier, he could make sixteen liters—or just over sixteen quarts—per day. By the end of the nineteenth century, that city was turning out ten million liters annually.

But by that point, the French wine industry was back on its feet, and the idea of banning or limiting alcohol in general was not nearly as appealing to winemakers as the idea of cutting out the green upstart from the Jura Mountains. Then came a final crisis near the end of the nineteenth century, one which divided France and poured gas on the anti-absinthe fire: the Dreyfus Affair.

In 1894, a French Army captain named Alfred Dreyfus was accused of selling military secrets to Germany and convicted of treason. (Decades later, the country was still suffering psychologically from its 1870 military defeat.) The case against Dreyfus was weak, judgment was rushed, and some of the evidence against him had been fabricated by his fellow officers. Over the next few years, arguments for or against Dreyfus—a French Jew—increased in rancor, approaching the level of a cold civil war. The antisemitic newspaper *La Libre Parole* led the charges against Dreyfus, while his supporters included the novelist Émile Zola, who published the broadside "J'accuse!" ("I accuse!") as an open letter to the president of the republic on the front page of the newspaper *L'Aurore* in 1898. That letter resulted in a new trial for Dreyfus the next year, which unfortunately finished with same verdict, after which the former captain was formally pardoned by the president in an attempt to heal a glaring wound that had cut straight across French society. A full formal exoneration would not arrive until 1906.

The injury was primarily caused by antisemitism: the resentment of Jewish people across France. And like the temperance movement that was growing in the United States, those agitating against absinthe in France started using baldly anti-Jewish messaging, too.

I'd seen something about this on Oxygenée, an old website where pre-bans were once listed for sale, I remembered, but that site had disappeared from the web not long after Christian's frauds were announced. However, I discovered that much of the old Oxygenée material was online at a new site called la Musée Virtuel de l'Absinthe, including a page about the anti-Jewish bigotry of the anti-absinthe crusaders. *La Libre Parole*, it noted, had led a vicious campaign against absinthe, focusing on Jewish-owned distilleries, including the leading maker, Pernod Fils. In 1894, a majority share of Pernod Fils had been bought by two brothers, Arthur and Edmond Weil-Picard, whose father had been a "Jewish banker," the paper noted; its editor, Édouard Drumont, called absinthe "a tool of the Jews," after having whined about "murderous absinthe" in his earlier, maniacal 1,200-page antisemitic polemic of 1886, *La France juive*, or *Jewish France*. The connection of the anti-absinthe movement with antisemitism and the widespread notion of "Jewish absinthe" got so bad that one distillery even sold what it called "Anti-Jewish Absinthe" on its label, which included a nationalist tagline, "France for the French," apparently in the fear that widespread anti-absinthe fervor might bring down the businesses of bigots, too. With the Dreyfus Affair having pushed antisemitism to the fore, everything was all cued up.

⋮

The Lanfray murders of August 28, 1905, were a gift to the anti-absinthe movement that had spread across Europe. Newspapers in every country reveled in the details: primarily, that Lanfray had drunk two glasses of absinthe before arguing with his wife, who neglected Lanfray's command to polish his boots. (Most reporters skipped an important point: during the course of the day, Lanfray had also consumed something like eleven glasses of red wine, one cognac and soda, a crème de menthe and at least two coffees with brandy.) After his wife's refusal, the former soldier Lanfray grabbed his Vetterli bolt-action army service rifle and shot her in the head, killing her almost instantly. He then shot his four-year-old daughter, Rose, when she entered the room, followed by his two-year-old daughter, Blanche, in her cradle. With the aid of a loop of string on the trigger, Lanfray then attempted to shoot himself, though he missed the desired target of his brain, hitting himself in the jaw instead. He carried Blanche's body out to the barn, where he lost consciousness. Alerted to the crimes by Lanfray's father, the police found the murderer and brought him to a nearby hospital, where he underwent surgery to remove the bullet from his jaw and eventually recovered, under police guard.

Those tragic events took place in the town of Commugny in the Swiss canton of Vaud, just south of Neuchâtel and the Val-de-Travers, where public outrage led that canton to ban the local sale of absinthe almost immediately, with the mayor of the town announcing that absinthe was "the principal cause of a series of bloody crimes in our country."

Lanfray's trial took place on February 23, 1906. Although the police had discovered that Lanfray regularly drank the equivalent of six to nine bottles of wine per day, Switzerland's leading psychiatrist, Dr. Albert Mahaim, offered a noteworthy professional opinion: "Without a doubt, it is the absinthe that he drank daily for years that gave Lanfray the ferociousness of temper and blind rages that made him shoot his wife for no reason, as well as his two poor children, whom he loved." The trial lasted just one day, and Lanfray was sentenced to life in prison. He committed suicide shortly afterward, hanging himself in his jail cell on February 26.

That might have ended the story for Lanfray, but with the quick ban on absinthe in Vaud, the anti-absinthe movement could taste blood, and Lanfray was one of its justifications. "L'absinthe rend fou" (or "absinthe makes people crazy") was a common refrain, while posters and banners called for the removal of Le péril vert— the green peril—from polite society. In Belgium, where Verlaine had shot Rimbaud during one of his absinthe binges, the drink was outlawed in 1906. Things moved slightly more slowly in France, though the newspaper Le Matin promoted a large anti-absinthe demonstration in Paris under the slogan "all for wine, against absinthe" in 1907.

After a massive advertising and political campaign, pressure from religious and commercial groups, a national referendum to ban the drink was held in Switzerland in 1908, where it passed by a wide margin. That same year, the anti-alcohol lobby in the French Senate stated its three main legislative aims: ending the longstanding right to home distillation, limiting the number of drinking establishments, and banning absinthe. The drink was blacklisted in the Netherlands in 1910, the same year the Swiss ban went into effect, and in the United States in 1912, though it managed to hold on in France until a temporary ban in 1914 at the start of yet another war with the Germans was followed by a definitive legal ban in 1915. Within just a few years, almost every country in Europe had banned la Fée

Verte, and after the Great War ended, the newly launched League of Nations even began to debate the merits of a global prohibition on a single type of spirit. The Green Fairy was dead.

$$\vdots$$

Or at least that was the case in France, the country that had drunk more absinthe than the rest of the world combined. However, there were a couple of small but important exceptions, including the newly independent nation of Czechoslovakia, which emerged from Austria-Hungary after the war ended in 1918 without ever having legally banned absinthe. Nor had Spain, much closer to France, where the old Edouard Pernod distillery from the Val-de-Travers had started making absinthe according to its woody pre-ban recipe in the Catalonian city of Tarragona in 1912. At first, the giant French Pernod—Pernod Fils—switched to making its wormwood-free substitute, Anis Pernod—the first pastis, which launched in 1918. Eventually, Pernod Fils took over the Tarragona distillery in Spain, changing the old Edouard-style recipe to the more anise-forward version of Pernod Fils for Spanish distribution in 1936. That production line stopped in 1939 with the fall of the Spanish Republic, only starting up again after World War II. Most collectors prefer the earlier, Edouard-style Tarragonas, which have real pre-ban character, though the Pernod Fils Tarragonas from the 1950s are also popular. The final Pernod Fils Tarragonas made after 1960 or so are not particularly beloved today, but like their predecessors, those bottles offered a vestigial hint of the Belle Époque's favorite spirit and helped guard our collective memory of absinthe. As for Czechoslovakia, Habu has identified at least one early Czech producer of real absinthe, Joseph Archleb in the

East Bohemian town of Dobruška, though unfortunately, no absintheurs have ever found a bottle. With absinthe, Czechoslovakia's
importance would not arrive after the Velvet Revolution in 1989,
when small distillers in the now standalone nation of the Czech
Republic would realize that there was nothing stopping them from
making absinthe in the 1990s, and thus kick off a global revival
nearly a century after Lanfray.

⋮

Leading up to the ban, it had been widely believed that absinthe
was different than other forms of alcohol: during the Lanfray trial,
a panel of leading Swiss doctors had stated that "more than all other
alcoholic beverages, absinthe exercises an irresistible temptation to
the drinker and compels him to drink too much." I didn't believe
the claims that absinthe was fundamentally different than other
types of alcohol, but there was obviously something special about
it. Historically, no other single type of spirit has been demonized
in quite the same way. The U.S. prohibition movement had also
deployed grossly racist, anti-Black, and antisemitic messages, focusing on the Jewish ownership of certain distilleries and stoking
widespread fear of crime by intoxicated African Americans, but its
stated and achieved goal was the total prohibition of all alcohol,
not a ban on just bourbon, gin, or rum. Historically, absinthe was
different, because we had treated it differently.

Beyond that, I could see that absinthe had changed people,
though maybe not in the way that the anti-absinthe crusaders
argued. Absinthe had changed Jean Lanfray, not from a peace-
ful farmer to a murderer—going by the amounts he'd drunk, that
transformation had been caused by wine—but from a real man to a

caricature, from a human being to the tool of a political movement. Absinthe had seemingly changed Magnan, too—his obsession over the drink had led to his own misdeeds.

But there was something in this that I needed to rethink, because I could see that a few of the lines didn't meet up. Christian wasn't like Lanfray, not really, or like Magnan. He had only been accused of ripping off his friends and fellow collectors, and he certainly hadn't been accused of anything like a triple homicide. And yet there was something similar about Christian and Lanfray, in that they had both damaged the absinthe culture of their day. Lanfray had been used as a blunt instrument, his story repeated in newspapers across the Continent, all arguing for a cause, while Christian's story appeared to have been hidden and mostly forgotten. But according to what I'd heard from Habu and others, the shadowy world of vintage absinthe collectors—the global absinthe underground—never really recovered from what Christian had done, even if no one was sure exactly how he'd done it.

Some of those secrets had to be in the Val-de-Travers. Absinthe had been born there and never died out, as generations of clandestine distillers had worked in secret to keep the Green Fairy alive. And at least one of them, I knew, had sold his absinthe to Christian in bulk.

THE HOMELAND
OF ABSINTHE

Ils ont force beaux lacs et force sources d'eau,
Force prez, force bois. J'ay du reste (Belleau)
Perdu le souvenir, tant ilz me firent boire.

—JOACHIM DU BELLAY

The forgeries I was trying to track down had all come out of London, but it had been reported that Christian had sourced some of the spirits he'd blended into those forgeries from Patrick Grand, a modern distiller in the Val-de-Travers. I wanted to get his side of the story, and learn whatever I could about how a drink could have had survived in its home region through ninety-five years of prohibition, which was had been legally enforced in Switzerland starting in 1910.

It was technically late autumn when I set out, though an unexpected storm had brought severe conditions across Central Europe, stranding both airline and railway passengers. My early morning train heading due south from the Czech capital was turned back at the border with Austria, due to snow and ice in the mountain passes between the two countries, which required a reschedule that sent me southeast to Vienna on a train that finally arrived two hours late. Fortunately, I'd built plenty of time into my rejigged itinerary and had hours to kill at Vienna's new Hauptbahnhof, where I ate a late supper of sausages, potato salad, and a couple of local beers before the station police cleared everyone out of the food court, and I moved to a bench to await my delayed train through the Alps and into Switzerland.

I had not taken a night train in over twenty-five years, and I seemed to be about that much older than the two other passengers in my compartment: a young man whose bottom-floor bunk faced mine, and a young woman who had booked the aerie-like top berth above us. Scheduled to leave at 11:26 p.m., the Hungarian-staffed train didn't even enter the Hauptbahnhof until 12:40 a.m., after which we quickly made our own not-quite-beds, turned out the lights and slept until dawn, when we opened our blackout window shade to find snow-capped mountain peaks rising high above us. A few hours later, we said *schöne Reise* and *auf Wiedersehen* to each other in Zürich, and a few minutes later I climbed aboard a fast train to the city of Neuchâtel in the far west of Switzerland.

German was the shared language when we started out, but as we moved west I heard more and more French, until the old tongue was less than a memory. During the summer I'd spent working in German-speaking Switzerland, I'd often heard German-speaking locals say that their French-speaking countrymen were also Swiss, just not quite as Swiss as they were. But by the time we disembarked at our terminus in Neuchâtel, the shoe was on the other foot. In many ways it felt a bit like France, perhaps due to the dulcet tones of conversation, though it also felt specifically Swiss: slightly better organized and generally a bit less messy than France. It took just a minute to buy my ticket for the local train from a pleasant Swiss Railways saleswoman, and a quarter of an hour later I was heading west into the Val-de-Travers.

Around Europe, it's often hard to discern a real difference between one region and its neighbor, where borders between communes, cantons, or districts are often ambiguous and invisible. I felt a clear delineation going into the Val-de-Travers, however—after the urban setting of Neuchâtel that faced the beautiful, turquoise waters of its namesake lake, the train passed through a quick series of tunnels through the heavy Jura Mountains, emerging in a narrow, dark, heavily wooded valley. There was little snow, and I could see the clear green waters of the Areuse river rushing into milky foam below us as the train continued and the valley opened up.

When I disembarked in Rousseau's former town of Môtiers, just a half hour from Neuchâtel, the sun had come out from the behind the clouds, illuminating the peaks and giving the valley's sense of scale—about fifty square miles in total, narrow but long in its east to west run up to the border with France.

I checked into a lovely bed-and-breakfast, A Côté, and went for a short walk to take some photographs. Around the corner, I found the Maison de l'Absinthe, a new museum that had opened after my last visit, which focused on the origins of the drink in the region, as well as the legends of the bootleg distillers—or *clandestins*—who had continued to produce absinthe during its near-century ban.

In the lobby, I met Odile Churchward-Gogniat, a member of the museum's founding board and a longtime friend from the absinthe groups online.

The idea of housing an absinthe museum in the building was originally floated as a joke, she explained. The building had been home to the regional tribunal, where any clandestine distillers caught by the police went before the judge. After a reorganization of the local government, the tribunal had moved to a new location, and the building stood empty. Dedicating a museum to illegal distillers in the very building where they'd received their sentences turned into a reality when la Maison de l'Absinthe opened to the public in 2014. It felt like a familiar thumbing of the nose from the common people to those with power, which paired well with the local sense of humor. That was partly why absinthe had been able to hang on during the ban. In a rural place like the Val-de-Travers, Odile said, people didn't want to be bossed around by folks from the big city.

"You know, we live in the far west. The people by the lakes always laugh at us, 'Those people from the mountains.' So it gives everybody here this feeling that, 'Ha, we'll show them,'" she said. "I think that's how the clandestine period survived so well."

It wasn't just about survival, although many of the clandestine distillers certainly started out after struggling to put food on the table. One of those was a real legend: Martha Charrère, widely known as just "La Martha," a distiller from the village of Les Bayards, who started making her own bootleg absinthe to support her family in the 1950s.

Other bootleggers went beyond mere survival, becoming well-to-do and quite famous in the process. Among the best-known was Roger Vaucher-Bähler, aka Le Poilu, who ended up getting caught after building a big house with a swimming pool for his family. Odile loved to visit, she said, because the Vaucher-Bählers owned a parrot and a mynah bird, and as a child she was mad about animals.

"I really liked them—I was at their house all the time and used their swimming pool," she recalled. "Nobody had private swimming pools in the 1950s in Switzerland—nobody. And a beautiful villa, and a big, American car, and he'd drive around with a cigar. He became a real show-off."

That showiness apparently attracted the interest of the police, who raided the Vaucher-Bähler villa several times without results. They studied the building more carefully and made measurements, eventually realizing that there was an unaccounted-for space in the middle of the cellar. Once one of the cellar shelves was emptied of its cans of fruit, a small lever allowed it to rotate, opening a hidden door to a tiny, closet-size space where Le Poilu kept his still. After he was caught, he was said to have escaped prison, possibly running off to Africa.

Other clandestine distillers worked hard to keep from getting arrested. A pair of clandestine distillers owned an auto body shop, using their clients' cars to hide their contraband. In what had once been the judge's chambers, the museum displayed several items that were used for smuggling, including a large vessel that could worn next to the stomach like a false belly, hidden under clothing. At some point, one local figured out how to put absinthe into cans, just like peaches or pineapple slices, which made it undetectable to the nose and eye.

Absinthe's popularity in the Val-de-Travers during its prohibition had led to the creation of the modern Swiss style of the drink: the colorless bleue. While absinthe was most famous during the Belle Époque for its green hue, that color made it easily to identify. But if Swiss clandestine distillers simply skipped the coloration step that turned the pure spirit green, the result would be perfectly clear, just like vodka, gin, or many other drinks, while still having the wormwood bitterness and sweet anise flavors absinthe was famous for. If you wanted to hide your moonshine in a clear glass bottle labeled "Machine Oil" (along with a sticker declaring "External Use Only") like the one displayed in the museum, a clear liquid was the only way to go.

That culture of contraband and smuggling seemed like the opposite of absinthe's glorious fin de siècle status: it was hard to reconcile absinthe labeled as an industrial lubricant with famous painters, writers, and can-can dancers at the Folies Bergère in Paris. For Odile, absinthe had very different connotations in the Val-de-Travers, at least by the time she was growing up in the 1950s.

"My dad always used to say absinthe fountains are for Japanese tourists," she said. "It was a poor man's drink, or a working man's drink, during the whole of the prohibition period." Back then, every village in the Val-de-Travers had cafés where laborers could stop for a drink after work, she recalled. "Workers would go there in their blue blouses, and they would sit on a stool, on an old table, with an old glass and a pitcher. Instead of an absinthe spoon, they would just use a fork. There was none of this fancy stuff."

The museum had several impressive antiques, including a famous bottle of Dubied Père et Fils absinthe dating from before the year 1848, which had been turned up by a celebrated vintage bottle hunter a few years earlier. I found even more great antiques at a nearby distillery, l'Absintherie du Père François, located inside the former Sandoz distillery: a sprawling, warehouse-like building on the other side of Môtiers. There, the revered producer François Bezençon—Père François himself—showed me around his collection of vintage posters, glasses, and other absinthe collectibles, primarily from the Belle Époque era. While he loved collecting antiques, he was not at all interested in drinking any spirits from before the ban.

"An absinthe is not a Bordeaux," he said carefully. "It doesn't age well. It loses a lot. The taste changes."

He had spent more than fifty years building his collection, but now that he was in his mid-eighties, he was pretty much done, he said. Unlike many of the modern absinthe distillers in the Val-de-Travers, François had never been a bootlegger. He had owned and run a successful wholesale drinks business, which required a license from the government. If he'd ever distilled before the ban was lifted, he said, he could have lost his business. Instead, he had waited until March 1, 2005—the first day that it was once again legal to distill absinthe in Switzerland. However, like most people in the valley, he had enjoyed drinking bootleg absinthe during its prohibition, he admitted.

He used two crutches to get around as we wandered through the rooms which displayed his antiques. The collection contained several small antique stills, or alembics, which were designed to sit atop the heavy wooden stoves that were once commonly used for cooking, making the job seem like any other domestic task. In fact, Odile had told me that people in the Val-de-Travers had often referred to clandestine absinthe distilling as "la lessive," meaning "laundry." If someone noticed the minty, herbal scent of absinthe hanging in the air, they might jokingly ask friends if they didn't also catch the smell of la Martha doing her laundry.

François Bezençon's museum was no longer open to the public, due to the growing popularity of the Maison de l'Absinthe, which got most of the tourists to the region. Until its closure, he had welcomed thousands of visitors. He was always surprised that many French visitors didn't seem to know what absinthe really was.

"In France, there was almost no absinthe during the prohibition. It wasn't like it was here. The French just lost their connection to it. The French who came here as tourists, sometimes they were even afraid of it. 'It's dangerous. It's actually poison.' You could see that they stopped drinking it. But here, we always kept drinking it, despite the ban."

He said that recipes had changed dramatically, even compared to the Belle Époque era. He had many recipes in his collection, including the books of the great Pernod Fils distillery from 1887 to 1915, which showed, he noted, that the amount of grand wormwood being used in each batch decreased by two-thirds from its early high, though he didn't explain if that was based on economic, regulatory, or gustatory concerns. In the Val-de-Travers, the shift from contraband to legal production had brought about much higher quality absinthe, as well as different flavors and aromas.

While he had never distilled absinthe himself before it was legal, he had occasionally sold some, off the books, through his drink business. The head of the local Coca-Cola office might call him when a drinks delivery was on its way. "'They're coming with the truck,' he would say. 'Give us six liters.' He just said 'six liters,' nothing else." In the Val-de-Travers, that was enough. Everyone there knew what that meant. "I knew plenty of clandestine distillers, so I'd go buy it from them, or I'd give them wine or something and we'd make a trade."

If the word "liters" had clearly meant "absinthe" in the Val-de-Travers, other code words helped the drink survive under cover, even out in public, during l'interdiction. On my first trip to the valley in

2013, a woman had told me that her parents had said she should always deny the family having any absinthe if someone called asking if they could buy it when she was a child. However, if they asked for *lapin*, or "rabbit," she could tell them to come pick it up.

Locals could get their hands on the drink in other ways, François remembered, as he poured me a glass of his own absinthe.

"They hid it in the cafés. They would serve you absinthe in the kitchen, or even just like I'm serving you this one—not very often, but sometimes. I occasionally drank absinthe in bistros here from cups for milk, because those are white, not translucent, and that way no one could see what you were drinking. I even once had a client who told me he tried to buy an absinthe at the bistro in the town of Travers. Someone had told him that if you want to buy absinthe, you ask for a milk. So he told the waiter, 'I would like some milk.'" His eyes twinkled. "And the waiter actually just brought him milk."

On my way out, I admired some of his antique posters, one of which announced the public vote regarding the potential ban on absinthe on July 5, 1908, while a large billboard next to the front door promoted the 72 percent alcohol, "non-oxygenated" absinthe from the A. Junod distillery. With la Maison de l'Absinthe doing its job in terms of educating tourists and his museum no longer functioning, he said he wasn't quite sure what to do with his collection.

"Young people are no longer interested in the old things," he said. "It's a pity."

⋮

François Bezençon could tell me nothing about the forgeries, but there was one distiller in the Val-de-Travers who had information. I'd met Patrick Grand in Pontarlier ten years earlier, under the very worst of circumstances: after drinking many great spirits throughout the day, including my very first pre-ban, I'd lost track of what I had consumed and ended up embarrassingly drunk. I didn't know Grand very well, but I'd learned that he was the kind of person who, years afterward, would enjoy reminding you of something like that, or bring it up with a laugh when he introduced you to others for the first time.

Grand had told me to meet him at the old church in Fleurier, the next village over from Môtiers, and when I got there the next day, I first saw a few wormwood plants struggling to survive in the pre-winter chill. Next to the entrance, a naked plastic manne-quin without arms or legs below the knees had been painted Kermit the Frog green, with "Fata," the name of one of Grand's absinthes, printed just above her bare, exposed breasts; the mocked-up fairy wings on her back were ripped and torn. Despite that green fairy's Fata branding, I wasn't completely sure I was in the right place, and I knocked on the church door a few times before Grand finally peeked out, holding his phone to his ear.

"Shut the door," he said, turning back inside.

It took him several minutes to finish his call, which gave me plenty of time to take in the scene. The church must have been deconsecrated, if only to go by the bottles, chairs, tables, poster re-productions, and—most conspicuously—a poster for Fata absinthe showing a cartoon of a naked woman on her hands and knees, fac-ing the viewer with her mouth opened all the way to her tonsils.

Grand paced around the room as he talked on the phone. He was broad-shouldered and stocky, built like a wrestler, about at the same point I was in middle age, sporting a gray sweater and gray jeans, with a puffy coat and a light-colored watch cap, even in-doors, where the space heater on the floor didn't seem to do jack.

He maintained the frenetic energy after he'd hung up, talking to me about how he'd gotten into absinthe. His father used to drink the clandestine version, but Grand himself hadn't appreciated it when he'd come of age in the 1980s.

"I was a hockey player, a good ice hockey player. We drank whiskey and Coke or whatever, but nothing forbidden. But the old people here were still drinking absinthe."

His father had originally purchased the building that now housed his distillery. At the time of that purchase in 1987, the deconsecrated church had come with two small alembics for distilling, which Grand's father had then sold off to Grand's hockey coach. When Grand started distilling himself after the ban ended in 2005, he'd tried to buy them back, but his coach's widow wanted too much money for them. Instead, he'd bought new stills from Portugal, which were housed in the church's former transept.

I told him that I was researching absinthe, primarily old absinthe, including the frauds that had come out of the U.K. a few years earlier. He shrugged, like the idea just wasn't very sexy.

"I love to taste modern absinthe because it's like perfume. I'm not interested in old absinthe, because it's like if you say, 'Do you want to make something with my grandma?' I would tell you no. With your sister or your wife? Yes. But grandma? It's finished for me."

He admired antique fountains and spoons in museums, he said, but he pointed out that you can simply take a plastic bottle filled with cold water and dribble that into your glass. For troubling an absinthe, that worked just as well.

"I love showing people that there are different ways of doing things."

One thing he admired about the old days, though, was the beautiful art that had been created. He pointed to some reproductions of old absinthe advertisements, a few of which I'd already seen in their original form at François Bezençon's distillery museum.

"I love the pictures. I love the creativity of the pre-ban era, the culture. It's incredible." He wanted to do the same thing himself, he said, with his brand, creating art and collectibles that related to the absinthe culture of today.

I asked him if the Fata fairy kneeling on the poster behind him was vomiting.

"No," he said. "She's just, uh, very thirsty."

While François Bezençon had made two kinds of absinthe for almost two decades, Grand had put out a variety of different recipes over the years, a business approach that matched his mile-a-minute approach to conversation. He wanted to have a YouTube channel, he said, and show different kinds of meals that used absinthe as a culinary ingredient. He didn't like that people sometimes said drinking absinthe could make you go crazy, because nobody said the same thing about ouzo, and ouzo and absinthe were very similar, and many people couldn't even tell them apart. Some French connoisseurs said the Swiss used too much anise and not enough wormwood in their recipes, and he didn't like that, but that was because of the amount of thujone in Swiss wormwood, and if they put in more, the spirit would surpass the legal limits. He grew his own wormwood, and he made me come outside to see the aromatic difference between a couple of the varieties that were dying in the cold. He was unhappy with the promotion of the Val-de-Travers region abroad, because the local tourism office had recently decided to stop using a logo with an absinthe fairy, and absinthe was the main thing the Val-de-Travers had going for it.

THE HOMELAND OF ABSINTHE

When I looked down at the recorder running on my phone, I calculated that he'd gone through twenty different topics of conversation in less than five minutes.

I tried to steer him back by asking what he remembered about absinthe's clandestine era. His father had owned a restaurant in the Val-de-Travers after moving from Lausanne, he said, where the family regularly returned to purchase food and drink from his previous suppliers. That allowed his father to help clandestine distillers source the alcohol they needed without attracting the attention of the authorities.

"When I was a kid, we went to Lausanne once a week to buy groceries, and we also bought alcohol for people here to distill, clandestine. Because if you buy alcohol here, everybody knows that you make absinthe. But if you buy it in another region, nobody knows."

Those distillers included La Martha, the legendary Martha Charrère, mother of the journalist and distiller Jean-Jacques Charrère, commonly known as Duvalon. Later, Grand was sometimes sent alone to pick up the finished product.

"I went once a week to buy absinthe from Martha Charrère. I remember how she opened the door, the old woman with this gray hair and cigarettes, and she always said, 'Hi, Little Grand. What do you want? You want absinthe? Come on in.'"

He had no interest in absinthe himself, he said, when he did his mandatory military service at the end of the 1980s, but everyone else in the Swiss Army asked if he could get them some once they learned he was from the Val-de-Travers. He usually brought canned absinthe back to his barracks, which camouflaged the spirit as would-be cans of peas and carrots. Other disguises were used for the drink's raw ingredients. To mask the strong scent of drying wormwood, many distillers kept their plants in the barn, he said, where the smells from their animals covered it up.

I asked him if he preferred the modern Swiss absinthe bleue or the classic verte, and he replied that he preferred bleue during the day and verte in the evening, with something special as a nightcap: his oak-aged absinthe, Grand No. 5.

He placed it on the table between us, a large square bottle with a square white label that parodied the traditional branding of Chanel No. 5 perfume. The liquid inside was brown, almost menacingly dark.

"This one is famous," I said. "I heard that Christian got a bunch of this one from you. He traded them for a couple of his pre-ban absinthes."

"Yeah," he said. "But those were fakes."

⋮

He'd come up with the idea for Grand No. 5 in the shower, he said, after having spotted one of his wife's perfume bottles on the shelf: its name matched up with his plan to add to his product line, which had just four absinthe recipes at the time. It was made in a sixty-liter French oak barrel, using a variation on the solera system used in sherry production: each time Grand made a new batch, he blended parts of it into barrels that contained different amounts of his previous batches, with every bottling including fractional shares from all the batches that had come before. When I sipped it, I got the bright, verdant aromas of a Swiss absinthe's typical anise and fennel, as well as the wormwood and a few other herbs. But it also had strong, oaky notes, and in that regard, it tasted more like whiskey or cognac than a great Swiss bleue, with pronounced tannic bitterness in the finish. It was bottled at a whiskey-like 45 percent alcohol, far less than the 65 percent of his verte, and he said he preferred to drink it without water, untroubled. When I tasted it, I couldn't imagine mistaking it for any other absinthe on the planet.

He hadn't known Christian as an online friend for long, he said, before Christian started contacting him through private messages, offering him pre-bans for sale, and asking repeatedly if he could buy Grand No. 5 in large quantities. Grand pulled up Christian's messages, and we read through them together. In one message, Christian said he didn't even need the bottles, just the liquid inside, which really felt like he was tipping his cards. In another, he suggested using the spirit in a blend to make something that tasted like a historic absinthe, taking one-third of Grand No. 5 with two-thirds of Grande blanche. He predicted that the resulting admixture would make for a "light, feuille morte, delicious absinthe," though he'd misspelled the French phrase and suggested the blend would be a "Grand Vintage," though I imagined "cuvée" would be more accurate, before he'd signed off with a winking emoji.

Grand frowned as he read through their conversations again. He pointed at the screen and shook his head.

"All the time he tries to sell me pre-ban absinthe. He started to be really direct."

In addition to pushing his own pre-ban bottles to Grand, Christian was practically begging for large quantities of Grand No. 5.

"He said to me, 'I would like to buy a barrel, one full barrel.'"

I was grateful to see the messages, if only because they made it clear that Grand had no idea what was going on with the forgeries at the time. For that matter, he wasn't at all interested in pre-ban bottles. When Christian asked him for five liters of Grand No. 5 in exchange for one pre-ban in 2017, Grand turned him down, writing, "You know that I'm not a fan of old absinthe."

Eventually, however, he relented, he said, trading an amount he couldn't remember—ten or fifteen bottles, he thought, though he wasn't sure—of Grand. No. 5 for two bottles of Christian's would-be pre-bans. He didn't care for it himself, but many of his absintheur pals were into it, and he imagined he might share those bottles with them. He couldn't remember what had happened to the other bottle, but one of the absinthes he'd received from Christian was on the shelf above us: a supposed pre-ban from an obscure nineteenth-century producer, Juillard & Babel. To my eyes, it looked convincing, but of course I knew very little about such collectibles.

After Christian had been publicly accused of fraud, Grand had followed up with him, asking to be reimbursed for the value of the bottles he'd sent. Christian sent him a rather self-righteous note in return, in which he admitted to making two forgeries, but claiming he'd never used any Grand No. 5 to make them.

> Hi Patrick, I'm just back on here after being kicked out of all the groups and heartbroken. I know my days in ab-sinthe are over after me selling two fake bottles, which I've since paid for on many levels and I'm sorry, but I've never done anything but enjoy the No. 5 that I PURCHASED from you. I have NEVER sold it on as something else. Let this be known: I absolutely owe you nothing.

At that point, the conversation ended. Like me, Grand had been blocked by Christian. It seemed like there was nothing else he could tell me.

⋮

I spent the next couple of days bouncing around, visiting distillers and trying to absorb more of the atmosphere. In the Maison de l'Absinthe, I'd seen a video in which the former moonshiner Francis Martin had admitted that he had been a "un clandestin" back in the day, before clarifying that he thought of it differently. "I prefer the term 'resistant,'" he said, making the act of distilling absinthe during its prohibition akin to fighting political oppression. The mountains and forests surrounding us certainly felt like a place for resistance fighters: the woods were dark and thick, with clouds frequently obscuring the tops of trees, though the wildly herbal scents from the forest were somehow always in the air.

That said, the story I was getting felt more ironic and humorous than oppressive or brutal: the people were not banned by the state from drinking alcohol, and in fact they'd often made their absinthe using alcohol they'd legally purchased from the Swiss government itself. As I understood it, they were also not banned from owning or growing wormwood plants, which thrived in the region, and of course anise and fennel were legal, too. But for ninety-five years they had been banned from producing, selling, or drinking legal alcohol with the flavors from those herbs in it. It was a ridiculous technicality that made no sense: all the ingredients that went into absinthe were legal. Combining them, however, was not.

In front of the Maison de l'Absinthe, I met the distiller Pierre-André Virgilio by chance, and took a picture of him in front of a delivery van bearing the name of his l'Herboriste absinthe, which echoed his previous career working as a druggist. In this part of Europe, druggists or pharmacists often prepared and sold herbal teas that people rely on as remedies, just as Americans turn to their boxes of antihistamines, decongestants, anti-inflammatories, eye-drops, and painkillers. I asked if he'd ever sold herbs to clandestine distillers during the interdiction.

"Oh yes, and in such quantities!" he said. "We sold anise by the ton back in those days."

I imagined that had to be an exaggeration, but I'd heard something similar on my previous visit from the distiller Christophe Racine, who owned the large absinthe shop at the main crossroads in Môtiers, not far from my bed and breakfast and just down the street from the museum. When I caught up with Racine again on my last afternoon in town, he told me that he'd done his training as an apprentice druggist with Pierre-André Virgilio. The Val-de-Travers was a close-knit place.

"We used to have a button on the cash register that said 'tisane,'" he recalled, using the French word for herbal tea. "When I first started my training, every single morning my job was to prepare sacks of herbs." By a "sack," he clarified, he meant a bag containing twenty kilograms of plant matter, or just under forty-five pounds. Every one of those sacks was sold as a tisane, or herbal tea. "It was pretty funny, because we sold tons of 'tisane,' but nobody drank tea."

He'd used his position at the drugstore to source the herbs for an uncle who distilled absinthe illegally and had started distilling on his own by the time he was seventeen, about a decade before the Swiss interdiction ended in 2005, even teaching some of the region's now-famous makers how to distill. He considered the ban of ninety-five years as "the era of research and development" for Swiss absinthe. The drink hadn't just survived the interdiction. It had blossomed.

"After the 1950s, absinthe really started to change. People began to put more herbs into it," he said. "In this valley, there were over 300 distillers. There was a lot of competition. Everybody wanted to have a standout absinthe. When you pass a recipe from father to son, the son starts to think that their recipe has stayed the same for twenty years, so maybe he should add his own touch to it."

With improved transportation, trade, and a better economy in the years after World War II, herbs and spices suddenly became much more affordable. "So he goes to discuss his recipe with a druggist or a pharmacist, and they tell him, 'Look, if you want it a little sweeter, you add licorice.' Before, we didn't have that, because it was expensive, but now we can use it. Or maybe someone else says, 'I would like it to be a little fresher.' So you can add coriander, to give it a lemony touch. We started to have a much wider range of taste. Recipes from before 1900 really started to change after 1950 or so."

Using an original recipe from his uncle and grandfather, Racine regularly produced one absinthe, La Fine du Clandestin, or "The Fine [Absinthe] of the Bootlegger," which aimed for a Swiss prohibition-era flavor profile, as well as modern recipes with even more herbal presence. Most of that, he said, came from the raw materials, especially when it came to the drink's namesake *Artemisia absinthium*.

He wheeled out a huge plastic barrel, and then brought out a small plate of what looked like dried grass. That plate contained modern pharmaceutical wormwood, he said, the same kind, usually sourced from Spain or Turkey, that had been purchased by distillers at pharmacies in the clandestine era. He told me to smell it. It had almost no aroma, just a hint of bitterness and some grassy notes.

He pulled the lid off the barrel.

"Now try this. It's the Swiss wormwood we use today."

Even without lowering my head, I was dizzyingly overwhelmed. An intense herbal aroma surrounded me, jungle-thick and somewhat sweet, like the aftertaste from a gulp of absinthe that was filling my head with the vapors of a dream.

He nodded at my reaction.

"Absinthe has changed."

⋮

Racine said he had very little interest in absinthe's Belle Époque era and he didn't buy old bottles, spoons, or labels himself. He did collect old alembics, or stills, and admitted that he was much more interested in the Swiss prohibition era than the many years of legal production that had come before it, having heard hundreds of stories about clandestine distillers before he'd joined his grandfather and uncle in the hobby. Prohibition in the United States had been the background for dozens of movies, he noted, but there were no movies set during the prohibition of absinthe in the Val-de-Travers. There were a few video interviews with former clandestine distillers playing on a loop in the Maison de l'Absinthe, but there still wasn't a single book about them, despite the abundance of great tales, like the time a distiller who had been brought to court told the judge that he would be a little late delivering the "liters" the judge had ordered from him.

"There was a time when the police confiscated a bunch of stills. They made a big raid on several distillers and put all the stills in a container at the railway station and locked the gates," he said. "The stills were scheduled to leave the station the next morning. So at night, a few people went to the station, picked the locks, and took their stills back."

One of the area's most famous bootleggers went by the nickname Le Teub.

"He was an ambulance driver, the very first ambulance in the Val-de-Travers. He put the absinthe in the ambulance, turned on the siren, and he could deliver absinthe wherever he wanted. He drove right past the customs and tax officers to buy alcohol with his sirens blaring."

He recalled how his grandparents had drunk absinthe in the stone cellar where they butchered rabbits, right next to where they kept their alembic.

"When they drank absinthe, he would open the cellar tap for ten or fifteen minutes, so that the water was quite cold. They drank out of the large glasses they used for lemonade. They didn't have an absinthe fountain, and they didn't have specific glasses. It was more about the moment."

He knew many families who made absinthe when he was growing up. Sometimes the kids didn't quite get the meaning of what was going on, especially the code words adults used in that era. When he was about ten, one of his friends had answered the phone. A man had asked if his father was home. The boy said no.

"Okay," the man replied. "Tell your father that tomorrow I'm coming to pick up some milk from the *génisse*." A génisse, or heifer, is a cow that hasn't had a calf yet, which meant that meant that it couldn't give milk. "And the little boy said, 'No, no, you're saying nonsense. Heifers don't have milk.' The man told him to tell his father anyway. And when his father came home, the boy said, 'Daddy, someone called for you, but he was crazy.'"

Cafés, he remembered, often served absinthe in glasses made from Bakelite, the most common of which were for Ovomaltine, a

Swiss kids' beverage rebranded as "Ovaltine" when it was brought over to the United States. That led to people simply ordering "an Ovomaltine" or "an Ovomaltine from the region" when they went out for a drink.

To my ears, it sounded like an entire culture of its own, clearly standing apart from the absinthe of Belle Époque Paris. It had its language and traditions, its own heroes and legends, like the tall man from Geneva who'd given Racine a huge tip when he'd first started his training as a druggist at the age of fifteen.

"He showed up in this enormous Mercedes, just gigantic, the kind of car you never saw around here back then. He told me to put the alcohol and the herbs in his trunk, and then he pulled out his wallet and gave me 100 francs. At the time, my salary was 300 francs a month. I was shocked. And then the man said, 'You're going to learn something here. I've been making absinthe for twenty years. I got caught and I had to pay a fine, in installments. Officially, I don't have any money, and I'm not paying anything toward my fine. I'm having a great life. And I'm still making absinthe.' When you're fifteen years old, that kind of thing hits you pretty hard."

I took as many notes about the clandestine era as I could while Racine recounted his stories. I was researching a book, I told him, which was partially about absinthe in general, but mostly about a man who had made a bunch of counterfeit pre-bans a few years earlier.

"Oh, I know something about that," he said. "The Englishman."

To my surprise, he'd learned about the forgeries through the former bootlegger Jean-Jacques Charrère, aka DuVallon, the son of La Martha. I'd never seen anyone connect the names Jean-Jacques

Charrère or DuVallon to Christian, but Racine was certain that Charrère had said he had been used by the absinthe forger Christian, without being aware of the frauds. Charrère had passed away a while earlier, so there was no way I could follow up with him myself, but Racine promised to try to find their old messages.

:

A pair of customers entered the store, so I moved away from the counter to let Racine ring up their orders. They were two young men in their early twenties, familiarly stocky and square-jawed in a way that most of the folks I'd met in the Val-de-Travers were not. I could see that they had both chosen bottles of La Fine du Clandestin, and when I heard them ask to pay by card in English, I pointed out that they were buying their absinthe from the very man who made it.

"We know, that's why we came here," the first one said.

They drove off, and Racine explained: a Czech factory regularly sent its employees to an associated business in the Val-de-Travers for training. When I stuck my head out, I saw a Škoda Octavia with Prague license plates pulling away in the traditional Czech style of driving: as if the driver had just robbed a bank. The Czech trainees in the region regularly bought absinthe from his shop, he said—another small connection between my adopted country and the drink's homeland.

Other customers entered the store during our conversation, usually buying a few bottles at a time. Most people just bought a bottle every few months, Racine said. It wasn't something people drank every day, and it wasn't a drink you would enjoy alone. It was meant to be enjoyed in company, with friends, which meant that it should be reserved for special occasions. Considering my experiences in Prague, I wondered if the visiting Czech workers in the Val-de-Travers felt the same way.

⋮

I had a much better sense of the valley and its residents now, as well as how Swiss absinthe had survived. I had even learned a few things about Christian, but there was still one more thing I wanted to see before catching my train back home. When I asked him for directions, Racine glanced down, quickly judged my hiking boots ("Ah oui, sans problème") and told me to follow the road in front of his shop out of town. I should be able to hear it, he said, and I would find it that way.

Following the road, I saw signs for new distillers whose names I didn't recognize, as well as an information board detailing Jean-Jacques Rousseau's time in the town. I passed a public fountain as large as a Jacuzzi, its corners and edges worn down by time, with a barely legible inscription crediting its construction to the beneficence of some king or other. Barns and stables along the way made the air heavy with manure, hay, and the wild scent of animal life—perfect, I realized, for hiding the perfume of drying wormwood or the heavy air from an alembic.

As the road climbed outside of the village, the landscape opened up, revealing the height of the mountains that surrounded us. Heavy white clouds rested among the treetops, pale white like the louche in a glass of absinthe, the dark green of the forests as deep and mysterious as antique glass. I passed the small electrical power plant Racine had mentioned and turned onto the path that followed the small stream that headed off the left, focusing on the far-off sound that was distant but still somehow deafening.

The creek next to the trail was only a yard or so wide, its fast-moving waters so clear they were nearly blue, and after a while I crossed it on a small footbridge with a protective handrail on one side. There the muddy trail climbed higher into the hills, following a large yellow blaze marked every so often onto pine trees, leading toward the rushing sound of the waterfall I couldn't see.

I'd been enjoying the reverie of time alone on a small trail through a thick forest, but the sound of footsteps approaching roused me from my thoughts. Running toward me was an elderly woman, to go by the contours of her face, though her pace and grace in motion was far better than mine: even moving quickly, she was sure on her feet, despite the slipperiness of the trail, and when she replied to my "bonjour" in kind she was clearly much less out of breath than I was, even though I was walking slowly. Like a deer through the woods, she was gone in an instant, and I began climbing up the lumber-reinforced steps that had been terraced into the hillside like flower boxes.

By this point, the roar was deafening, and the steps climbed alongside a steep runoff stream from the cataract. I noticed other markers, brassy-gold ovals bearing a few lines of script, cemented into the ground every few meters, the last of which said "So far from you" in French, not far from the small, shallow pool at the bottom of the waterfall.

It fell from high above, more than a hundred feet up, hitting the rocks at several points on the way down, turning into a milky foam before it emptied at my feet. On the far side of the pool, a cave entrance offered a refuge in the rocks, while the mist of falling water thickened the air around me.

There might not be a fountain of youth, but it felt like there must be something in the water or the air here, something that made the plants that grew here somehow different than elsewhere. Over eons, uncountable volumes of herbs like grand wormwood, veronica, and pontica had all grown from this source, before dying and decomposing into the geological strata that later served as its filter. At the foot of the waterfall, I could smell the resiny scents of the pine forest, as well as a trace of floral and herbal notes, strange and unrecognizable. I moved toward the runoff stream, knelt toward the flowing water and scooped some into my hand.

Its temperature surprised me, far colder than I'd imagined, and my hand shook slightly as I raised it to my lips. I had expected sweetness, but that was wrong: the taste of the water was more elemental, without a hint of sweet or salt, with no trace of minerality or vegetation, so delicious and refreshing that I immediately plunged my hand back into the frozen waters and tried it again. It felt like I was tasting something real, in its purest and most original form.

CHAPTER
6

THE ABSINTHE
UNDERGROUND

Can you understand the happiness I get out of my absinthe?
I yearn for it; and when I drink it I savor every drop, and
afterwards I feel my soul swimming in ineffable happiness.
—W. SOMERSET MAUGHAM

I f it were true, as Christian had told me, that he had been collecting absinthe for twenty-seven years, that meant that he would
have been part of the global absinthe underground before the
drink became legal again in Switzerland in 2005, ahead of its sub-
sequent return to polite society in France and the United States. I'd
heard that the culture at the time was fun and clubhouse-wild, especially in places where the drink was still illegal.

Cary René Bonnecaze was part of the stateside underground
scene around the time when I was legally drinking Hill's no-E

Absinth in Prague and subsequently imagining that I'd looked at my own brain. A drummer, Cary was a founding member of the Baton Rouge alternative band Better Than Ezra, though he'd since left the group around the time he'd gotten into absinthe and its antiques in New Orleans around the turn of the millennium—several years before U.S. consumers could legally buy the drink again in 2007. I called him a few days after my return from the Val-de-Travers, asking what the New Orleans absinthe scene was like in those days. His initial recollection was a dimly lit dive on a quiet street in the French Quarter that had a secret sign to let insiders know when illicit absinthe was available.

"They used to have a candle behind the bar," he said. "When they were serving absinthe, the candle was lit—it was like 'The coast is clear.' If it was not lit, we would basically just walk right by, because there would be a cop in there or something. It was just such a weird time. No one knew what kind of trouble you could get into."

At the time, gray-market bottles were regularly coming in from Europe. Newspaper articles noted that European absinthe was widely available in the United States, though still illegal. I was going back to the States at least once a year at that point, and I often brought a bottle of Hill's with me to impress—or, effectively, poison—my friends in California.

In 2000, Cary launched his antique store, Vive la France, on Royal Street in the French Quarter, selling original homewares and reproductions with a French flair. As he built up his own collection of absinthe paraphernalia, he started selling more and more material related to the drink, eventually creating a shop inside Vive la France that he called La Maison de l'Absinthe, whose popularity eventually caused it to subsume Vive la France entirely. Its success was probably due to its location a few blocks from the famous Old Absinthe House on Bourbon Street. Talking to Cary, I guessed that another part of its success was due to his own enthusiasm for the drink's culture and history. His voice was sweet and southern-slow, the vocal equivalent of a sugary aperitif you'd want to sip in small doses. As he talked, he apologized for jumping from subject to subject, though to my ear his conversational leaps seemed spaced out and languid, like those of a lazy bullfrog.

"The whole thing of it just being so forbidden, that was the exciting part for me," he said. "The whole joy for me just always centered around one thing, and that was the antiques. It was so crazy to own something that someone used in drinking absinthe so long ago."

As Cary got further into spoons, glasses, and fountains, he spent more and more time online, mostly just as a reader, on websites like the Wormwood Society. It wasn't just interesting that absinthe was semi- or even completely illegal at the time. There was also a huge amount of education going on, as absintheurs began to piece together basic knowledge about the drink. Most of the world had banned absinthe for a century, which meant that many elements from absinthe culture had to be rediscovered, relearned, and understood anew. If it wasn't supposed to be lit on fire, how was quality absinthe really supposed to be served? How do you correctly use an absinthe spoon? That information was only just coming out, and much of it was being shared online.

"You have to realize that no one alive today was alive back in the day during absinthe, much less drinking it," he said. "Even for collectors and people who have been around the block, there's no one who's able to say, 'This is how it was done.'"

A good example was the small device called a *balancier,* a popular Belle Époque collectible that you could find on French eBay or Le Bon Coin, a French announcements site. Collectors understood that a balancier—also known as an *auto-verseur,* meaning "self-pourer," as well as sometimes called a "see-saw" in English—was a small vessel that was supposed to sit on top of a glass of absinthe and dribble two streams of cold water into the spirit in a hypnotic, tick-tock rhythm in order to trouble the drink and create the louche. At the time, the popular understanding was that a balancier should be placed above an absinthe spoon holding a sugar cube, the cone-shaped reservoir should be filled with ice and water, and one of the balancier's two streams of water should be directed to drip onto the sugar cube. Only that's probably not how it was used in its heyday.

It was Eric, an active French absinthe collector and dealer, who shared the correct procedure. The original balanciers were made of metal, and thus relatively indestructible. And while Belle Époque magazines might have focused on how the beau monde in Paris loved its absinthe, those articles almost always omitted details on how the drink was served. Eventually, however, Eric uncovered an antique balancier, still in its original packaging, which contained instructions on how to use it. In the golden age of absinthe, they didn't put an absinthe spoon and sugar cube under a balancier.

"It actually specifically says that the sugar goes inside of the cone," Cary said.

The online absinthe community grew busier, as did the underground settings where gray-market absinthe was being served stateside. As a seller of absinthe paraphernalia, Cary could clearly see where the drink was most popular at the time: in Seattle, San Francisco, New York, and New Orleans.

"Looking through our sales and our most popular target cities, those were the main places that people drank absinthe," he said. "But all of a sudden, just before it became legal, all of a sudden it started to blow up, and a *lot* of other people flooded in."

Many of the new arrivals suffered from misinformation, he remembers.

"At some point, everyone getting into it thought it made you go crazy. That was part of the lore."

Thanks to his business, Cary got a small, advanced warning about the coming legalization of absinthe in the United States. In addition to retail sales, his company La Maison d'Absinthe also offered bulk purchasers the chance to buy branded versions of its reproductions that showed off a product logo or the name of their restaurant or café. After a heads-up phone call from fellow Louisianan Ted Breaux, Cary started to receive massive orders for absinthe spoons and other reproductions bearing the brand name Lucid, which didn't exist on the market at the time; a Google search he did turned up absolutely nothing. But then in May 2007, Breaux's partners at Viridian spirits introduced Lucid, which they called the first legal and authentic absinthe to be sold in the United States since World War I. It was correctly made with grand worm-wood using one of the recipes that Breaux, a former chemist, had pieced together through his own research, distilled in France on a traditional copper alembic at Distillerie Combier, an 1834 distill-ery that was "literally a museum," according to a wildly popular curtain-raiser profile in *The New Yorker* the previous year. Lucid got around the legal regulations of the federal Bureau of Alcohol, Tobacco, Firearms, and Explosives, it was said, by producing an *Artemisia absinthium*–based spirit that had less than ten milligrams of thujone per liter, which effectively counted as thujone-free. And of course, it didn't hurt matters that absinthe had already returned to legal status in other countries that competed with the United States in terms of trade.

As absinthe gained a newly legal buzz, its popularity blossomed.

In 2007 alone, *The New York Times* ran articles devoted to absinthe in its Arts, Fashion, Your Money, and Food sections, with many more pieces—including reviews and tasting notes—over the next two years. A new generation of collectors was born, and prices for absinthe antiques shot up, especially among buyers in the United States. A traditional absinthe spoon with a wormwood-leaf pattern has long been a bestseller at Cary's shop, in the form of an $8 stainless-steel reproduction of the nineteenth-century antique, or a gold-plated version for $14. But in 2007, a particularly sought-after original antique spoon sold in one of the online groups for more than $5,000.

The culture was swooning. Absinthe was hot. New fans were joining the groups daily. People were just starting to find things and learn how they were supposed to be used, after the world had lost that knowledge for almost a hundred years.

"It was awesome," he said.

⋮

In his telling, Cary was really an absinthe collector and not really a drinker, more interested in the accoutrements and paraphernalia than the once-banned spirit that had inspired it. When he spoke, it was hard to tell if he remembered being happiest when he received an antique he'd ordered, or while he was waiting for that package to

arrive, tracking its journey toward him online. He described opening a newly arrived antique as a high far beyond that of a kid a
Christmas.

"I bought a lot," he said. "I have a *huge* collection."

Vintage posters, fountains, glasses, and balanciers: he bought
them all. Multiple copies of any antiques—a second Absinthe
Terminus advertising poster in near-new condition, a third or
fourth Pontarlier glass from the nineteenth century—could go on
to brighten his shelves in the French Quarter, at least for a minute.

"Anything that I had extras of in my collection, I would sell at
the store, and we sold those like crazy," he said. "You cannot find
almost any absinthe antiques in the U.S."

Even American-made absinthe collectibles—the few original
antiques that were known to have been made before the ban—were
extremely hard to find in their country of origin. One of Cary's
trophy purchases, he told me, was one of only two known copies
of a pre-ban spoon made for New York's legendary Café Lafayette.
Although it had been produced by Reed & Barton, a silversmith
founded in Massachusetts in 1824, Cary had to buy the spoon from
a dealer in Europe.

At that time he was primarily focused on antiques and not the
spirit itself, but eventually Cary started buying pre-bans as well.
About half of those, he said, ended up coming from Christian.

"He approached me a few times, just to let me know that he's
got some samples of this or that," he said. "The funny thing is that
I was *the* perfect target for him."

That was because of the way he approached and appreciated
pre-ban absinthe, he explained. Unlike many absinthe fans, Cary

didn't particularly enjoy opening historic bottles. When I sipped my
first pre-ban at the Guy distillery, my pupils dilated and my pulse
raced as my mind toyed with the idea that I was possibly drinking
the same spirit that Oscar Wilde or Pablo Picasso might have tasted.
But for Cary, an intact pre-ban bottle was the thing in itself: a pristine, perfect-condition antique to be enjoyed visually. The way he
saw it, opening an old bottle basically ruined it.

"All of my pre-ban bottles, I've never opened one. Because the
way I look at it is, if you open a bottle, it's dead. I can drink it—I
can share it with friends and I love the fact if that we're drinking
something that's a hundred and twenty or a hundred and fifty years
old, but to me, it's dead. Right now, it's living, when it's closed with
the original cork and everything. I absolutely love that."

That obsessive respect for the sealed bottle was extended even
to the parted-out, shot-sized samples that Cary first started buying
from Christian. But he didn't just pick up the small samples. He
soon progressed to buying full pre-ban bottles: some from Christian,
some from other dealers. The nature of seeing a historic bottle as
its own aesthetic object, independent of whatever spirit was sealed
inside it, meant that he didn't seem to differentiate between the
two groups of bottles, not even during our call, several years after
he realized that he'd been defrauded. When I asked how many pre-
bans he owned, he said "about twenty-five." When I asked if that
included the ones from Christian, he corrected himself and said that
he had about a dozen.

In hindsight, he said, his compulsion to buy new bottles might
have helped the community finally start following Christian's sales.
Cary believed that Christian kept offering rarer and rarer finds to

catch his eye. But it was the rareness of those claimed discoveries that also made a small group of absinthe collectors start to wonder how Christian could possibly turn up such obscure bottles. They included a legendary French absinthe dealer by the name of Patrick Roussel, as well as Eric, neither of whom had ever seen many of the bottles that Christian claimed to have found.

"He was coming up with so many different absinthes," Cary said. "He knew I was going to buy them. It's just the collector side of me."

⋮

Christian might have paid special attention to Cary, but he gave his time to just about every aspect of the underground absinthe scene in that era, a popular member of most of the major absinthe groups and websites. He attended real-life festivals, like the Fête de l'Absinthe in the Val-de-Travers, and at the Absinthiades in Pontarlier, where he and I eventually met. He even showed up at bar events in London whenever Ted Breaux was in town promoting his absinthe Jade. Pretty much all the collectors, Cary says, trusted Christian, at least initially.

"Everyone that I could possibly think of, we've all bought absinthe from Christian," he says. "I mean he was as well liked and as well known as anyone."

From an earlier conversation, I knew that Cary had been hurt by the betrayal of someone he'd always considered a friend, and I didn't want to plumb that wound more than I needed to. Instead I asked him one last time about the absinthe underground, when people were finding rare antiques and figuring out how they were used. It was a period with a lot of very positive vibes, he said.

"I guess you could compare it to the U.S. in the 1950s, you know? Everything was wonderful after the war. It was a good time. There was a bit of creativity in everyone. And no one ever thought that that you would have someone come in and just lie and forge these things."

THE PALAZZO CACHE

In his right hand he held a small tumbler; the wan light filtering in through the ground glass of the door fell upon its cloudy green contents, giving them a strange, unearthly gleam.

—M.E.M. DAVIS

As I started piecing together these two stories—how Christian had created his forgeries and how the absinthe community had figured that out—I heard several references to something called the Palazzo Cache, always divorced of any backstory or context, like a local bogeyman or village ghost whose existence was so widely accepted that it required no explanation. Like many ghost stories, the name was often spoken in a lowered voice, as if the speaker didn't want any outsiders to hear about it. After hearing it mentioned so often, however quietly, I wanted to learn more. What I didn't understand was how difficult that might be.

Most absintheurs seemed to agree that the Palazzo Cache comprised some thirty—or perhaps fifty, or maybe even over a hundred—bottles of Pernod Fils, and possibly other absinthes, dating from before the ban ended production in France in 1915. They were discovered in the cellar of a palazzo, possibly while it was under reconstruction, somewhere in the north of Italy. The palazzo itself was never named, and indeed no absintheurs even claimed to know its true location, but the consensus held that it was a former hotel which had welcomed artists and bons vivants from across Europe in the late nineteenth and early twentieth centuries. Bottles from the cache and related finds were an important part of the absinthe collector market for several years, peaking between 2012 and 2016, after which they seemed to have disappeared, leaving a hole that was often recalled with what seemed to be a sense of mourning.

Whenever I asked absintheurs about the Palazzo Cache, everyone seemed afraid of saying too much. The picture that emerged was cloudy, composed of shadows and half-formed images that hinted at other characters, different locations, and earlier activities outside the frame. No one seemed willing to share verifiable details, which I found frustrating. But as I pieced together the story, I realized that there was a good reason for that. What most people didn't know was that the first reports of a cache from a palazzo in Italy started much earlier, beginning with a short post on an Italian absinthe forum in the fall of 2006.

⋮

"Ciao, ragazzi. I found some old absinthe. How can I go about selling it?"

That was the first message posted by Sergio, a newly registered user on an Italian absinthe forum, in late 2006. One of those who immediately responded was Stefano Rossoni, an enthusiast who would later go on to become famous in the absinthe world for distilling his own vintage-inspired spirits, including two highly revered recipes, L'Italienne and La Grenouille. In private messages, Sergio confirmed to Stefano exactly what was under discussion: a large, unopened bottle of absinthe, apparently dating from before the ban. The two agreed to meet in person, along with a man called Eugenio, a dealer and collector then considered the premier absinthe connoisseur in all of Italy. Sergio said he was coming from Trieste, at the very edge of the country's northeastern border, though there was some mention of Venice as well; the locations seemed to be kept vague on purpose. With Stefano located in Brescia and Eugenio in nearby Mantova, both in north-central Italy, they chose a spot midway between Brescia and Venice: a bar called Tres Deseos in Verona, where they met one Saturday in late 2006.

Instead of just one pre-ban bottle, Sergio showed up with two: a one-liter bottle of Pernod Fils and a tiny, 375-milliliter bottle of Gustave Déchanet Fils. Pernod Fils is, of course, the most famous absinthe brand of all time. Déchanet is pretty obscure, even among connoisseurs.

Eugenio confirmed that the two bottles were genuine, originating from before the 1915 ban. Admiring them, Stefano asked where they had come from. Sergio told him that he ran a business that cleaned out old houses and cellars and resold valuable bottles, usually wine.

"Sergio said he found those two absinthe bottles in a cellar somewhere in a northeastern city—I want to say Udine or Pordenone," Stefano recalled. "He knew they were valuable, but he had no idea what they were really worth."

That part made sense to me: Udine and Pordenone have famous Venetian palaces. The prices they decided upon in Verona were way out of whack, however: just 300 euros for the small Déchanet, or about $350, Stefano said, and only 600 euros for the large Pernod. Despite his interest, the two bottles didn't go home with him. Eugenio was literally in his element: the dingy bar Tres Deseos was a client of his spirits business. Perhaps because of that, or because of his status as the country's premier absinthe expert, Eugenio insisted on buying both bottles himself, which Stefano still seemed to regret. A short while later, Eugenio reported that he'd sold them on to David Nathan-Maister, a London-based absinthe dealer and the author of *The Absinthe Encyclopedia*.

Those bottles were the first hints of what would later become known as the Palazzo Cache, though I found out later that some connoisseurs only use that term for a very specific subset of Italian-sourced bottles. As more bottles from the Palazzo Cache and related troves came to the surface, weird new details about their origin were unearthed with them.

⋮

A few months after the meeting in Verona, Sergio emailed Stefano. This time he included a startling list of pre-ban bottles he was offering for sale, ranging from well-known brands like Pernod Fils and Edouard Pernod to rare marques like Gempp Pernod, Jules Pernod, Premier Fils, and Absinthe Cusenier Oxygénée. They were said to have been found in the cellar of a bar in Venice.

"Sergio said that it was kind of a miracle that the bottles were in such good shape, considering that the cellar was below water level," Stefano said.

Having apparently been appraised of the true value of historic bottles by Eugenio and Nathan-Maister, Sergio was looking to sell these new bottles for something closer to the regular retail price: 1,500 to 1,700 euros each, or about $2,000 to $2,300 at the time, depending on the brand. Perhaps remembering what had happened at the bar in Verona, he wanted to offer Stefano the first shot at them.

Though sorely tempted, Stefano wasn't comfortable buying unverified historic bottles at anything close to retail prices. He passed, thinking he'd never see them again. But the next year, he was able to taste samples of pre-ban Gempp Pernod and Jules Pernod from bottles that Nathan-Maister brought to that year's Fête de l'Absinthe, the summer absinthe festival in the Val-de-Travers. At the time, he was sure that those samples were the ones that Sergio had offered him a year earlier.

"The Jules Pernod was phenomenal," Stefano said. "One of the best pre-bans I tasted."

⋮

Sergio wasn't the only crepuscular character involved with the Palazzo Cache. As word spread about the bottles coming out of Italy, a woman who called herself Alessandra began reaching out to users on English-language absinthe forums, offering new bottles for sale from the collection. She introduced herself as Sergio's girlfriend, adding that she was helping him with the sales. Some of the bottles she wanted to sell were decorated with artwork—small sketches and drawings. The hotel with the absinthe collection, she explained, had welcomed artists, writers, and other cultural figures, who had enjoyed its well-stocked cellar. Sometimes those artists made sketches that were then glued onto various bottles. One of the decorated bottles was reported to have been bought by Nathan-Maister. Another was bought by Mira Müller, a Swiss collector who befriended Alessandra, at least to a degree. I knew Mira tangentially from some of the private absinthe groups, where we had a handful of mutual friends. When I reached out, she agreed to tell me about the Palazzo Cache, and we scheduled a call one evening in early winter. Throughout the call, she spoke slowly, as if she were choosing quite carefully what she wanted to reveal.

"The story goes that the hotel that ordered all the absinthe from Pernod Fils did so because they were frequented by lots of artists," she said. "They partied, discussed, drank lots of absinthes, and some of the drawings were put on some absinthe bottles and stored in the cellar."

Mira only briefly mentioned the art-decorated bottles, as if she didn't want to share too much. Instead, she gave me a typically fuzzy outline of what the Palazzo Cache might contain, which only added to my interest.

"It's a bit mysterious, because the seller was quite anonymous," she said.

By "the seller," she did not mean Alessandra and Sergio, who only had access to an old hotel in Venice, which was regularly flooded by water from the lagoon. She meant the owners, though she wouldn't tell me exactly who they were. "It's owned by a very rich family, and Alessandra had personal contact [with] them, and they went there from time to time to search the cellar for valuable bottles and sold them."

When I asked her if she had any idea why the family sold them so secretively, she laughed.

"Yes. There are some speculations."

She wouldn't go further, though I imagined many people might have assumed tax evasion or the involvement of organized crime, to say nothing of a famously wealthy family's entirely justifiable desire for privacy. For that matter, it could be that the family member who was selling off the bottles wasn't in fact authorized to do so, or even that the property wasn't the family's to begin with. If you thought about it, you could come up with dozens of reasons, and none of them got you any closer to knowing where the palazzo was or which family owned it.

Alessandra and Sergio had started out selling historic absinthe, she said, by offering dealers like Eric their vintage bottles, which they had initially sourced from old hotels close to Italy's border with Austria. That corresponded with Stefano Rossoni's comment about the first bottles hailing from Udine or Pordenone. However, Alessandra and Sergio weren't happy with the lowball prices the established absinthe dealers wanted to pay. When Alessandra discovered the bottles that came to be known as the Palazzo Cache, she decided to sell them directly, without going through dealers like Eric. In the closed community of absinthe collectors, that wasn't easy.

"Nobody knew her and she didn't have a reputation," Mira said. In addition, some of Alessandra's former business partners threw up roadblocks, writing in a private forum post that it was probably just a scam, and not authentic pre-ban absinthe.

"She had a real hard time selling the bottles," she said. "But they were real."

Part of the doubt stemmed from the bottles themselves. All the Palazzo Cache bottles contained just one kind of spirit: pre-ban Pernod Fils, dating from right before production ended. But instead of a standard Pernod Fils bottle with an embossed stamp in the glass, bottles from the Palazzo Cache were just standard Italian wine bottles, with no "Pernod Fils" stamp. Bizarrely, each was fitted with an authentic Pernod Fils cork that appeared to be sealed with the distillery's own wax. Perhaps because of the coming illegality of its product, the theory went, the Pernod Fils distillery had offered the hotel its absinthe in bulk, as well as the wax and corks. Even though they were just wine bottles without labels, Mira said, they all looked beautiful, often covered with what looked like a century's worth of sediment.

"They were so pretty. There was a lot of residue—ash or dust—on the bottles. As soon as you saw a bottle, you instantly knew it was from the Palazzo Cache."

Mira believed that the Palazzo Cache contained around sixty bottles in total. She had purchased a few herself, and tasted several others. Each was remarkable.

"At first, right when you opened it, it was really, really wonderful." She laughed. "I'm not all that keen on absinthe, to be honest—it's the story that interests me. But this was really nice. On one side, it was clearly an old absinthe. On the other side, it was remarkably fresh, with a lot of aroma and floral notes. But it also very quickly disappeared—once the bottle was opened, you had to drink it quickly. It didn't get better."

The antique refilled wine bottles of Pernod Fils were sometimes sold at fire-sale prices. The least Mira paid Alessandra for a Palazzo Cache bottle was 500 euros.

"Somehow she needed money, and she needed it really fast. She was almost desperate, so she sold it for much less than she could have if she had listed it on eBay. This was very strange."

I asked if she knew why, or if she knew more about the Italian family, but I got no response. Instead, she said that it might be a good idea for me to talk to others and get back to her.

"You will hear a lot of guesswork," she said. "It's quite a complicated story. Lots of things are very unclear—like why, for example, they never told their real name."

⋮

The first bottles that emerged from the Palazzo Cache made big waves in the absinthe community, like any bottle of pre-ban absinthe. When a find was purchased and delivered, buyers often shared photographs in private online groups. Some bottles, like most of those Cary purchased, were left intact. Others were opened and enjoyed, often shared among various friends, either in person or remotely, sent via post or other delivery services. While an average one-liter bottle—containing 1,000 milliliters, or about thirty-five ounces—might cost some 2,000 euros (about $2,700 at the time), a small sample from that bottle could be much more affordable: a fifty-milliliter (or 1.75-ounce) shot might go for as little as 100 euros, a proportional price per volume, if the sharer was feeling generous, though prices occasionally went as high as 300 or 400 euros.

People who knew Christian remembered sharing several samples with him from the Palazzo Cache and other historic bottles that they had purchased: fifty milliliters of pre-ban Pernod Fils from here, 100 milliliters of Gempp Pernod from there, followed by others as they became available. They would arrive in the small dark apothecary bottles preferred by the absinthe community, often with a handwritten label that specified the year and maker, tucked inside a well-padded envelope or small box delivered by Royal Mail or FedEx. Many samples were labelled "Palazzo" or "P. C.," as if that alone guaranteed the sample's authenticity and provenance.

⋮

Although Mira had mentioned the decorated bottles that Alessandra had sold in addition to the Palazzo Cache bottles, I had never heard anyone else say anything about them. A few weeks later, however, Mira reached out to ask how my research into the Palazzo Cache was going. After we exchanged a few messages, she offered to send a picture of her purchase.

It was a large bottle of J. François Pernot Absinthe, still sealed with its original wax, the liquid level having settled well into the bottle's shoulder due to evaporation. Instead of a normal J. François Pernot label, a fading piece of paper had been glued to the glass. On it was an Expressionist-style sketch, apparently in charcoal, depicting a man smoking a cigarette and looking forlornly off to his right. The paper was torn and worn in parts, with beautiful browning and discoloration. At the top I could see a few words in script.

"The artist is Ernst Ludwig Kirchner," Mira said. "The drawing is a self-portrait."

A founder of the group Die Brücke, or The Bridge, Ernst Ludwig Kirchner had helped launch the Expressionist movement. Today, his works are held in museums like the Guggenheim, the Pinakothek der Moderne, and the National Gallery of Art. When I zoomed in on the handwriting at the top of the bottle, next to a couple of holes and the foxing of more than a century, I could see what clearly seemed to be his signature.

⋮

Of course, the Palazzo Cache was not the only source of historic bottles. Adrian Mørk, a painter and absinthe lover from Trollheim, Norway—literally, "the home of trolls"—became obsessed with buying vintage absinthes, including Palazzo Cache bottles. Following a tip from Mira, I reached out to him. I first located his website, which includes a gallery of his paintings—some quite good, though dreamy and fantasy-inspired—and an email address. He blew off our first arranged interview, but eventually we worked out our schedules and managed to talk about collecting historic absinthe on the phone. In a way, absinthe really did lead to insanity, he said.

"I spent more or less all my money for a few years," he said. "As soon as I got started, I got hooked. I did go a little crazy for a little while."

His method was to scour auction sites in various countries. In part, he was trying to find bargains, since small historic samples from established dealers felt too expensive, with a small sample of 1/20 of the bottle's volume sometimes costing as much as 1/5 of the price of a full bottle. And the full bottles were not cheap.

"If you go to a reputable source, usually you would pay from $1,800 to $3,500 per bottle," he said. "But if you go rogue and you start searching and try to stumble across something from an auction . . . Well, I ended up spending less than half for most of my bottles. It's a bit more of a risk on your own, because you have to be sure that you're buying something legitimate."

One of his best finds hadn't come from an auction—or even from a place that is normally associated with absinthe. Instead, he scored a true rarity, a pre-ban bottle of Legler-Pernod White

Absinthe, hidden inside a wall in an old house in Massachusetts. It was a rare uncolored blanche, a forerunner of the modern Swiss bleue style, from before 1915.

"I stumbled across it from a guy running a blog about renovating houses," he said. "I was lucky stumbling across it, because his blog wasn't about bottles or anything like that, it was a renovation blog. So was just like a random update: 'Hey, I found some bottles.' I sent him an email asking if he wanted to sell."

Mørk's collection included several other obscure bottles, including an example of a pre-ban Pernod Fils that was damaged during World War II.

"There's an article or chapter on it in most of the absinthe history books. After the ban, I think there were some 6,000 bottles that were shipped to the Netherlands. What happened was the Allies bombed the building and all the bottles were destroyed, except for just a few. And I managed to stumble across one of them. I have no idea what it's worth, because I own the only bottle I know of in existence that is still intact."

He rarely used eBay, he said, because so many of its users were specifically looking for absinthe. Instead, he found success by haunting smaller, regional auction sites in places like Portugal and Spain.

"I did end up finding quite a lot of bottles, but I was looking in the same places where the pros were looking. I even met them in passing. As in, if I lost an auction, I would see the same bottle end up on their sites."

He had held or seen some twenty bottles from the Palazzo Cache and had tasted at least six of them. All, he said, were impeccable.

⋮

Perhaps because of the way Stefano Rossoni had explained the origins of the Palazzo Cache, I had a bad habit of thinking of—and sometime referring to—all historic bottles from Italy as Palazzo Cache bottles, including those from brands other than Pernod Fils. For her part, Mira had mentioned her Kirchner-adorned bottle while we were discussing the Palazzo Cache. But in a later conversation, she went out of her way to correct me on the distinction, after which she said something about Christian that shook me.

I had asked her for more information about something she had mentioned: that as the bottles had run out, Alessandra and Sergio had eventually sold a fake Palazzo Cache bottle—to the dealer Eric, of all people, after which she'd disappeared.

Something like that had ended up happening, she said, but it wasn't a Palazzo Cache bottle.

"The Palazzo Cache bottles are only the wine bottles filled with Pernod Fils that Alessandra found in the palazzo cellar. None of those bottles were fakes. Until then it was unheard of that Pernod Fils had ever filled bottles other than their own, so it wouldn't have made sense to fake something like this."

Instead, she clarified, that forged bottle was a different, would-be pre-ban, though it somehow had a modern label on it. It was sealed with a badly faked cork—new, but burned, to discolor it in imitation of age; figuring out how to make new corks look old was one of the main problems absinthe counterfeiters faced. Bizarrely, this bottle with a modern label appeared to contain some kind of old absinthe, though no one could tell what it was.

In total, she believed, Alessandra had sold two fakes, though it wasn't clear who had counterfeited them. Alessandra claimed that she had purchased those forgeries from other collectors in Italy, and not from the wealthy Italian family who owned the palazzo, from which dozens of legitimate bottles, including the one with the Kirchner sketch, had been sold. I tried to imagine the size of a palazzo cellar below water level with so many bottles that a scout like Alessandra could keep finding sought-after wares, even after many visits. The Palazzo Cache, she said, was just something that Alessandra found in the cellar, under layers of other bottles.

I could practically smell the mold and hear the waves in the canals. I imagined that I could see the dim light of the collection—hundreds and hundreds of bottles, some of them covered with price-less artworks. A question from Mira pulled me back to the surface.

"Did you get to talk to Christian?"

I realized that this meant that she'd read the short article about Christian's forgeries that I had published in VinePair, although she and I hadn't ever talked about that article, or about Christian at all. And I remembered that Adrian Mørk had brought up Christian, too, calling him "that asshole you wrote about." There was a good chance, I realized, that many of the absintheurs were communicating about me and my research in private.

"Him? No. We met once, but he won't answer me now," I said. I thought about if for a second and decided to extend an invitation, as if Christian could somehow receive it through Mira. Perhaps they were still in contact. "I'd love to hear his story."

"I wrote to him a few times," she said. For her, the sketchy part was that he could barely write in what was supposed to be his native language.

At this point I had to reflect on Mira's background, as well as my own. I knew that Mira was Swiss and was fluent in German as well as English. More to the point, I was aware that for years she had also lived and studied abroad, learning another language there. As someone who has also studied a few foreign languages, I knew not to underestimate the insight of a language learner. Those of us who study languages often have a particular ear for weird accents or nuances of grammar in our new languages. We might make mistakes that native speakers don't make, but we notice very different, sometimes overlooked errors in the languages we study. It is a handicap to be a language learner, but it is also often a superpower. I had no doubt that Mira was right about Christian, though I had no idea what to make of that.

It sounded like she'd had enough contact with him to be a good judge. When she was living in northern Europe, she explained, she used to organize an annual gathering for local absintheurs. One year she invited Christian, since he claimed that he was visiting family in the region at the time, and he agreed to come.

"Of course he never showed up," she said. Despite his supposed connection, he didn't speak the local language well.

⋮

The idea that Christian didn't speak his supposed native language well made me wonder about him. Was he actually English? Was the foreign-sounding part of his double surname a complete fiction?

But at the same time, it also made him seem a bit more understandable, or at least more relatable. I don't speak Greek, my mother's first language, very well at all, and feel a face-flushing sense of failed duty when someone speaks Greek to me and I can't respond, having an idea of what their words mean but not knowing the words I should use in response. While traveling in Greece, I have felt both deeply connected to and disconnected from both the culture and language, as well as an occasional sense of what I can only call shame. I imagined that Christian might have felt the same way in his family's homeland: unable to speak, yet aware that he somehow should; not local, and yet not completely foreign either. A sense of shame, I decided, might be part of the motivation behind his fraud.

⋮

I brushed off any attempts to psychoanalyze Christian from afar and turned my focus back to the story of the palazzo, finally discovering some explanation for all the secrecy during a long phone conversation with Wolfgang Klotz, a German collector who was said to have purchased the largest share of Palazzo bottles. He was clearly reluctant to speak with me, but he relented when I reminded him that we'd met years earlier at the Absinthiades. In truth, it turned out that we hadn't: I had simply confused him with someone else. We did have several real-life shared friends, however, and eventually he agreed to speak very late at night, once he'd gotten his infant son into bed.

When I asked what kind of historic absinthes he had, he was coy, as if he wasn't sure where to begin. His collection of vintage absinthes was so large, he explained, he no longer knew exactly what was in it. He had at least one historic absinthe bottle from every year as far back as 1880, in addition to a full run of the Tarragona absinthes from when Pernod moved its production to Spain after the ban in France. He was most proud of owning the oldest known bottle of Dubied, the very first commercial absinthe distillery. He didn't just have good luck, he said. It was more than that.

"I'm a bit special," he explained. He paused and I could hear him take a drink, which I imagined to be absinthe. "I like to say that it's not that I search for bottles, or that I'm looking for them. It's more like the bottles like to come to me."

That wasn't how it worked when he first developed his interest in historic absinthe starting in 2007, he said. Initially, he tried as hard as he could to find vintage bottles, with no luck. Eventually, something flipped.

"I searched and searched, but I didn't find any bottles," he said. "And then at one point, people started coming to me, saying 'Oh, I have this bottle, I have that bottle.' They sent me so many offers that I have trouble with the money to buy them all."

He had been involved in sharing samples from historic bottles with Christian and other absintheurs, but since the discovery of Christian's forgeries he'd given that up.

"I am not doing that anymore, because there was a big problem with fake absinthes, and with good friends who made fakes," he said. He paused, quietly taking another sip. "I was also accused in the beginning, that I made fakes, or that I helped people to make fakes. They say, 'Oh, we have some people who make fakes. Maybe Wolfgang is one of them.'"

That passed, he said, although some collectors still seemed to doubt the authenticity of his collection. His responses were laconic for most of our conversation, and he briefly went completely silent after he brought up Christian's forgeries, but he started speaking more freely when I asked about the Palazzo Cache.

He confirmed most of the details I'd heard from Mira and Stefano but went even further when I gave him space to speak. Wolfgang started talking about the family behind the Palazzo Cache and explained how they'd ended up with their store of bottles.

"A lot of it is more of a secret," he said. "But in the end, what I can say from the seller who handles these bottles is that the family is a big family from Italy. A very, very rich family. They have some hotels, some restaurants. It's one of the richest families in Italy. They originally had some businesses with herbs and fruits—they handled everything. And so I think they had some direct contact to Pernod and to distillers in the Val-de-Travers."

What we know, he explained, was that Pernod Fils sent a train to Italy when the ban came into effect. In the train were many bottles, as well as several demijohns containing the last French-made, pre-ban absinthe from the Pernod Fils distillery in Pontarlier. Those demijohns have been the source of the Palazzo Cache bottles, and their discovery helped collectors understand how things were done at Pernod.

One of the most confusing aspects of the Palazzo Cache, he explained, was that many of the bottles were very different from one another in terms of taste, aroma, and color. If this is Pernod, tasters wondered, why is it clearly different from other Pernod bottles from the same era? The reason for that was another aspect of the culture around the drink that had been lost: Pernod Fils was a blended spirit. The distillery's method was much like the solera system used in making sherry, he said, where new batches were continuously mixed into old batches, ensuring a uniformity of flavor over years. Because the Palazzo Cache consisted of the last batches of unblended spirits, the bottles didn't always have the same consistency or character as Pernod's blended absinthe. Tasting the Palazzo Cache bottles allowed connoisseurs to sample the building blocks of Pernod Fils, the raw material from which the great spirit was constructed. "So you have a different kind of Pernod Fils. Different colorations. Different tastes. And they all aged differently."

The Palazzo Cache included standard wine bottles, he said, but also other bottles. His own collection contained Palazzo Cache bottles in various sizes, shapes, and colors, ranging from dark glass to completely transparent. The family had said that there were about 100 Palazzo Cache bottles, but Wolfgang thought the number was closer to 400. He repeated the story I'd already heard about the bottles with artwork, like Mira's Guggenheim-worthy Kirchner bottle, as well as the idea of the palazzo hotel attracting cultural figures of the fin de siècle and early twentieth century.

"The sellers say that a lot of artists, Hemingway and other people we know, like Sigmund Freud and Thomas Mann, they also came to this place and drank bottles from this Palazzo Cache," he said. "That's what the sellers say. But it makes a lot of sense, because we found some bottles with art on the bottle—a drawing or something they put around the glass."

He'd never been to the palazzo himself, but he had close enough contacts that he had tried to arrange a visit several times. It simply hadn't worked out. "The family wants to keep everything as a secret."

I asked if the cellar with the Palazzo Cache was in a hotel in Venice, as I'd been told, and his response revealed something that finally put all the secrecy and vagueness into relief. We were speaking English, but Wolfgang kept saying "Keller," the German word for cellar, which left little chance for me to misunderstand or mishear him.

"Yes, this keller was in a hotel in Venice," he said. He paused for a moment, taking another drink, and then spoke quite quickly, as if he couldn't stop the words from spilling out. "But there are more kellers. There are kellers from hotels, there are kellers from restaurants, there are family kellers, private kellers, there are many more kellers. There are a lot of kellers, and they are all full of spirits."

All of these kellers—meaning cellars—were owned by the same wealthy Italian family behind the Palazzo Cache, he said, and their trove of vintage absinthes was not something that had been sold off in 2012 or even by 2016, the point when most absintheurs believed the Palazzo Cache was exhausted. It was still ongoing, he assured me, which is why no one who knew anything wanted to reveal much about it. No one wanted to get cut off from the source.

The secretive Italian family behind the Palazzo Cache, he said, is still regularly selling pre-ban absinthes to a select group of collectors even today.

REMAKING
HISTORY

Absinthe, ô ma liqueur alerte,
Il me semble quand je te bois
Boire l'âme des jeunes bois
Pendant la belle saison verte.
—RAOUL PONCHON

S pirits are often said to be unable to express a sense of terroir
or regionality, the characteristics of which are believed to
be destroyed by the intensity of distillation, but I got a very
specific sense of place and location as I approached the Žufánek
family distillery a couple of weeks after my return from the Val-de-
Travers. Time, however, started to go a bit fuzzy.

A couple of hours after setting out from my home in Prague,
I drove by the fields where the Battle of Austerlitz—also known
as the Battle of the Three Emperors—had taken place, and found
myself thinking of the French, Austrian, and Russian soldiers who

must have been looking at a similar landscape, and comparably nasty early winter weather, on very nearly the same date back in 1805. Rolling hills and open meadows were lashed with freezing rain, which turned to flurries as I climbed through the Chřiby Mountains, a far-western range of Eastern Europe's legendary Carpathians, moving closer and closer to the Czech Republic's border with Slovakia. I pondered some of the strange place names along the way, seeing signs for the village of Hluk, meaning "noise," and Otrokovice, which seemed to mean "Slaveville," before I rounded a big curve in the road and saw the familiar capital-Z-but-also-a-percent-symbol logo of Lihovar Žufánek, the Žufánek distillery. Not far away, I found the house where Martin Žufánek had told me to park.

We'd first met ten years earlier at the Absinthiades festival in Pontarlier, when I had joined up with Martin and Habu, and it strangely seemed like the time in between hadn't touched Martin. That said, he had since become much better known in the Czech lands, emerging as one of the country's culinary celebrities. In the Czech Republic's eastern half of Moravia, the hilly Slovácko region where he lived and worked is mostly known as a traditional wine region, and indeed, I'd spotted a number of wine cellars, decorated with Moravian folk prints of flowers, as well as grape clusters and leaves, along the route. However, Martin and the Žufánek family distillery had become so well known in the previous decade that I imagined distillation must be a larger part of the region's identity by now, though of course it was also part of its past. My wife and I had long cherished the meruňkovice, or apricot brandy, made by her good friend's father in not-too-far-off Kyjov, and on the way over I'd seen that there was a museum devoted the history of folk distilling in the nearby town of Vlčnov.

The Žufánek distillery was the opposite of historic and folksy, however: shiny and new, contemporary and cutting-edge, just like Martin's newly built house. He welcomed me inside with a handshake and a bowl of an elegant Japanese white tea, looking almost exactly like he had a decade earlier in France: quite tall, ursine but friendly and gentle, boyish, and shy. He was comfortable and easily conversational in English, though he occasionally mixed a few German words in, too—an understandable quirk, given the relative closeness of the Austrian border some thirty-five miles away. I found myself thinking about time and place, and how that related to the production of spirits, especially in the case of what I believed to be Martin's most interesting product: a celebrated recreation of Dubied Père et Fils absinthe, following a recipe that dated back to 1798 or so.

It had been Major Dubied who had supposedly taken a patent medicine recipe from Dr. Pierre Ordinaire, a French Army deserter, and commercialized it in partnership with his son Marcelin and son-in-law Henri-Louis Pernod, before Pernod launched his own distillery in Couvet, expanded production across the border in Pontarlier in 1805, and eventually became the world's largest producer.

The Žufánek distillery wasn't quite at that level, but it had enjoyed a lot of success with its absinthes, many of which had historic inspirations, and had most recently become locally famous for its cocktail-friendly gins, which bore the amusing names OMG and OMFG, as well as its bestselling traditional fruit brandies, backed up by a few oddball spirits that were mostly unknown outside of

Central Europe. But to me the historic Dubied recreation felt like Martin's biggest achievement: something new that tasted old, and a drink which captured the imagination of real connoisseurs.

⋮

Žufánek absinthe wasn't quite like that at the beginning, he explained with a laugh.

"The first batches of my absinthe were undrinkable, if I compare them to what we are distilling today. But you have to start somewhere."

I asked him to tell me the full story of the historic recreation that he'd called Dubied 1798–Žufánek 2018. I knew a bit of the tale already: it was a limited edition that had completely sold out within a few hours of its release, based on a historic recipe from Dubied that Martin had tracked down. But according to Martin, a recipe itself wasn't all that important. Not even for something as simple as a Czech potato salad.

"A recipe is just a recipe. It's just a few words," he said. "If I give you the recipe for a bramborový salát and the same recipe to different person, the result will be different."

Those gaps in procedure had created the most difficulties when he'd first started, he said. Authentic absinthe recipes are not too hard to get. Modern absinthe memorabilia collectors have tons of the historic recipes, at least in terms of the ingredients, and I'd seen several of them displayed on the walls of the Maison de l'Absinthe in the Val-de-Travers. The instructions, however, are usually missing. If you're coming from an absinthe distilling family, you could probably guess most of the steps in the process. But that wasn't the case when Martin started releasing his versions in 2008.

"It was quite funny, because I didn't know anything about absinthe," he said. "Absinthe isn't a traditional drink for the Czech Republic. My grandfather didn't even know what absinthe was. So I started with the books, obviously, researching, and I found some recipes. The problem is that you are able to find almost any recipe for absinthe, but nobody kept the distilling protocol written down. A father would give it to his kids, showing them the way he had learned it."

A similar kind of parent-child tutelage was how the Žufánek distillery had come about: Martin had originally learned how to make the Czech plum brandy *slivovice,* which English speakers usually refer to by the German word, slivovitz, from his father. Much like the father of my wife's friend in Kyjov and the clandestin distillers in the Val-de-Travers, Martin's father had been an illegal producer of high-quality spirits for personal use, during both the communist and early post-communist eras. While Martin had learned from his father how to cut the heads, hearts, and tails for fruit brandies, he had no idea how absinthe was made. And it showed.

"It was a self-learning curve which took almost five years," he said. "It's all about the distilling protocol, the temperatures, very small details, which I had to learn. Nobody taught me that."

Even today, he said, most distillers hold their cards close to their chests.

"Distillers are just little bitches. Nobody's sharing secrets. Commercial distillers are not willing to share any information," he said. The case was quite different for small brewers, he thought. "When you meet people who are making beer, they share everything. 'Hey you have to use this, that.' Temperatures, ingredients, everything.

But distillers? Jesus, distillers keep their secrets. They are not willing to share any information. Not even in France or Switzerland."

As a result, everything Martin learned about absinthe came through trial and error. Using wormwood, anise, fennel, and other herbs was quite unlike working with the plums in slivovitz.

"When you are macerating herbs in a pure spirit, it is very different than fermenting a mash of plums," he said. "The first batch of absinthe I macerated for like a week. It was bitter as hell. The same with the coloring. When you are coloring absinthe, it takes minutes, maybe even just an hour, but my first batch was colored for about fourteen days." The resulting spirit had wildly over-extracted herbal flavors. "It was like if you are making tea, and you leave the tea bag in it for a week. It was horrible."

After a few years, things started to go right with the absinthe Martin called Saint Antoine around the year 2011.

"The first success was with the third batch of Saint Antoine. It was three years after the first batch," he said. "I sent out the samples to the whole world—U.S. drinkers, French drinkers, even Japanese drinkers. They all said, 'Oh, finally. The first Czech absinthe which is drinkable.'"

Today, he said, bottles of his first good absinthe taste a bit like absinthes from before the 1915 ban.

"It's aged. It's smooth. The biggest characteristic of pre-ban absinthe is that you basically can't say 'This is anise, this is fennel, this is wormwood,'" he said. "All three of those components merge into one brand new flavor. You can't make that from the distillation. It needs time for the anise, fennel, and the wormwood to blend together. It takes at least ten years."

⋮

That got my mind spinning over the strange nature of historical reproductions. Modern distillers like Martin were trying to make absinthes that taste like pre-ban absinthes, but the only examples of pre-ban absinthes we have as points of reference are over a hundred years old, and which have thus been changed by the passing of time. But in the pre-ban era, I asked, wouldn't drinkers have been enjoying fresh absinthe, which would thus have been more like a modern absinthe today?

Martin's eyes flashed.

"Exactly! This is my point. They were drinking something that is more like modern absinthe," he said. "We are now drinking pre-ban absinthe and thinking, 'This must have tasted the same a hundred years ago,' but that's completely false."

It's hard for an absinthe to achieve that character, he thought, without spending a century in the bottle. Mira had said that the aroma of the Palazzo bottles faded quickly once they were opened, and François Bezençon had told me that absinthe didn't age like fine wine. But for Martin, time clearly helped tame and integrate absinthe's complex flavors and aromas.

"The biggest challenge is to recreate the current aroma and taste, which needs a hundred years to change. It is completely different when you make a fresh absinthe, compared to an aged absinthe." However, there are methods, he said, that can make a new absinthe taste old. And not just techniques, but also ingredients.

"There are some herbs," he said. He paused to consider his words, and for a second I got the impression he was considering how much he wanted to share with me—distillers being little bitches, after all.

A moment later he nodded to himself and continued.

"It's like 'speedy aging' or something," he said. "There are some herbs, which if you put into the coloration process, the aroma of those herbs can recreate the aroma of a pre-ban absinthe. But it takes a big portion of time, experience, and trial and error. Basically, what I'm saying, is that every distiller of absinthe these days is trying to recreate the tastes and aromas of hundred-year-old absinthe, but it is almost impossible. It's damn crazy, because you can't speed up time. Herbal spirits, like absinthe, age in the bottle. It's not like whiskey. It ages, and it gets better and better every year."

⋮

That might be true, but there was something particular about the Dubied process in terms of aging. Distillers might be unwilling to share information, and he might have complained about the secrecy himself, but I got the clear impression that Martin was probably holding a few things back. That said, he was remarkably open when he started telling the story of how the Dubied recreation came about. It started, he said, when Wolfgang Klotz found two bottles of Dubied, although he didn't even know exactly what they were at the time.

"He just said, 'Look, this is something very old.' Even he didn't know the rarity of the bottles. He offered me one of the bottles for around 3,000 euros, which is super cheap if I compare it with today."

Martin passed on the offer, not recognizing the bottle, after which the Maison de l'Absinthe museum in the Val-de-Travers agreed to the purchase for its collection. That purchase authenticated the bottles as some of the oldest pre-bans known to exist. Although the exact year of production is unclear, the labels stated that some of the bottles came from "Fürstenthum Neuenburg," an old German name for the principality—literally "a land run by a prince"—of the modern Swiss canton of Neuchâtel, which stopped being a royal state in the year 1848. They could have been made earlier, but they couldn't have been made after Europe's great revolutionary year, a full half-century after Dubied first started making absinthe commercially in or around 1798.

With the absinthe authenticated by the museum, the only thing left was to taste it.

"Wolfgang opened the second bottle and he prepared about fifteen samples. He sent one to me, some to some French guys, a few others around the world," Martin said. "It was really good. I tried it and said, 'Okay, this is the historic moment.' And then I started with the research."

He began trying to learn everything he could about the Dubied family and their distillery. There were actual Dubied recipes that people had found in the archives, one of which Martin ended up reproducing as art on his absinthe's label. But there were plenty of weird threads to follow, including a direct link from Dubied to the very origins of the drink. It's generally believed that Dubied was among the first to popularize absinthe commercially, though he didn't end up quite as famous as his son-in-law Henri-Louis Pernod. But the Dubied family didn't die out, Martin said. Instead, they emigrated.

"Through a friend of mine who lives in Canada, I found some descendants of Dubied, which is the truth," he said. "The guy is around seventy nowadays and he only speaks French, so I sent an email to the friend of mine in English, saying, 'Hey, I'm a big fan of absinthe from the Czech Republic. I'm hugely interested in the history of your family. Do you have any information in your archives about your family? Do you know that you were producing absinthe about 200 years ago?' And the old man sent me some papers, invoices and stuff like that, the financial books, and there was a recipe. The

original recipe, written by hand by Mr. Dubied. And it was different
from the one which is in circulation which everybody knows."

And it was not just a list of ingredients.

"It was the first time I ever saw a written protocol of how to
make absinthe," he said. "Every time, as I said, I just found the
recipe, but the missing piece was the protocol and the coloration
process. I found the process, handwritten, which said, 'Take this,
steep it in the clear absinthe at this temperature.' Like, the *exact*
protocol. It was the crucial piece of information I needed. The
coloration process was the missing puzzle piece."

When he started to describe the process, it seemed to connect to
the concept of "speedy aging" he'd mentioned a few minutes earlier.

"It's completely different. There are even some herbs which
I haven't found in any other absinthe recipe before," he said.
"Nowadays, when you distill an absinthe, it's clear like slivovitz, and
you put herbs in it, you let it macerate like a tea, you take the herbs
away, and you are done. But his coloring protocol was very different."

It was unlike anything he'd ever heard of before, he said, a series
of steps which involved splitting the batch of absinthe in two, coloring each part separately with different herbs, and then blending
them back together.

"He was coloring for very different times, at very different temperatures," Martin continued. "It was very complicated. But when I
tried it, that was it. Something came out of the coloring herbs which
I wouldn't be able to get using the traditional method."

It wasn't just the color, he said. The Dubied recipe's unique coloring instructions changed the absinthe's taste and aroma. It made
the absinthe taste like it had been aged, even when it was coming
straight out of the still.

"It was already old, like maybe six years old, just directly after I finished the coloration process," he said. "It already tasted like an aged absinthe, which was crazy." The aromas and flavors of the herbs used for coloration, he said, had already blended into a cohesive whole.

"If you are coloring absinthe, you are generally using fresh hyssop and petit wormwood. And when you take the herbs out of the absinthe, you can taste it and say, "Okay, there is the fresh hyssop and there is the fresh petit wormwood. But this special coloration process made the freshness disappear. It was like old hyssop, like old wormwood. It was more gentle. There was no sharp note of the fresh spirit or the fresh herbs. It was blended together and already balanced.

"This is quite hard to achieve, because fresh absinthe is unbalanced. It is harsh and wild, and you need a lot of time, maybe six months to let it settle and balance. But this was already balanced."

⋮

I asked if we could visit the distillery, so we grabbed our coats and walked toward the big gates bearing the company's name. I knew Martin wasn't telling me everything, but he had told me what he could: that the techniques and possibly the unusual herbal ingredient or ingredients of a special coloration process had helped to create an absinthe that tasted "old," like a pre-ban absinthe, even when it was fresh. He claimed that process had come from a handwritten recipe he'd received from a Dubied descendant in Canada, though I wondered silently if that was the truth. But even if it wasn't the full story, I knew Martin's description of the resulting absinthe as tasting like a pre-ban was probably accurate. He knew his way around pre-bans, though he said that he hadn't purchased any in a while.

"It is quite hard these days, because most of the bottles are already sold off to collectors or even drunk," he said. "I've got maybe two bottles left, but I used to have ten bottles of pre-ban absinthe. The problem is that I'm actually drinking it. I think Wolfgang is the same. Wolfgang has the biggest collection of pre-ban absinthe, and he's drinking it like there's no tomorrow."

As we approached the distillery, I saw plum orchards covering most of the rolling hills around us. They all belonged to the distillery, Martin said, and were the source of the fruit the company used to make its most important product, a classic Czech slivovice. In several other ways, his distillery seemed deeply connected to its setting there at the far eastern edge of the Czech Republic, close to the Austrian and Slovak borders, where "folk distilling" and winemaking—both amateur and professional—were commonplace activities. Unlike most Swiss distillers, he sometimes made his own base spirit for absinthe from wine, just like many of the great pre-bans.

"For our most expensive absinthes, I'm using a brandy, a wine spirit, which I distill myself," he said. "And this is crucial, because you can change the variety of the wine. I found that the best wine for my distillations is Grüner Veltliner, which I buy just four kilometers from here, from a friend of mine who has a winery in the next village."

Because his family traditionally made mead from the honey that came from their beehives, he was also able to distill that to make a "mead base" absinthe, which had ruffled the feathers of many tradition-minded absintheurs.

"They all said, 'Oh, this is not the original absinthe. It tastes

great, but hey, let's be honest: this is not absinthe,'" he recalled. But
for him, using mead to make the base spirit for an absinthe was akin
to something from another field he knew well, mixology, in which
bartenders commonly offered their own riffs on classic recipes.

"A mead base is like an absinthe 'twist,'" he said. "When you are
distilling absinthe and you are following the recipes, you basically
get the same result as every other distillery who is doing the same
job, using the same recipes and working in the same style." It can
be boring, he said, to taste fifty absinthes that were all made in the
same way. "I said, 'Okay, the recipe is basically done. You have to
use anise, fennel, wormwood. You can't change that, but you can
change the base spirit for it. And I found that if you put sweet anise
into a spirit made from honey wine, it blends perfectly. It is still
absinthe, but with a different approach."

That jazz-like sense of riffing on a classic didn't impress most
modern absinthe lovers, who tended toward established patterns.
After the initial success of the third St. Antoine distilling, Martin
made La Grenouille with Rossoni, an absinthe inspired by the herbs
of southern Europe. Taking its name from the 1869 Renoir painting
La Grenouillère and the beautiful young women who frequented
the public swimming pool of the same name, it contained a number
of plants that were not typical for classic absinthe. That also didn't
go over well with modern absintheurs.

"Absinthe fans are super into tradition," he said. "When we
distilled La Grenouille, they said, 'Oh, Jesus Christ, this is too
much floral, this is too Mediterranean. This is not absinthe.'"

Over-adherence to tradition might be annoying, but he noted that
Czech drinkers often feel the same way about their favorite spirits.

"It is the same with the fruit brandies," he said. "You can't make a slivovitz with ginger or a slivovitz with something else. Slivovitz needs to be just plum brandy. No twist allowed."

The air thickened with the sweet, jammy scent of fermenting plums as we entered the distillery cellar. Martin showed me a wall of shelves containing hundreds of bottles of various sizes and types, some with other, older brands on them. They were the archive of the spirits his father had made, not quite legally, long before the Žufánek distillery was a tax-paying enterprise, back when Martin was a child.

"I still remember the taste and aroma of the slivovitz," he said. "It's in the DNA of the people of this region. When you are a kid and you have like troubles with your stomach, you get slivovitz on a teaspoon. Even at four or five years old. It's just super traditional." It was not, however, something you would regularly buy: slivovitz was just something that people in his region made at home.

After the fall of communism, however, they started to encounter commercial versions. Ironically, tasting those early commercial versions is what inspired the Žufánek family to found their distillery as a legal enterprise.

"The commercial slivovitz was terrible. It was like a fruit spirit, mixed with a potato spirit. It was crazy bad. When we asked ourselves, 'Hey, what about distilling it commercially, with the same quality as a homemade product?' that changed everything. It also changed the whole market in the Czech Republic, because nobody had even thought about doing the same thing."

The Žufánek's legal distillery opened in 2000, focusing first on slivovice and *hruškovice*, Czech pear brandy. Other traditional drinks followed, including *kontušovka*, a traditional spirit from

Poland that was mentioned among the many other drinks in the classic novel *The Good Soldier Švejk*. A bit like absinthe, *kontuš-kovka* includes anise, fennel and wormwood, as well as mint and cardamom, though it is slightly sweetened, while absinthe is generally not. Another of Martin's unusual spirits, oskerušovice, is distilled from sorb, *Cormus domestica,* also known as the service tree, an Old World fruit I'd never even heard of before he'd told me he was working with it.

Like absinthe, those spirits don't form a huge part of the business at Lihovar Žufánek—the distillery mostly sells the slivovice and hruškovice, followed by Martin's mixology-friendly gins—but the fun part of having a family-owned distillery is that you can make your own decisions.

"We're a small distillery. We don't have a board of managers sitting behind the table and doing like public research and saying, 'Hey, people want kontušovka.' Nobody told me that. I just made it because I wanted to taste it. I wanted to drink it myself. So I did it, and we are still making it."

As a curious drinker, I was very glad they did. From a friend in the area, I'd heard that many locals had initially shied away from the Žufáneks' slivovitz: it was a commercial version, after all, which couldn't possibly be good in the mind of most people here, when compared to the homemade stuff. But Žufánek's bottles contained the best non-homemade versions of slivovitz I'd ever tasted. Rich with spicy, cooked-fruit flavors, they were oceans ahead of most of the country's biggest brands, the most famous of which, R. Jelínek, was located less than an hour away, in the same plum-filled region where Martin lived.

⋮

The distillery had originally launched with Czech-made equipment, but Martin wanted to show me the high-quality German stills to which the distillery had upgraded. Moving to the Arnold Holstein stills, he said, had made a big difference on everything from slivovice to absinthe. He had distilled the same recipe on the two different stills and found that he ended up with two very different spirits.

Another important difference, he said, was where the ingredients came from. Commodity plums from large farms in Poland might measure thirteen degrees on the Brix scale, meaning they only contained about 13 percent sugar. But with its own orchards, the Žufánek distillery didn't need to buy plums, and it frequently had a surplus that it sold to others. The quality of the fruit was much higher, too.

"If you look around, there's plum trees all around us. And when we were picking up the plums three or four months ago, they had twenty-eight degrees of sugar," he said. "It's a completely different league. If you distill a slivovice using your own fruit, the result is completely different." While it was self-sufficient for most fruit, the distillery did have to buy apricots, he said, and also brought in Williams pears from France for a few special products.

Other ingredients took much of his attention.

"When I started the absinthe, I got really passionate about it. It was driving me mad. For example, it took me six years to find the best source for anise. I tried anise from Serbia, Turkey, Italy . . . it took six years to find the right one. The same with fennel. The same with wormwood. With Czech distilleries, they just go to the warehouse for herbs and buy what's in stock, because they think 'anise is anise,' and nobody cares about where it comes from. But the origin makes a huge difference. Absinthe made with anise from

Turkey was completely different to my current absinthe, which has anise from Andalusia, which is perfect—it's fruity and smooth."

It not only took a lot of time and attention, he said. It also took a lot of money.

"Do you know how many kilos of ingredients I throw away? Not just anise, but juniper. Everything. I returned 500 kilos of juniper to the supplier last year. He asked me, 'Why? This is the juniper that everybody is using here in Czech Republic.' And I said, 'No, it is crazy bad quality. I can't distill it.'"

When I asked what most people didn't understand about how he distilled spirits, he lowered his head for a half-minute before answering.

"The biggest thing is that for every product and every distillation, I put my own taste first. I'm basically distilling everything for myself, so it needs to reflect my style, and my taste."

That is not the case for some distillers he knew, some of whom make absinthe, even though they hate the spirit. One Czech distillery had been badly hurt by that approach. "They basically fucked up a batch of absinthe and didn't even notice it, because nobody was drinking it at the distillery, and the customers told them, 'This is undrinkable. What happened?"

The Žufánek family distillery had benefited from his hands-on approach, though there were some downsides. Martin wasn't going to produce a version of the popular Czech ersatz rum *tuzemák*, he said, because he doesn't drink it himself.

"It sounds like a cliché, but every absinthe, every gin, everything here is produced the best way I can do it."

He showed me the oak barrels holding what he called his first

and last whiskey. He'd distilled one batch of single malt before realizing that he wanted to stick with what he knew.

"I want to make perfect fruit brandy, perfect gin, and perfect
absinthe. After this, I'm going to leave whiskey to the other guys."

⋮

I had come out to ask Martin how spirits could express a sense of
place and what it meant to recreate historic absinthes, but there
was more on my mind. I knew that absinthe was deeply connected
to the Val-de-Travers, but Martin had managed to connect it to the
wild beauty of the Slovácko wine region and the western edge of the
Carpathian Mountains, just like his slivovice. But I also had to ask
Martin about Christian, which I'd left to the end for reasons that
became obvious once I brought up the forgeries.

"Oh, Jesus Christ," he sighed. He seemed to collapse slightly, a
big man who suddenly became quite a bit smaller. Then he nodded
and began telling me everything he remembered.

⋮

Martin and Christian knew each other for years online, before meeting a couple of times in person, including in London. Martin remembered him as both funny and generous. When they'd gone out together
at restaurants and bars in SoHo, Christian had insisted on paying.

"He was like a big friend, like an open-hearted man," he said.
"He was super friendly. His wife was super friendly. He liked to
share. He shared a lot of information."

They'd spent time together, along with their wives, at the
absinthe festival in Pontarlier. They had DMed each other regularly
for years, sharing their interests and news. At first Martin had

trouble finding those messages, but after a minute he was able to pull them all up on his phone. They seemed to include scores of shots of Christian's wrist.

"We shared a hobby of collecting watches," Martin said, looking through the images. "He was sending me a lot of pictures of new Rolexes." Considering what I'd heard about Christian, I wondered how many of those he owned, and how many he just photographed while he was out shopping.

In addition, Christian had regularly sent Martin pictures of obscure absinthes he claimed to have found.

"Oh my God," he said quietly, rereading his messages. "He was showing up with bottles like crazy. So many bottles."

Over the years, Martin had ended up purchasing three of those would-be pre-bans from Christian, he said—two Edouard Pernods and one A. Junod. He pulled up a picture of an Edouard, which Christian was offering in the message for the "reduced price" of £1,900.

"I bought this bottle from him. I opened it and it was terrible. It was bitter. The cork looked brand new, but like it had been slightly toasted on a burner or something." He handed me the phone. "He did a really good job with the wax seal, all the dirt and everything."

After that, Martin didn't buy any more pre-bans from Christian, feeling both disappointed in the quality and ever so slightly suspicious. But Christian kept offering the chance to buy new pre-bans through their message history. One of his final offers to Martin was for a true rarity—Sevas et Compagnie 72% Grand Absinthe du Bourgoin—from early 2019, right before the reports of his forgeries broke. "'In case you are interested, buddy,'" Martin read aloud.

He sighed, as if he recognized now how ridiculous it sounded. "Nobody in the absinthe world had ever found one of these bottles before. Nobody had ever seen so many different bottles. It was insane, a new bottle every week. If he had been selling two bottles a year, nobody would have caught him. But selling a different bottle every week was crazy. I don't know what happened in his mind."

⋮

As a committed pre-ban drinker, rather than a mere collector, Martin had only a few authentic pre-bans left, which were stored in what looked like the distillery's meeting room. They were a bunch of loners, Martin said, and the distillery itself didn't have a visitors' center, despite its fame, though I imagined more than a couple dozen guests could pack in there just fine. The long back wall was covered with hundreds of bottles, both from Žufánek and from its competitors; he said he wanted to support his industry, even if he didn't like to drink some of the bottles he purchased.

On the far right, the shelves bore antique absinthe fountains and old bottles, including two Dubieds he'd purchased from Wolfgang, as well as pre-bans from Romans and Pernod, and at least one post-ban Pernod from Spain. Martin cradled one of the Dubieds lovingly as I took a couple of photographs. When I asked its price, he didn't blink. He'd paid 5,000 euros.

It was the passion of absinthe collectors that had most surprised him, he said, when he first encountered the absinthe underground.

"It is so expensive, the glasses and spoons and everything, and the people in it are such diehard fans, just crazy serious about all the antiques," he said. "I've never seen such committed fans in the world of fruit brandies. Not even with whiskeys. Just with absinthe."

I asked him how much he'd lost on the fake bottles he'd bought from Christian, and he had to revise his estimate a couple of times as he added them up mentally, eventually ending up at about 7,000 euros.

"I lost a huge amount of money, but shit happens. It was a good lesson."

I wanted to know what he thought might have motivated Christian. Martin thought it mostly had to do with arrogance, or with proving his superiority.

"He was so . . . what's the English word?" he asked. *"On si myslí, že je tak dobrý.* He thought he was so good he could trick every absinthe drinker, because he made some blends and sent them to America. And so he said, 'Okay, I can do this.'"

But Martin thought the money certainly must have something to do it.

"He made a small fortune on it," he said. "But he basically ruined the whole absinthe community. He ruined absinthe collecting, I believe, because nobody is buying pre-ban bottles these days."

He paused and almost smiled as he thought of something. "It was so sad. The best part was that one of the bottles I bought from him included my own absinthe." After going back to the pre-bans he'd purchased from Christian, Martin was sure one of them contained some Justifiée et Ancienne, a Žufánek absinthe which took its French name from a classic KLF house track, and which appeared have been mixed with portions of Grand No. 5 and other spirits. I asked Martin how he knew, and he gave a look like the answer was both disappointing and obvious.

"I recognized it," he said.

To me, including a distiller's own absinthe in the blend you sold to him as a pre-ban spoke to arrogance, if not megalomania, but it also hinted at a kind of death wish, as if Christian had a desire to get caught. I'd heard that he'd even sent samples to Jan Hartmann, a young scientist in Germany who studied old spirits in a high-tech laboratory, which made it seem like he wanted to see how close he could get to the flame before it finally burned his fingers.

But even if what was going on in Christian's brain was hard to guess, he had told Martin he'd done it for the money. Martin pulled up an email on his phone, which he let me photograph before skimming through it again.

"He basically said that he faked an absinthe, but only once."

It read as follows:

> Hi Martin,
> I saw your mail on my old account and wanted to contact you and let you know what's really happened.
> I did very recently fake a Constant Pernot and fill up an old Pernod Fils to sell out of desperation for money (The Edouard is real and different to the bottle Cary thinks it is—Which I also own).—Something I'm very ashamed of and embarrassed that I could stoop that low. I've never done this before.
> Ashamedly I sold the Pernot to Cary. I have since offered to refund him, but he was insistent that nothing from me could be real anymore after that sadly.
> I've since been shunned out of all the groups and had so much grief that I've had to leave FB.
> I'm heartbroken that I made such a cardinal error.

I'm heartbroken that I can no longer be part of the
community or buy and sell anything. And saddened for
any feelings of betrayal.
Before this recent event I have NEVER sold fake
absinthe to anyone. I am a genuine collector.
Every bottle you've ever had from me is GENUINE I
promise you.
Christian

That was another clear admission of guilt from Christian for at
least one forgery, though I'd heard that the group of amateur absinthe detectives had assembled plenty of evidence for others.

In the end, Martin had written one more time to ask Christian
how he could do such a thing.

"In the final message I sent to him I said, 'I thought we were
friends. I spent a lot of time with you. We had a lot of conversations.
How can you do such a thing to your friends? To trick everybody?'
He never replied. I don't know if it's some kind of a mental issue.
He just blocked me."

He paused for a minute to consider his words.

"It was all a big disappointment. And it really needs to be written
down, because the story is unique."

LES COLLECTIONNEURS

Je suis d'une génération qui buvait en public la délectable
liqueur et non ses contrefaçons.

—ERNEST TISSERAND

I wanted to know more about the collector's mentality, what
drove people to buy old bottles for thousands of dollars, as
well as try to understand why Christian, whoever he was, had
done what he had done. When we'd talked on the phone, Wolfgang
Klotz had shared a good amount with me, but I could tell he was
holding back more than a few things. He'd known Christian well
for years and ranked as one of the most prolific European collectors of antique bottles, famous for finding caches of Tarragonas
or standalone pre-ban rarities that went far beyond Pernod Fils.

As such, more than a few absintheurs had believed that he might have had something to do with the frauds, though that speculation had waned after the allegations broke. When I asked people about him, he was generally seen as a collector's collector, an eccentric German with an absolute mania for old spirits. And he was friendly, even to someone who was effectively a stranger. When I wrote a few months later and asked if I could come see his collection, he said absolutely.

I also wanted to talk to Mira in person, if I could, to hear more about the Palazzo Cache and learn how collectors thought. In a lucky coincidence, a travel article I'd pitched more than twelve months earlier was given a green light early in the new year by my editors at the *Times*, which meant that I could have some of my travel expenses paid by the Gray Lady. My article would be about the food in dining cars on European trains, which hit its apex on the Gourmino gourmet train that rolls through the Albula Alps on the scenic railway line between Chur and St. Moritz. It was on the wrong side of Switzerland if I wanted to go back to the Val-de-Travers, to the south and east instead of the north and west, but it was perfect for getting me back to Zürich, where I met Mira Müller the evening before my Gourmino ride in a busy grocery store and café near the city's main train station.

⋮

Zürich had changed noticeably since I'd spent a summer in college stocking shelves in a grocery store in a small town not too far away. On my way to meet Mira I heard English almost everywhere on the street, which was certainly not the case back in the dirty nineties. As one of several languages she knew, Mira's English was good but very careful and thus a bit slow, and she occasionally took a few seconds to choose her words. Because she naturally spoke very quietly and the space was echoey and bustling, I often had to lean forward to catch what she was saying.

She'd enjoyed being part of the absinthe underground, she said, after a sip of tea, though she repeated that she enjoyed the cultural elements and the history more than the taste of absinthe itself. That set her apart from many collectors of vintage bottles.

"Many people buy pre-bans because they want to drink them," she said. "They want to make it part of their lives, part of their own bodies." We spent a minute trying to find the English equivalent of *Einverleibung*, or "incorporation," in the sense of taking something foreign into one's own space or one's own body. That was what a lot of collectors wanted, in her eyes. They wanted it to be inside them, to make it part of them—not just the spirit, but its history and aura, as well.

Her bottle with the Kirchner painting was a very different story. She had recently loaned it out to the Kirchner Museum in Davos, she said, where it had been part of an exhibition dedicated to the artist's possessions shortly before his suicide.

"It's something that should be looked at like a time capsule. It's from another time. It's also a bit of a liability, because you have responsibilities for something that is beautiful, and I didn't feel it was safe at our place."

It wasn't the only artwork bottle that had come out of Italy, she reminded me: the other one she'd mentioned was decorated with a signed drawing by the French post-impressionist Maurice Utrillo. There was also a rumor of another Kirchner drawing in the personal collection of the famous family behind the Italian bottles, supposedly in color, though that one had never been seen by any outsiders.

She'd purchased her Kirchner bottles after helping Alessandra find homes for many of the finds from the cache, though she hadn't received any proceeds from those sales herself. But Mira had wanted to help, she said, because she'd seen Alessandra face an uphill struggle in the boys' club of absinthe collecting. Plus it had been thrilling to watch what was coming out of the old cellars. But that volunteer work had been trying, and expensive: Alessandra had once not come through with a bottle for a buyer who had already paid for it, and since Mira had set up the transaction, she'd reimbursed the buyer herself.

"In the beginning, I didn't believe that I would ever see such a bottle in real life. And then suddenly I found out that there are lots of bottles. It's just a question of how much you want to pay."

Some of the bottles had quirks, as did their collectors. One bottle came with a vintage dead housefly, preserved forever in the spirit inside, which went into the collection of the Norwegian painter, Adrian Mørk. Eventually, the supply of Palazzo Cache wine bottles that had been filled from a Pernod Fils demijohn was reportedly exhausted, and Alessandra got out of the vintage absinthe trade. They were no longer in contact, Mira said.

It had seemed strange that those who had questioned Alessandra's integrity were the same absinthe authorities who had had previously championed Christian as the real deal. Eric had gone out of his way to say that people should not trust Alessandra. Once I added up all the stories, I guessed I could see why. But Christian had gotten a very different treatment from Eric.

"He was the one who introduced Christian as an expert," Mira recalled. In online groups, Eric had told absintheurs that Christian was even better than he was in terms of his skill in evaluating absinthe, saying that no one alive had tasted so many pre-bans.

Christian had never been in contact with Mira's sources in Italy, she said, so any forgeries associated with him probably had a different origin. For herself, she'd been glad not to have worked with him. She rattled off the things about him that rubbed her the wrong way: that he claimed to be from northern Europe but was not able to speak or write properly in any language from the region, that he did not fulfill a promise to ask his sister in to pick up some antiques near where she lived, or that he would swear that he was coming to an event, like the absinthe meet-up, and then not show up.

"You never knew what was true or not," she recalled. "But I didn't ever believe that he would come."

He was invited to that gathering in part because of his roots, and because the northern European absintheurs were all curious about the mysterious nineteenth-century absinthe "essence" he claimed to have. Unfortunately, they never got to find out if it was real or not, and no one from that group had ever tasted it.

I asked if it was true that Christian was connected to the wealthy family behind a famous toy company, as he had told people.

"No way," she said. "No way. I think he's just a liar. He's a compulsive liar."

Because she'd seen the end of the palazzo bottles, she'd been surprised by Christian's ability to keep coming up with new finds.

"I never trusted him, because he was so over-the-top. He opened pre-bans on birthdays, the rarest of pre-bans, and just drank them," she said. "I always wondered, 'Are there really so many?' Because I'd heard from Alessandra that there were not many left."

When I asked why Christian might have done what he had done, she sounded quite certain.

"It was a game for him," she said. "He needed to trick people."

After a moment, she inhaled quickly in a slight gasp. There was something she had just remembered, a detail that no one else had mentioned. The news that Christian had sold fraudulent absinthes spread quickly through multiple private Facebook groups. And afterward, Christian had used Facebook to let everyone in the absinthe world know what he really thought of them.

"When it went public, he changed his profile picture on Facebook to him grinning like a maniac. It was like he thought it was funny, that he's making fun of all these people. He was laughing in the face of anyone who looked at his picture. I just thought, 'He knows what he did. There's no remorse.'"

$$\vdots$$

The corrupting influence of money in the absinthe world went way beyond Christian, Alessandra, and a few fraudulent bottles from Italy, Mira said. Even legitimate dealers could be ruthless, as I'd heard muttered in the Val-de-Travers, especially regarding absinthe antiques. Alessandra had been frustrated to see dealers, after buying palazzo bottles directly from her, selling them on their own websites at prices many times higher than what she'd received. The same held for things like absinthe spoons, Mira said, some of which you could find for just a few euros from a non-specialist, or for as much as 800 euros from a famous absinthe antiques dealer.

"I really didn't understand," she said. "If you just went to a French market or just even googled an antiques website, then you could find all this stuff much cheaper."

⋮

The next day I had plenty of time to brood over Mira's take on the absinthe world and the collector mentality, as well as the influence of money. After the early train to Chur, I enjoyed a breakfast of smoked trout, Prosecco, coffee, and toasted croissants on the Gourmino as it plowed through the snowfields and forests of the upper Engadin valley, watching families with sleds disembark at several of the small stations along the Albula's miles-long sleigh route. Afterward, I wandered lazily around the glitzy shops in St. Moritz, half-blinded by the late winter sun, gawking at the horse-racing track that had been set up on the frozen, snow-covered lake. While seated on a comfy couch in front of large-scale Symbolist paintings in a small hilltop museum dedicated to the artist Giovanni Segantini, I thought up a few questions for Wolfgang Klotz. Then I wandered back in time to order a three-course lunch on the Gourmino's return trip to Chur.

Sometimes, I had to admit, travel writing does not suck.

After a night in my hotel back in Zürich, I was ready to leave Switzerland again. In addition to the Gourmino, my article included reviews of meals on Czech, Austrian, and German railways, which had enabled me to schedule the rest of my trip through Wolfgang Klotz's part of southwestern Germany, not too far from Heidelberg, just a couple of hours away from Zürich on a dining-car-equipped, high-speed ICE train. The German warmed-up dining-car experience was a big step down from the Gourmino, also short of the hearty from-scratch cooking offered by Česke dráhy, but I couldn't complain. However, when I joined Wolfgang and his family in their favorite small-town pizzeria that afternoon, my appetite was gone. I recalled the questions I had for Wolfgang and asked him how he managed to find so many old bottles.

"At first, I really had to hunt," he said slowly. "But now the bottles find me."

He was small and wiry, with rather intense eyes, which I hadn't expected from hearing his voice over the phone. The man with whom I'd spoken had been mysterious and not terribly forthcoming, and—from his voice—I'd imagined a tall, dark man, one who might be holding several secrets. There is a different quality to meeting a person in real life, compared to talking to a voice over the phone, and another quality altogether to meeting someone with those who know him best: the people who trust him completely. Seeing the young father together with his toddler son and wife, I got a good read of Wolfgang Klotz quite quickly. If he thought he could lie to me, I was sure I would feel it immediately.

I'd heard a few stories about how he had come up with rare bottles beyond the Palazzo Cache. Habu had told me that collectors like Wolfgang sometimes bought old business papers from famous distilleries at absinthe festivals, searching for orders from before the ban to hotels or large estates. Then, armed with the information that Hotel X or Château Y had purchased four cases of absinthe back in 1914 or whenever, the collector would reach out to the location in question to ask if any of those bottles were still around, and if by chance they might be available for purchase. It sounded like the buck-wildest of wild goose chases, a breadcrumb trail that would have to have gone stale over the course of more than a hundred years, but apparently, it occasionally worked.

It was even easier, he said, if you just asked sellers of interesting bottles if they had anything else.

"On eBay, if I see that they have this bottle, and they have that bottle, I think that maybe they have other bottles that they're going to put up for auction later. And when I contact them, I just say, 'Look, I won this auction, so you know I'm good for it. What else do you have? Do you have any absinthe? What do you want for that? Name your price.'"

When I listened to my voice memos from that day, I was struck by how quickly Wolfgang was speaking, and how tightly excited his voice became when the subject turned to absinthe. We spoke in English, unless we came up to an expression or idea that worked better in German, and the words flowed with ease: he was a natural conversation-carrier, and clearly very happy to talk about his favorite things. But he interrupted himself, often, to take care of his son or converse with his wife. Their boy was slightly ill and consequently very whiny, frequently needing attention, which both Wolfgang and his wife provided happily, patiently, with clear kindness. At that point, my own kids were in the older and far surlier years of middle school and high school, but I easily remembered how challenging it was to have a crying toddler who needed care, and I couldn't help but notice Wolfgang's patience.

After we finished, Wolfgang and I headed to their home, while his wife took their boy for a walk. They lived on the second floor of a small, squat apartment building in a quiet residential neighborhood. As soon as we entered from street level, he showed me the ground-floor storage units—above-ground cellars—where he kept his bottles.

There seemed to be thousands, at a quick guess, many still in their shipping boxes, a vast selection that spanned the entire world of spirts, from rum to cognac. Only a small percentage of the collection appeared to be from within the last twenty or thirty years, while a surprisingly large share dated from the nineteenth century, including many bottles from the early commercial offerings of Chartreuse, starting with its first year, 1840. He grabbed a few that he'd been wanting to open, locked the cellars with a key and we headed upstairs to his dining room table.

He spent many late evenings there at the table, working on his laptop, he said, searching online sites for collectibles all around the world, haunting the small, local auction sites he hoped other collectors hadn't yet discovered. He had plenty of absinthe, but for our tasting he wanted to start with a bottle of Lagavulin 12 from the 1970s, which he asked me to open. I poured a small amount in a couple of thistle-shaped tasting glasses, a crate of which he had at the ready, and we let them air for a moment.

He told me he liked to leave a bit of spirit in a glass overnight and taste it again the next day, and I admitted that I often did the same thing: I'd noticed that it helped me identify the less-obvious characteristics of a drink after finding them in the stale and oxidized sample, as if the ruined version, with its overstated faults, could help you understand the structure of the pristine drink. He felt the same way. Sometimes he could identify the scent of an absinthe even before a bottle was opened, he said, and could pick up the aromas of the place where it had been stored when tasting the spirit later.

"You can smell the cellar in the absinthe itself. And if you put an absinthe in this cellar, or that cellar, the aging of that absinthe is completely different."

As we sipped the Scotch, he talked about how the phenolic aromas of peat smoke can dissipate over time, while the aromas of the grain might develop and grow over the years. We moved on to the next bottle, a Domaine de Latapie Premier Grand Cru Armagnac that dated from 1914, but which had only been bottled after World War II, followed by an intense, thick, and inky Jamaican rum from 1889. We were sampling very small amounts, just spoonfuls, really, but the experience was intoxicating in other ways. I had the sense of not just looking into the past or studying it from a reserved, academic distance, as I had with literature in Paris, but of tasting something so intense and strange that it did not feel like the bottle had passed through the centuries into our present day. Instead, the elixir in the bottle seemed to carry us backward into the past from which it had come.

I had no idea of the value of the bottles we were opening, which made me wonder what kind of budget Wolfgang might have to play with. Later, when I looked up the price of a Chayriques Frères Rhum de la Jamaïque Récolte 1889, I found a bottle listed for just over $7,000, though it had a shoddier appearance than the one Wolfgang opened for us, carefully negotiating its broken, 134-year-old cork like he'd done it a hundred times, which I suddenly realized might well be the case. A bottle of Armagnac similar to the one we tasted was available for around $1,350, while replacing the Lagavulin from the 1970s would barely cost $1,000. Wolfgang was a young father, just thirty-eight years old and—like me—very clearly not a millionaire, so how did he end up being able to open bottles worth almost ten grand on a lazy Sunday afternoon?

A lot of it came through trades, he said. He had a service job with a city nearby, more in the hedge-trimming than the issuing-permits line, which provided a steady income, though probably not at the $7,000-bottle level. However, his ability to turn up valuable discoveries had put him in contact with other collectors, who traded things around quite freely.

"Sometimes I buy bigger lots that include stuff I don't need. I'm looking for spirits, but sometimes I also find wine. I give the wines to the wine collectors and the wine collectors give me spirits. It's perfect for everyone."

Many of his scores financed other purchases, as well as basic expenses. On a trip to Spain with his wife, he recalled, he'd found enough underpriced Tarragonas to pay for that vacation and several others after he'd resold some to other collectors. On another trip, he'd bought a bottle of pre-ban absinthe for 50 euros which he sold later for 2,800 euros. When he had extras, he kept them, building up his collection until it was overflowing and he'd effectively lost track of what it contained. He had no catalogue or list, physical or digital, of what he owned beyond his own memory.

"You have so much, you can't find anything," he said with a shrug. He drummed the table and smiled slyly. "Would you like to taste some pre-ban absinthes?"

⋮

We headed back to the cellar and he waded through his stacks like a disorganized bibliomaniac. I took a few photos and made some video clips as evidence, though I have trouble believing they were real. There were rum bottles bearing outdated caricatures of women of color—Rhum Negrita, Ron Morita, Ron la Mora and the like—from the sixties and seventies, guessing by the typefaces. There were shelves filled with bottles of Punt e Mes, Cinzano Elixir China, Baudino, Mirafiore and other vermouths, including a very old, huge-format bottle of Martini & Rossi that stood almost twice as tall and over twice as wide as the standard bottle. All the vermouths were unopened, though many of the spirits had been opened and recorked. There were wine racks filled with bottles I couldn't identify lying on their sides, matched by weird drinks like Doppio Kummel and St. Raphaël Quinquina. And then there were the absinthes.

My eyes were working just fine, but even on the second trip to the cellar my brain was having trouble processing what they were taking in. One shelf was dedicated solely to pre-ban Pernod Fils, as far as I could tell, holding thirty bottles from that brand alone. The next shelf up bore nineteenth-century brands I'd never heard of like Bardinet, as well as a clutch of at least four Dubied bottles, one of which clearly said that it had been made in the Neuenburg principality, just like the one in the Maison d'Absinthe. That meant that it dated from before 1848, while his later-production Dubied Duvals had been dated to 1873 and 1884, he said. All the known Dubieds in the world were Wolfgang's discoveries, and all had come from the same cache, including the one I'd seen in the Maison d'Absinthe in Môtiers.

I spotted a bottle of Žufánek's Justifiée et Ancienne among Wolfgang's collection of modern makers, whose contemporary branding contrasted sharply with the historic spirits. There were shelves of Pernod Tarragona, Rigal, Terravill and other Spanish *absenta* brands from the mid-twentieth century, with boxes and boxes of the shot-size sample bottles that absintheurs used to share their finds with their friends around the world.

I asked about the Palazzo Cache, and he pointed to a shelf where a number of what looked like wine bottles stood, all in different

sizes. The spirit inside the true palazzo bottles filled from the demijohn of Pernod Fils had a particular color, he said: it was almost
pinkish, and unlike any other pre-ban anyone had seen. He was
still buying from the people behind the Palazzo Cache, he said, but
he now wanted to go directly to the family who owned them, since
a few of the recent bottles offered by Sergio had been "extremely
questionable," which I took to mean fake. Fortunately, some of the
earlier bottles he'd purchased had labels that indicated the name of
the family that was selling them, as well as an indication of their exact origin, which sounded like an address. When I asked, he apologized, but he didn't want to say more.

"Because they have such nice bottles, it's better to keep it all
a secret. If the family hears anything, like if we make it public or
something, then it's all over."

I let that thread drop and he handed me a wine bottle with an
ersatz label of brown paper that had a sketch of a bearded man on
it. It reminded me of Mira's Kirchner bottle, though this was much
more of a scribble, with what looked like the words "Aprile 1917"
and the cryptic phrase "from my telling story" in English, scrawled
out in the calligraphic slices of a fountain pen along the label's flat
upright edge. It wasn't signed, and Wolfgang had made it seem like
just another bottle, but I suddenly felt clumsy and awkward with it
in my hands, and I couldn't stop myself from letting out a sigh once
it was safely back on the shelf. I set it next to another decorated
bottle, with an Expressionist-style caricature of a young man with
a loose white shirt, saw-blade cheekbones, and complicated, up-
style haircut like that had been something worn by Ian McCulloch
in his 1980s prime, though it had probably been painted at least
seventy years earlier.

Wolfgang continued digging through his boxes for several minutes, making clinking sounds with the antique glass like a chorus
of wind chimes, until he had selected several candidates for tasting
and we walked back upstairs to his apartment. In the meantime, his
wife and son had returned and were happily playing, all bundled
up, in the fresh winter air on the terrace. There was no snow in this
part of Germany, but it was quite cool outside, which helped with
his son's illness, Wolfgang explained.

In the hallway, I admired two large advertising placards for
Terminus and Absinthe Parisienne, both in nearly new condition,
the latter of which had a suggestive tagline, "Drink it and you'll see,"
apparently uttered by an old man to a young woman with an hour-
glass figure and a gasp-worthy neckline. Other antiques seemed to
hide just about everywhere. From a box on the counter, Wolfgang
dug out a handwritten letter addressed to "Mon cher Pernod" at
the Pernod distillery in Couvet on October 2, 1811. To my eyes, it
looked like a pleading request for financial assistance.

He readied a set of tasting glasses and explained that we would
be starting our tasting with a real rarity, a so-called "essence" of
absinthe, much like the one Mira had mentioned. This version had
been produced by the U.K.'s Bush & Co. sometime around the year
1890, he said: effectively a liquid concentrate of all the aromatic
herbs in absinthe, a few drops of which you could add to any neutral alcohol to create a serving of absinthe.

That description made me think of something like instant coffee, but the result was far more flavorful than a mug of Nescafé
Gold. A bizarre freshness hit me first, tasting and smelling like
a very recent production, pastis-like in its overall approach with
some head-spinning aromatics, despite its age, before finishing with

a pronounced herbal astringency. I'd never encountered absinthe essence before, nor had I heard of any U.K. producers from before the ban. I asked where he'd found it.

"This is from Christian," he said.

I tried to control my face, but I must have looked he'd just announced that we were drinking pure poison. I looked at it again, studying the perfectly opalescent glass that had been drawn from one of the small sample bottles that the absintheurs used to share scores amongst themselves. It was for sure real, he added, and when I asked how he knew, he made it sound like it was obvious.

"You can taste it. You just know."

I imagined that might be possible for an experienced taster, and I guessed that a truly rare pre-ban collectible like an absinthe essence might be harder to fake than the more common versions of the spirit, though I'd heard Mira herself express doubt about this particular sample, since it was associated with Christian. I certainly couldn't tell by the taste myself. And I knew there were plenty of fakes around, even beyond any frauds connected to Christian. Wolfgang admitted that he had been fooled into purchasing a few over the years.

"This is the game we play. If everything goes right, they send you pictures from the bottle, the label, everything, and you can look at all the details and you decide. Sometimes you can make a really good deal, and you have the big win. And the next time you have to lose."

There were a lot of fraudulent historic spirits of all kinds coming out of Italy, he said, extremely well-made examples that were effectively professional forgeries, probably put out by organized groups. But authentic pre-ban absinthes stood out as clearly real when they were tasted by cognoscenti. Perhaps that was why Christian hadn't ever sold any fakes to Wolfgang.

His open-plan apartment was relatively new, but the living room area next to our tasting table had an old-fashioned tile stove for heating in the corner. On it stood several antique absinthe fountains, though we were troubling our spirits in a less posh, more practical way: using a half-frozen, 1-liter bottle of Black Forest spring water with a loosened cap that allowed it to release an icy dribble into the glass.

I'd never tried a Tarragona, and since Wolfgang had them in spades, he opened one from the 1920s, the very same spirit Hemingway would have consumed before fighting bulls or composing a few lines of deathless prose. I'd imagined that the quality had gone downhill after the move from France to Spain, but what I tasted was full of black pepper, mint, and grassy herbs. Although they were not as sought-after as pre-bans absinthes, Wolfgang said that the early Tarragonas were among his favorites. In general, he liked to buy Tarragonas when they were under-priced, around 50 or 100 euros, though he'd go up to 400 euros for an early bottling like the one we were trying. Compared to the going price of 3,000 euros for a pre-ban, I could see the appeal of a Tarragona, especially when I considered the possible margins of buying late-era bottles for under 100 euros. Specialist absinthe shops retail late-era Tarragonas around $1,200. If Wolfgang could buy one for 50 and sell it to a retailer for 600—euros or dollars, it didn't really matter—he'd have more than half a grand to play with, even while leaving the retailer with a healthy potential margin of his own. If Wolfgang could buy a box of them, as he said he had more than once, he might end up with $10,000 at his disposal. Suddenly, the

ability to amass a stellar collection of antique bottles as a munici-
pal employee almost made sense.

We moved on to a modern absinthe that he thought might be
important for me to try: a Segarra 45 from an inspired producer,
Julian Segarra in Spain.

"He has vineyards and he grows his own grapes. He makes
wine and then distills the wine base for the spirit," Wolfgang explained. "He even grows his own herbs or uses local wild herbs.
Totally crazy."

It was delicious, but for me it didn't quite compare to the early
Tarragona. Although I didn't tell Wolfgang, it struck me as simple
and not cohesive, as if I could taste the wormwood, anise, and fennel separately, in an echo of what Martin Žufánek had said. There
was an advantage to spirits with a century on them, I guessed.

The next bottle seemed to bear that out. It was gorgeous to
look at, with a beautiful label that showed little evidence of over
a hundred years in the cellar, bearing a bright white cross on a
red field over a small five-pointed star and the proud name of
Absinthe Supérieure Premier Fils à Romans. It was from around
1910, Wolfgang said, pouring me a generous portion and passing
the semi-frozen bottle of water for me to trouble the spirit with as
I saw fit.

I couldn't get over the varying fruitiness of it, as well as the
fullness I felt in each sip. The aromatics seemed to expand in
the mouth, offering new flavors and scents, one after another. It
contained a special herb, Wolfgang said, which took us a while
to figure out, though eventually we got to the correct name. In
addition to wormwood, fennel, and anise, we were also tasting
Acorus calamus, or sweet flag, a possibly toxic wild plant that had

been banned from commercial use in food and drink in the United States by the FDA in 1968. If sweet flag was what had made the pre-ban Premier Fils taste so delicious, they should probably reconsider.

⋮

I took a minute to photograph the bottle, and we took another break to look through some of Wolfgang's antiques. On the tile stove stood one of the largest corkscrews I'd ever seen, suitable for a giant bottle like the large-format vermouth I'd spotted in the cellar.

There was also an antique home bar: a set of three ornate glass carafes whose stoppers could be locked with a key, presumably so the household's servants couldn't get into them. Beyond the personal letter from 1811, Wolfgang had acquired Pernod collectibles, including a collection of a variety of stamps, presumably originally used for labels, in whose backward letters I could read the words "Pernod SA Couvet (Suisse)," "Pernod Couvet" and even "Maison à Tarragone." I leafed through a torn, late-nineteenth-century company catalogue, whose color lithograph cover displayed a drawing of a long line of Maison Pernod Fils employees, both men and women, walking out of the stately distillery building in Pontarlier.

Wolfgang's son came in again, whining slightly, and Wolfgang took time to play with him while I wrote down notes. I could tell Wolfgang was being honest with me in his responses to my questions, far more so than he had been on the phone, and I certainly felt like I could trust him, though there were one or two things that still kind of threw me off. He'd been accused of being part of the fakes, but, like Mira, I didn't believe that was the case. Or perhaps that impression was just the result of drinking together, and I was being naive.

I asked if he knew anyone else with a larger collection of pre-bans, and he had to say no, but admitted that he'd lost a bit of interest in it in recent years. While he didn't blame Christian directly for that, it seemed like that might have been the case. He'd stopped selling absinthe to collectors in the wake of what he called "Christian-gate," and had instead focused on his plans to make his own distillery someday, hoping to produce new spirits that were aligned with his tastes.

When I asked what he remembered about when the news of the forgeries had broken, he said he hadn't realized really what was going on at the time, because he'd been immediately kicked out of most of the private Facebook absinthe groups along with Christian. Mira and a few other absintheurs had pointed out that the evidence didn't connect Wolfgang to the forgeries, after which he'd been unbanned, but the absinthe world had changed after that. Maybe his relationship to absinthe had changed, too. But there were things about the vintage bottles that he adored, he said, like the very last pre-ban he wanted me to try, whose foxed and age-stained label proudly declared "Picard & Cie." and its city of origin, Marseille.

It was a rarity among rarities, a pre-ban absinthe blanche, much like the one bought by Mørk that a homeowner had found hidden in the walls of a house in Massachusetts, showing the historic roots of Swiss bleues. They were hard to find, he said, but they did exist.

He told me to pour as much as I liked, and I noticed that he'd replaced the bottle's vintage cork with a new one. When I troubled the spirit with ice water, it turned white almost immediately, and a moment later I caught a strong blackberry-leaf aroma rising from the glass, followed by a peppery, bitter finish. It wasn't my favorite sip of the evening—that prize went to the stellar Premier Fils—but it was a great spirit to end on, putting the modern Swiss absinthes I'd tasted into a new context.

It was time for me to go, and after I said goodbye to his wife and son, Wolfgang walked me to the local train station. I'd finagled a work trip into the chance to see a spellbinding collection of bottles, as haphazard and chaotically arranged as that was, and the afternoon had ended up being one of the most interesting drinking experiences of my entire life. Before I left, I wanted to hear what Wolfgang thought about Christian. They weren't in contact, he said, and he had no desire to speak to Christian ever again. I asked if he knew why Christian done what he was accused of. He didn't know, but he was sure it wasn't because of money.

"He comes from a good family, and I think he has enough money, because he had expensive guitars and other expensive stuff. I think it was just for the feeling that he can do it."

I asked what he meant, and he told me that he thought Christian wanted to make fakes simply to mess with people, which seemed to jibe with Mira's story about the laughing image on Facebook. The way he put it made it sound more deeply psychological than anything else, and I guessed it was plausible.

As for Christian really being rich, I wasn't sure, but Wolfgang said that he'd heard that Christian had some very wealthy relatives who had founded a famous toy company.

"One of his family members was the creator, I think."

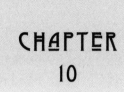

SEEDS
OF DOUBT

In hindsight, it's easy to say that there were plenty of reasons to doubt Christian early on, though most of those only became clear afterward, like reading back through a failed dinner recipe and realizing that, as printed, it doesn't include a crucial cooking step or list several important ingredients. When Anthony Sacco started getting into absinthe and joining private groups dedicated to the drink around 2015, Christian was seen as one of the world's great authorities on the spirit, someone who could answer his questions as a newbie. But there were things that struck Anthony as kind of weird at the time, I learned when I called him at his home in Chicago to ask him about the first time he thought the vibe was off. The earliest indications had nothing to do with absinthe, he said, but rather guitars, as Christian liked to post showy videos of himself tearing up the frets on social media channels.

"He was playing Yngwie Malmsteen licks, like super-fast neoclassical stuff. He would just be *ripping* it," Anthony said. "I got to be honest, he's not terrible."

Christian's playing might have been fast and accurate, but a wonky description on one of his videos caught Anthony's eye: Christian posted that a clip showed him playing what he called his new (old) '69 Fender Stratocaster. The headstock for Fender Stratocasters from 1969 has a particular shape, as well as a new branding and lettering, which Anthony remembered as noticeably different from earlier years, especially those models produced until 1964. When he watched Christian's video, he didn't see the '69 headstock he was looking for.

"It's probably the ugliest headstock that was ever on a Stratocaster. They're bulbous. They have different details. Like when you see Jimi Hendrix at Woodstock, that's a '69 Strat. It's got a huge headstock on it. The guitar he was playing was very clearly a '64-style headstock. I was like, 'What the fuck?' If you're going to say it's something, fine. Say it's something else. Don't say it's that one. And that got me thinking, 'God, what else is he lying about?'"

On the screen, I could see a handful of vintage guitars in the background of Anthony's room as he shared a photo that showed what the Fender headstocks looked like, along with a still from Christian's video. To my eye, Anthony was correct: Christian's guitar was different. The part around the tuners had a relatively straight bottom edge under the rounded loop at the end, not a curve, and it had much smaller "Stratocaster" lettering than the big branding from 1969. I'd owned a Stratocaster since I was a teenager, and its headstock looked just like the one Christian was playing.

When I asked about his background, Anthony described himself as "a collector of all kinds of things" who had studied the history of art and architecture at DePaul. With that background, I imagined he must have had a lot in common with Christian. And indeed Anthony had looked up to Christian as an authority figure in the absinthe world, when he first joined some of the same private groups I'd been in.

"Christian had been around since the early days of the forums online, back in the late '90s and early 2000s," he said. "Everybody knew him from way, way back in the day, and he was very well tied in."

Although the incorrect guitar year caught Anthony's attention, he knew it didn't matter, and he didn't mention it to anyone else at first. But there was another bad vibe when Anthony later tried to buy an expensive, early-nineteenth-century glass from Christian, who was doing a lot of business selling absinthe antiques to group members: it arrived with a chip missing from its so-called "lemon-squeezer" base. Christian refused to offer a refund, as the damage must have happened en route. But that wasn't likely, Anthony pointed out, since the missing chip of glass wasn't in the box. After some haggling, they reached a compromise, with Christian refunding part of Anthony's payment and Anthony using that amount to have the glass repaired by an expert near him. Despite working out a deal, it left a bad impression.

However, not everything about Christian was negative. Christian was damn funny, Anthony said, and had once given him a joke nickname—"the Pennywise Gopher," due to a shaggy haircut and cool slouch in Anthony's profile picture—that he found so funny he didn't even feel bad about it.

Although Anthony had since moved on, he said, he'd enjoyed being part of the absinthe underground, and bought shares of many pre-ban bottles that prolific collectors like Adrian Mørk were parting out, generally paying around $200 for a fifty-milliliter shot, as he remembered it. (That would nominally value a 1-liter antique bottle at four grand, though low "shoulder" bottle levels due to evaporation usually put the partitioner's net closer to $3,600, he said.) His own biggest find had been a full bottle of pre-ban Pernod Fils that he had bought out of the cellar of a bourbon-making family in Kentucky, an unopened gem which still bore the original English-language label identifying it as "Green" that had been slapped onto pre-ban French exports to the United States. Though he'd enjoyed a lot of that one himself, he's shared a good amount of it, shot by shot, with other collectors. The community was like that in those days.

Maybe it was because Anthony had joined the absinthe underground relatively late, he saw things differently, with fresh eyes, instead of the semi-blind vision of the long-term resident. Or perhaps it was Anthony's own education in art history. But over time, he started to notice something about the videos and photos of Christian opening pre-ban bottles, which he posted quite frequently.

"You would never see the top shot of the original cork in the bottle, with the foil on top and the wax," he said. "He would be very careful never to show that, and then whenever he did take a picture of the bottle, it would always be a replacement cork. Or there were a couple of cases where he had set his shredded-up cork on the bottle opener. The angles of the shots were always oriented so that you couldn't really see the upper neck. And they always had some kind of edit on them."

That struck Anthony as strange, especially for someone who was supposed to work in photography. And it wasn't just unboxing videos, he recalled. Christian was obviously editing the photos of his antiques, too. When Christian posted a photo of a nineteenth-century ouraline vessel, a type of glass that was famous for glowing slightly in ultraviolet light, thanks to the uranium that had been incorporated into it, Anthony could clearly see a black haze surrounding it—a relic of the filters Christian had used to goose up the image.

"It was like, dude, we all know what that glass looks like. It's not a big deal. You don't have to make it look like it's Ghostbusters ectoplasm or something."

There were a few other things that struck Anthony as strange at the time, and which seem even more so now. Christian regularly posted publicly that Grand No. 5 tasted like a pre-ban absinthe. That could have been a clever attempt to prepare the ground ahead of a battle, a way to precondition would-be suckers to expect that a pre-ban absinthe—in this case, a counterfeit one—would taste a lot like Grand No. 5, since that was part of the mix the forger was going to put into the bottle. But when I thought about it, it reminded me more of the times I'd accidentally tipped my cards by saying what I was secretly thinking, like if I made a dumb joke about wanting to marry the elegant woman who would later become my wife right after we'd met, before we'd even started dating. Was this criminal mastermind operating at a similarly stupid level?

It was one of those frequent comments about Grand No. 5 that had led Anthony to message Christian for the first time early in

2017, asking which pre-ban Christian thought tasted so much like Grand No. 5. "Pernod Fils, mon ami," Christian had replied.

In hindsight, Anthony's follow-up question reads as bizarrely on-target, a bullet shot straight through a bigger bullet. Had Christian had ever tried—or would it be possible—to make a contemporary absinthe taste old, he asked, or like it had been barrel-aged?

Christian suggested adding charred oak chips to the bottle for a week and microwaving it. "I've not tried this, but someone I know did, and I tasted it," he wrote. (As Anthony read the message, I felt my eyes open wide. Was this guy in sixth grade? "Someone I know," like when kids say "Someone I know *likes* you," that kind of thing?) That oaked-and-microwave spirit was quite good, Christian wrote, though not quite at the level of a true pre-ban. He then added some advice.

"Also, once filtered, you'd probably want to rest it for five years," he wrote. "There's just no way of faking age."

Anthony raised his eyes from Christian's old messages and laughed.

"Like, that's a *very* specific amount of time. If you hadn't done it, how do you know it would take exactly five years? It's clear that he was already working through this stuff. He had a whole process."

⋮

Anthony kept his doubts to himself for a long time, he said, but he eventually brought up two discrepancies in Christian's claims regarding his guitars to Scott MacDonald, with whom I'd shared the pre-ban at the Guy distillery in Pontarlier in 2013. Scott was the author of the book *Absinthe Antiques* and ran his own online absinthe group, but more importantly, he was working as a luthier, a maker of bespoke, high-end acoustic and electric guitars.

Anthony remembered that his suggestion to Scott didn't go over perfectly well, though it sounded like he might have planted the first seeds of doubt, or given them water if those seeds were already in the ground.

"All of my stuff was kind of circumstantial, but I was the first one to say that something's up with him—that this, psychologically, doesn't really add up, and that there's something to be concerned about with him," he said. "Scott told me I was nuts at first. And then he did a complete one-eighty."

A
SIMPLE TASTE

Incorrect dates on old guitars and weird comments hinting how to make forgeries might have raised an early eyebrow, but there's nothing quite like tasting a bad drink to make it clear that something is off. Like smelling smoke and feeling panic, tastes and smells communicate directly with our hearts.

By all accounts, Scott MacDonald had a very good palate. When we'd met at the festival in Pontarlier, I'd heard him make comments to François Guy, the fourth-generation owner of Distillerie Guy, about the proper amount of sweet fennel character in absinthe (not much, in Scott's opinion, if I remembered his recommendation

correctly). Reading through his old reviews on the Wormwood
Society, even his earliest tasting notes were confident and clear, devoid of extravagance, verbosity, or woolliness: "A warm rich anise,
alpine florals and light spice. During the louche, it opens up, and
the wormwood becomes more clear. Very nice."

I knew that part of what had happened with Christian was an
early warning from someone in the absinthe community, long before any proof was offered by the small group of amateur absinthe
detectives. I wasn't surprised to discover that Scott was the one
who had made that warning. When I called him the next week to
ask about him it, he started out by telling me how he'd developed
his sense of taste for absinthe, after first getting into the spirit in
2010. A French producer, Distillerie Paul Devoille, had put out a
tasting kit that contained individual herbal distillates, which allowed absintheurs to sample the many, often-similar components
of the spirit separately.

"You could taste grand wormwood alone. You could taste green
anise alone. You could taste fennel *doux* alone. You could taste angelica by itself. You could taste coriander by itself," he said. "That
really changed everything for me."

We'd met during Scott's first trip to the Absinthiades in France,
in 2013. He'd gone back many times since, also attending the festivals in Switzerland, sometimes serving on the juries that judged
the spirits in festival competitions. He had even been named an
"ambassador" of absinthe, an honor in recognition of those who
have made important contributions to promote the spirit, one of just
three Americans with that title, the distiller Ted Breaux being another. To this day, he said, absinthe makers still send him samples
asking for his opinion. In short, Scott knew absinthe, especially the

modern versions of the spirit, and his ability to taste was the real deal. And at one point, long before anyone said anything about Christian, Scott raised a supposed pre-ban to his lips and knew that something was wrong.

⋮

It was supposed to be a Pernod Fils, sent from a well-regarded absinthe dealer in Europe to a high-profile collector in the United States, who had then shared a sample from it with Scott. When he tasted the spirit, he knew exactly what it was, and it was not hundred-year-old absinthe.

"I noticed right away that there was a very recognizable base from a French distillery in there," he said. (He didn't want to tell me which maker the spirit came from, lest someone else take that information and attempt to do the same.) With a bottle from the modern French distillery in hand, he did a side-by-side comparison with the supposed Pernod Fils.

"The color, the aroma, the taste, the finish, everything *exact*, with one tiny little difference," he said. "I think he might've put a little bit of Tarragona in there, just for that little bit of separation, to make it slightly different."

Scott didn't make his initial opinion public, but he was sure of what he had found in the glass. It was still a couple of years before Christian's forgeries came to light, just the first taste that something was wrong, but that was enough to activate Scott's spidey-sense. With just one sip, he knew that forged absinthes were getting around.

⋮

By that point, I too had learned that fake bottles were circulating. Soon after I'd published my article about the absinthe trail in *The New York Times,* a reader had contacted me through the email address on my website. Would I be interested in buying an old bottle of absinthe they had in their closet?

Even to my inexperienced eye, it was not a very attractive purchase, though the seller sounded more like a slightly confused senior citizen than a clever scammer, which obviously might have been part of the con. I dutifully shared the photos in an email to the dealer Eric, who was posting pictures of absinthe forgeries in one of the main Facebook groups.

The bottle was funny, he replied, because it was so badly put together. The label was from Pernod Fils, but the bottle's stamped glass clearly said that it was from a different producer, Edouard Pernod, while the sticker on the bottle's neck had the name of Lecomte & Fils. Inside, some kind of greenish liquid stood at the low shoulder level, just below the bottle stamp, and a photo of a seal over the cork that didn't look at all right.

When he thought about it, Eric said, he might have spotted this very bottle on eBay or another site just a few months earlier. But when he'd noticed that bottle up for sale, it was empty.

⋮

Scott didn't know how the counterfeit Pernod Fils he'd tasted had gotten to the dealer who'd sent it to his collector friend in the United States, but it was enough to make it clear that the fake absinthe was coming from the other side of the Atlantic. There were other reminders, like Eric's occasional warning posts on Facebook, as well as sketchy vintage items that sometimes showed up on European auction sites. But in 2018, another counterfeit pre-ban reached Scott, and this time, it had a clear lineage.

"This was before it broke, but we all knew something was going on. From time to time on French eBay you would see a questionable seal on a vintage bottle," he said. "And then I was sent a sample by somebody who got it from Christian, and I tasted it. Right away, I knew that it was a fake. Absolutely."

Even for someone with a healthy amount of self-confidence, it wasn't easy to declare that Christian was the source of fakes: the man was a cornerstone of the absinthe world, a trusted authority on both antiques and spirits who was described as having tasted more pre-bans than anyone else alive. But Scott felt he had to do something, so he posted a vague warning in one of the groups, saying only that he had just tasted something that was clearly a counterfeit, that fake pre-bans were out there, and that collectors needed to be careful going forward. He made a point of not mentioning Christian by name. But he did highlight a few dealers he trusted, and Christian's name wasn't on that list. To be fair, Christian wasn't really a vintage absinthe dealer in the same way that Eric or the leading French dealer Patrick Roussel were. But the omission was noticed.

It didn't take long for Christian to contact him. He firmly denied any wrongdoing, but his attempt to sound friendly and relaxed seemed strained.

"I got an email from Christian saying, 'Hey brother, love ya, I heard you're accusing me publicly of this and that. I heard you're telling people that I'm faking absinthe. I would never do that. Lots of love, Christian,'" Scott recalled. "He was just boldly lying to my face, with lots of smiley faces and 'love.'"

Although Scott hadn't accused Christian publicly, others saw it that way. Several collectors rushed to defend a group leader whom they thought was being unfairly impugned. Scott's warning created the first big schism in the absinthe underground.

"Christian was so beloved, and he'd been so 'generous' with sending things, and he was playing such a great game," Scott said. "I posted it and became a pariah. I didn't use Christian's name. I just said, 'I know a fake when I taste it, and this is a blend of modern absinthes.' Half the community eviscerated me."

That was in early 2018, nearly a full year before all hell broke loose. It made for a pretty tense festival season. When Scott went to the Absinthiades later that year, several of his former friends barely spoke to him. That hurt.

To be fair, I knew Scott could be kind of argumentative, even somewhat pushy. There are various types of people you encounter when you do interviews, and Scott is a particular species: the person who thinks carefully about the angle of your article before he or she speaks. I found him extremely friendly and very easy to understand, sympathetic in the way the French use *sympa* to mean "likable," the kind of person whose speech patterns and lines of thinking don't take me a long time to get used to. But I could also see how he might rub some the wrong way or come off as overly self-confident. Personally, I probably wouldn't tell a distiller to use less fennel.

⋮

Friendships might have been frayed and fault lines were clearly surfacing, but the absinthe community kept going, in part because of the wonderful times they'd had in the past. Scott had been particularly active in bottle shares, as when Eric got in touch after finding some sought-after pre-bans walled up in an old house in France.

"Somebody was rebuilding their kitchen, and they found five or six bottles of Premier Fils that had been there for probably a hundred years. Eric offered me one of those bottles for an incredibly fair price."

Even at a reduced rate, a full bottle still wasn't easy to afford, especially when you have a family. But Scott found nine others who could join him in the purchase, and he split the price into ten equal chunks.

"We each spent about $200 and bought the bottle, and I decanted everything and sent everybody off their samples. We all got 60 milliliters or whatever. And for my trouble, when it was all done, I kept the bottle as sort of my gratuity for doing all the work."

Those shared purchases might have inadvertently helped Christian, Scott believed, since a would-be fraudster could follow the shared sales online and start to think things through. The most obvious evidence for any fraudulent pre-ban absinthe would be on the bottle: incorrect labels, new corks that didn't look nearly old enough, the wrong foil seal, the wrong wax seal, or some other aspect of the packaging. But when ten people shared the bottle, only one of them would ever have a chance to inspect that evidence. That could improve your odds substantially.

"If ten people are buying a bottle, but only one person sees it, and if that one person isn't looking for those things, you just fooled ten people, not one," Scott said. "Most of them will never even see the bottle itself. So how are they going to know if it's a fake or not?"

The bottle shares offered another form of inspiration, since a potential fraudster could see how quickly things were moving. Lists for potential bottle shares filled up on the same day, sometimes within minutes. And once absintheurs started sharing the cost of pre-bans, it became obvious that many more of them were going to be sold, now that the metaphorical bottleneck of the high price was eliminated. If you had ideas about selling absinthe, you could see exactly what people were buying and for what prices. The absinthe underground was thirsty for pre-ban absinthe, obviously willing to pay for it, and someone was going to have to fill that void.

Another thing to consider: when bottles were shared, they were usually split into individual, single-drink portions that were almost always consumed by their purchasers—you could see them posting their tasting notes, sometimes even noting their regret that their historic sample was gone forever. Unlike the type of collector who bought a bottle and never opened it, or who opened a historic bottle and only took a single drink, generally nothing remained inside the shared bottles, not that anyone was even talking about proving fraud by examining the spirit itself at that point.

Of course, there were a few knowledgeable people who joined the bottle-sharing groups. But most of the real cognoscenti, people who really knew what a pre-ban Edouard Pernod was supposed to taste like, owned their own bottles. They'd already tasted most absinthes and knew what they were like: the collector Patrick Roussel, for example, had no need to join a shared purchase of Pernod Fils organized by a bunch of Americans. And while some of the purchasers had decent palates, they were obviously in the minority. You could see it: many of the newbies who posted tasting notes from bottle shares got the names wrong, or the flavor descriptors

wrong, or absolutely everything wrong. The odds were in your fa-
vor. Novices trying samples simply didn't know what they were
doing, and they didn't know what they were tasting. Or as Scott put
it, in an attempt to explain how a potential absinthe fraudster might
have seen things at the time:

"What's in those vials is whatever they tell them it is."

⋮

Scott might have been burned by the experience of calling out the
fake absinthes that were starting to spread through the community,
and some of his former friends no longer talked to him. But by
making that post, he'd hit the radar of a small group of absinthe
connoisseurs who had been doing some important detective work
in recent months. Soon afterward they invited him to join a shared
folder online, where they had a collection of photos they thought
he should see.

Henri Privat-Livemont's 1896
poster for Absinthe Robette,
the pinnacle of Art Nouveau
absinthe advertisements.

"Drink it, you will see after." This late
nineteenth-century poster for Absinthe
Parisienne by P. Gélis-Didot and Louis
Maltéste plays up the healthy ("santé")
angle of the spirit, with a strong dose of
the period's pervasive male gaze.

Many French soldiers became
familiar with absinthe while serving
in the country's overseas colonies.
The artist Lucien Lefèvre echoed that
connection to the spirit in his 1895
illustration for Absinthe Mugnier.

Uncolored or "white" absinthes from the pre-ban era are extremely hard to find. Among other rarities, Wolfgang Klotz tracked down a pre-ban white from the Picard distillery in Marseille.

Due to evaporation, many unopened pre-ban bottles are frequently found at the low shoulder level. Chips, cracks, and other unique marks make it possible to identify individual bottles, often just from photographs.

"You have so much, you can't find anything." Wolfgang Klotz's cellars include hundreds of vintage vermouths, rums, and pre-ban absinthes, plus scores of post-ban Pernod Fils bottles from Spain.

The distiller Martin Žufánek with a bottle of pre-ban Dubied absinthe. The term "Fürstenthum Neuenburg" on the label indicates that it was produced before 1848.

Quentin (left) and and Patrick (right) Roussel, behind the bar in their private absinthe museum. The hundreds of antiques on display in their collection are all originals, with zero duplicates.

Best-known among Czechs for his traditional fruit brandies and innovative gins, Martin Žufánek gained fame in the absinthe world for his takes on the Green Fairy. His recreation of one of the first commercial absinthes, Dubied Père et Fils, sold out the day it was released.

A corner of the Roussels' private absinthe museum in Nantes. The fountain promoting the beneficial ("bienfaisante") nature of Terminus Absinthe hints toward the growing health concerns over the spirit in its heyday.

During the clandestin era in the Val-de-Travers, many of the region's illicit absinthe distillers used stovetop alembics, like this example from François Bezençon's antique collection.

In many Belle Époque paintings, absinthe drinkers were portrayed as rakish, dissolute, or fully debauched. In *La Buveuse d'absinthe*, Albert Emmanuel Bertrand depicts the absinthe-inspired reverie of an elegant young lady.

The leading illustrator of bohemian Paris, Henri de Toulouse-Lautrec was intimately familiar with absinthe. In *Monsieur Boileau at the Café*, a glass of absinthe in the foreground serves as a counterbalance to the seated central figure.

UN CATALOGUE RAISONNÉ

Il faut bien être sur ses gardes pour reconnaître la fausse monnaie que donne un ami.

—HONORÉ DE BALZAC

Absinthe's sense of place might be firmly grounded in Switzerland's Val-de-Travers and Pontarlier in France, but the drink had long since moved on to other homes: Paris, of course, as well as Spain, with lighter connections to the Czech lands, Italy, and a few other places. But when I set out trying to learn more about the absinthe forger, I did not expect that I would need to put the western French city of Nantes on my list. For many, Nantes probably sounds like a sleepy university town where you might book a romantic weekend holiday, and where you'd possibly end up feeling like you should have gone somewhere else. But in the

world of absinthe collectibles, it has an oversize position, thanks to
the collector and dealer Patrick Roussel, one of the group of amateur detectives who had identified the counterfeit pre-ban absinthes.
He knew more about absinthe antiques than anyone else, and he
could tell me how the group had caught Christian.

I was lucky to find a direct flight from Prague, though my return
trip would have to be routed through the hell of Charles de Gaulle.
Nantes Atlantique Airport felt much smaller than I expected, and
within five minutes of leaving the plane I had found the bus stop
and purchased my ticket into town. With over 300,000 inhabitants,
Nantes was supposed to be the sixth largest city in France, but it felt
more like a village, at least until the airport bus dropped us off at a
tram station, where I crossed the slow-moving waters of the Loire
into Nantes *centre ville*.

There were tons of students around when I exited the tram,
crowding the French tacos shop and other fast-food restaurants
nearby, but I found a half-empty crêperie and considered my goals
for the trip over a buckwheat galette filled with a fried egg, cheese,
and thick, coiled wheels of slightly stinky andouille sausage. After
the meal, I wandered through the old city on foot, admiring its
timbered houses and puzzling through a few bilingual signs in
French and Breton, before I boarded another tram, sped past the
imposing buildings and high defensive walls of the Château des
Ducs de Bretagne, and headed east toward the small commune of
Sainte-Luce-sur-Loire.

If I had any regrets about not having enough time to tour the
historic sites in Nantes, they disappeared after I got to Patrick's
place. At first, however, I thought I'd made some kind of mis-
take. Sainte-Luce-sur-Loire felt like the last suburban village at

the very end of the universe, and for several minutes I couldn't find Patrick's address. But then the welcoming aquiline face of a middle-aged man waved, beckoning me down a long drive, and I stepped into what Patrick described as the world's largest collection of absinthe antiques.

There were so many things to look at it was hard to know where to start. Two rooms that were attached to the Roussel home contained nothing but absinthe collectibles, all of which were original pre-ban items, from a variety of producers. On one wall, a fat peasant man with a pipe promoted Gempp Pernod on a poster the size of a kitchen table. On the back of the door, a shiny enamel sign promoted the same "absinthe supérieur" brand with a calendar for the year 1907. There were absinthe-branded plates and glasses on the walls, as well as scores, if not hundreds of antique absinthe spoons. A section of the first room had been set up as a café, with absinthe-branded tables, chairs, and matchstick holders, along with a chalk sign showing which bottles were available to drink. This was all Patrick's personal collection, he said, although he also sold antiques to others, and none of the items I was seeing in this collection were duplicates. If you think you know something about the history of absinthe, staring at a hundred-year-old clock pumping Bailly's "extra-purifiée" spirit or a vintage Peton & Jeannot chalkboard drink menu will quickly rid you of your excess self-confidence.

Patrick introduced me to his son, Quentin, and they took turns telling me the origins of some of the pieces in their collection. Dealing antiques was not Patrick's real job—he was recently retired, after a long career in the French Army—but it was substantially more than a hobby, which had started simply enough, when he'd purchased a single vintage absinthe spoon at the time of Quentin's birth some thirty-one years earlier. Today, they dealt in absinthe collectibles as both a hobby and a business, though Quentin spent most of his time at his job in educational administration.

They were a daunting pair. Patrick had a face like that of a bird of prey, perhaps more of an owl than an eagle, and an air of the patient observation such animals display before launching an attack. As a former soldier, he seemed ordered and organized, prepared for any eventuality, and observed the scene like a raptor waiting for a vole to emerge from its den. In contrast, Quentin seemed like he might be younger than thirty-one, but in my pictures he has a starkly mischievous look in his eye, hinting at what might be my favorite expression of intelligence, the kind that finds many aspects of modern life to be worthy of a smirk, if not a laugh.

I expressed amazement at their antiques, and asked if it wasn't true that pre-ban bottles were getting much harder to find.

"Yes, there will be fewer and fewer, especially if people keep drinking them, but there will always be some bottles coming out. There are always wine cellars being cleared out, every year, from châteaux or homes, and there are good bottles coming out on the market every year. For example, for myself, I'm going to receive a bottle of absinthe tomorrow. It's not an exceptional bottle, but I'm sure that it's real."

I asked if it was really that easy. Apparently it was for Patrick, though it wasn't always that way.

"When you're known, yes—it works like that. But when a collector starts out, it's very difficult to find things. And if you want to find things, it's necessary not to go too fast. That's important. Above all, you have to learn."

As a collector himself, he had an understanding of the obsession that can overtake someone who was interested in absinthe and its antiques. The worst thing, he said, was for collectors to decide that they wanted things now, quickly, simply because they had money and they wanted to buy something with it.

"To be a collector, you have to learn your subject matter," he said. "You should start with things that cost five euros, ten euros—just small things that are not worth a lot, and you start to understand. And after learning to understand, you can buy more expensive things, and you can start to progress. You start to collect at a different level."

Not everyone does it that way, he added.

"I've known a few collectors. I knew a banker who had some money. He told me, 'I want all the spoons.' At the time, I told him that's not how you do it. You buy a few, you go slowly, you start to learn what they're for, what their history was, and so forth. But I'll tell you what happened: he bought everything. He gave us thousands of euros. And after the spoons, he wanted all the pitchers and all the glasses. He bought and bought and bought. And then, after three or four years, he was done. He had a collection, but he didn't know anything about the history. So he couldn't move forward with it. You have to make progress with your knowledge."

He gestured around the room.

"This isn't a collection from one or two years. I've been collecting for thirty-one years. And I still don't know everything."

For example, there were the matchstick holders, *pyrogènes*, which were generally ceramic. At the end of the nineteenth century, pyrogènes bearing the name of absinthe brands were given away by distilleries as promotional material, sitting on top of café and cabaret tables to remind customers to choose absinthe Premier Fils or some other brand for their next glass.

"Personally, I originally thought there might be maybe thirty different kinds," Patrick said. "And then you find out there were hundreds."

In part, those hundreds of variations spoke to the changing views on absinthe in its time, Quentin added. He gestured toward the large Gempp Pernod poster with the happy peasant man I'd spotted when I'd first arrived. In faint letters, the smoke from his pipe spelled out "C'est ma santé," or "It's my health."

"If you appreciate these differences, you start to wonder why they're there," he said. "In the case of 'It's my health,' that's because there was a time when it became important for producers to argue that absinthe was actually good for your health, because people were starting to say that absinthe was very unhealthy."

A similar shift could be seen on a series of small posters promoting the Oxygenée brand. Early posters often said "Absinthe Cusenier," Quentin showed me, followed by the word "oxygenée," meaning "oxygenated," in much smaller letters. Later, the brand "Oxygenée" became larger and larger.

"Eventually, they removed the word 'absinthe' entirely. Look at this little thing." He handed me a thick circle, roughly the diameter of a poker chip, with a clear lid through which I could see three tiny yet functional dice, as well as a small bottle painted on the dice board they sat upon. "It's a game called '421'—the goal is to throw a four, a two and a one at the same time. It says 'Oxygenée Cusenier.' If you look really, really closely, you can see that on the label of the bottle down there, there is one very tiny reference to 'absinthe.' Otherwise, it doesn't even have the word 'absinthe' on it. Just 'Oxygenée Cusenier.'" He smiled. "And these little pocket games? We didn't even know they existed a short while ago."

Patrick nodded.

"Originally, this one was in really bad shape. I took it apart and completely restored it. And then one of my friends found another, four or five years later, basically new, in perfect shape. No one even had them recorded as absinthe antiques, and that's why we're able to find them. It's a similar story with the old bottles."

$$\vdots$$

Although Patrick was famous among drinkers for sourcing remarkable pre-ban spirits, his focus had always been primarily on antiques, even to the point of obsession.

"Once I decide to own something, sometimes it takes me years to get it." The best example was his favorite spoon: the rarest absinthe spoon in the world. "It's known that there is just one example, and it has a huge history. It's not prettier than any others, and it's made from regular metal, but it is unique."

When he set it on the bar, it looked fairly shiny for a piece of nineteenth-century silverware, with a symmetrically pointed tip that looked more like a dagger or a bayonet than a spoon. Halfway down, its blade extended into a large rectangle where a sugar cube could sit, atop flowery Art Nouveau cutout designs that would let the water and dissolved sugar drip through. Leaves and a thistle stood behind a shield that read "Garnison de Nancy," under which a stylized ribbon carried the motto "Qui s'y frotte s'y pique"— literally, "Whoever rubs it gets pricked," which could be poetically translated as "If you go looking for trouble, you'll find it." At the bottom of the handle, the large letters C and M were interwoven in another ornate cutout design. It was from the French military garrison in the eastern city of Nancy, he said, sourced from its old *cercle militaire*, or mess hall.

"This was the officer's mess, the place where all the officers of the Nancy garrison met in the evenings," he said. As such, the spoon had a personal connection for him. "I was an officer in the French army, and I served in Nancy. My son Quentin was born in Nancy. I served under the colors of this regiment. I wore a thistle on my uniform—that thistle, there. And 'Qui s'y frotte s'y pique,' that was the motto of my regiment in Nancy. There were a lot of things that made this really meaningful for me. It just had to be mine someday."

But with just one known example, that simply wasn't possible. Another collector had it for twenty years while Patrick waited, and that other collector simply wouldn't sell it.

"But then, one day, he said, 'Hey, you should come by and have a drink soon.'"

The collector who had held the spoon for two decades suddenly needed a bit of money, he said, and wasn't so interested in collecting. *Et voilà*. The collector was happy that the spoon from the garrison was going to a good home, glad to have a much-needed infusion of cash, and Patrick was grateful that he finally had a spoon he'd wanted for twenty years. But for a true collector, the feeling doesn't last long.

"Once I got it, the very next day I had to move on to something else."

Unlike the spoon, he wasn't even aware of the existence of his other favorites before buying them, like the pocket dice game. He was particularly proud of the stained-glass window in the second room, which stood roughly two feet high by two feet wide, also promoting the Oxygenée brand. In lead-framed cut glass, it depicted a Belle Époque woman with a generous décolletage carrying a tray with an absinthe bottle—only the O of its brand name was visible—as well as a glass and a carafe of water. In flowing orange letters against a green background, it read "Absinthe Oxygenée," with the phrase "en vente ici," meaning "sold here," at the very top.

"One day, a guy sent me a picture of that. It was a bad photo, taken in full sunlight against a white wall, and it wasn't very visible. He said that it was a stained glass window, and asked if I was interested. But until then, no one in the absinthe antiques world had ever talked about stained-glass windows."

The man was Swiss, though not from the Val-de-Travers, and he claimed that he'd bought it from a bistro that had recently been forced to close and sell everything. It was an original artwork, he said.

Patrick told the man he'd think it over, and showed the picture to Quentin, who believed they'd seen it somewhere before. Over the next few days, the two searched through all their books on absinthe antiques without finding a single reference. Eventually, one of them came up with an old postcard from a *guinguette*, a type of countryside tavern or dance hall that was popular in the late nineteenth century, when their locations outside of the city limits allowed guinguettes to offer drinks at low prices. Like the spoon, it came from the same city in Lorraine where Patrick had once served.

"The guinguette was where people went to dance on Sundays," he said. "This one was just outside of Nancy. On the postcard you could see that it had, all around, absolutely huge stained-glass windows, advertising absinthe, beer, water, the salon—just giant advertising windows." Those windows stood more than four meters in height, or about thirteen feet tall, and in the very middle of the postcard was one that looked exactly like the one the Swiss seller was offering. It was not even close to the right size, however.

"I thought it had to be a reproduction, that the guy was trying to sell us something that was made last year."

Patrick asked for more photos before he could agree to the purchase, and while the seller was getting those ready, the Roussels continued with their research. They found that the original windows from the guinguette had been destroyed in the 1980s, but there were photos of plexiglass copies of the originals in the Musée de l'École de Nancy, the regional Art Nouveau museum. With that, Patrick was able to confirm that the one being offered was a perfect scale model, an exact match in every proportion, of the original window that had been made by a glass worker called Berger. He also learned that window makers like Berger generally created scale models of their larger works before they embarked on their productions. What was being offered for sale was not an original, nineteenth-century advertisement promoting Oxygenée absinthe, Patrick realized, but the workshop model for that advertisement.

The seller wanted cash, and Patrick wanted a customs declaration and an invoice for taxes and legal clarity. For the sake of convenience, they agreed to meet at the train station in Lyon, where Patrick handed over an envelope which the seller took into a bathroom stall to count privately. When Patrick returned to Nantes with the window, he learned that museums all over France had already refused to buy it for budget reasons—it was simply too expensive. In a happy twist, he also discovered that it fit perfectly inside the window frame facing his collection's second room.

"It was like it was meant to be here."

⋮

Although his obsessive heart was focused on antiques, he also had luck with bottles, though he wanted me to understand that when pre-bans were found, they were almost always Pernod Fils.

"I did have the good luck to find a cache of Berger absinthe— twenty bottles," he said. I'd heard versions of that story already, as it was a near-legend in the absinthe underground: a few years earlier, Patrick had purchased a slew of C. F. Berger pre-bans, all from the year 1913, all in remarkable condition. The source appeared to be a family of French colonials who had returned from Algeria with everything they owned, including the remains of the family wine and spirits cellar, around 1961.

"It's easy to find a bottle of Pernod Fils. Still—every year, fifteen or twenty bottles of vintage Pernod Fils hit the market. But with other brands, it's much more complicated. The smaller the production, the harder they are to find. Berger was an excellent absinthe, higher quality than Pernod Fils. But in terms of volume, they made much, much less. And above all, when you find bottles, they're always close the date of the ban—they're almost always between 1910 and 1915. Wolfgang did find some bottles from around 1850, but that was an exceptional case."

Although he was based in the far west of France and had picked up a couple of his favorite antiques near Nancy in the east, he'd had the best luck in the south, he said, around Marseille and the port cities from which the old distilleries had once shipped their products. He'd found his case of Berger bottles from 1913 and many more down there.

Other good bottles could be found in Spain, he said, where the Tarragona Pernods are still regularly available. He'd once found a group of twenty-five Tarragonas himself, and Wolfgang had been able to source boxes and boxes of them, he said.

"But that's about it. It's really mostly just Pernod Fils—the other brands are really rare. And that's how we brought down Christian."

⋮

In fact, the wide variety of Christian's would-be finds had raised Patrick's and Eric's suspicions, just as Cary believed. The proof had come much later. But their early intuition was important. Logically, it bugged them.

"Personally, as a collector, I can't come up with a different absinthe every month," he said. "You can go years without finding an unusual brand—it's just Pernod Fils, Pernod Fils, Pernod Fils. But Christian was selling a different brand of absinthe every *single* month. Every month the bottle changed. And that started to concern us."

Along with Eric and another dealer, Thibault, Patrick started to keep track of empty bottles from the pre-ban era that were being listed on auction sites like eBay in France and elsewhere, creating a shared folder on the internet where they could post pictures and record the sales. At first, they didn't know what they were going to do with it, but they thought it might come in handy.

Patrick started to notice other suspicious aspects of Christian's bottles, like the stamps. Historically, most distillers had packaged their spirits in generic bottles that had been made for the mass market, which they customized by marking them with a piece of molten glass that they stamped with their own brand. Atop the cork was a wax seal, which had another stamp that bore the brand's name, although the wax stamps and the glass stamps were not the same.

From one of the drawers of antiques, Quentin pulled out one of each for Pernod Fils, pointing out the differences in size and design. From a couple of the pictures Christian had posted online, Patrick thought the bottle stamps and the wax stamps looked too similar, as if Christian might have used the three-dimensional impression of the stamped glass to make his own stamps for the wax.

But for Patrick, the crucial moment came when his friend Patrick Grand casually mentioned that Christian had traded two pre-ban bottles for what he remembered as fifteen bottles of Grand No. 5. For a price-vs-cost-focused antiques seller like Patrick Roussel, the math simply didn't add up.

"How much does a bottle of Grand No. 5 cost? But an absinthe from before the ban? That's 2,000 or 3,000 euros all on its own. That's when I said, 'This doesn't make sense.' And then Patrick showed me the bottles."

If the variety of the bottles Christian claimed to have found had raised Patrick Roussel's suspicions, as well as the iffy wax in some of the pictures, visiting Patrick Grand at his distillery in the Val-de-Travers provided immediate confirmation. On the two bottles, the labels were at the wrong height.

"He made mistakes. He made *gluing* mistakes," he said. Antique dealers like Patrick relied heavily on information from the Institut national de la propriété industrielle (INPI), the French national institute for industrial property. Even today, they use information that was registered with the INPI more than a century ago to authenticate antiques or identify a year of production, brand, or maker. Crucially, the INPI archives also contain precise information on product design.

"The height and position of the label on the bottle was always registered when they filed the patent. 'The label is two centimeters from the bottom.' It's clearly noted and very well defined," Patrick said.

Christian had purchased plenty of antiques from Patrick over the years, including a number of old absinthe spoons and vintage glassware. But he'd also purchased many examples of another type of collectible: unused bottle labels, which dealers track down by the dozens in the archives of old distilleries or through print auctions, and which absinthe aficionados then obsess over, rate, and store in books, much like baseball cards for Americans. Those labels must have been what Christian had fixed onto the empty, generally label-free bottles he'd picked up on French eBay, Patrick reasoned. And while he didn't know what was inside the bottles Christian had sent to Switzerland, it couldn't be authentic. Patrick could see that Christian's absinthes looked wrong, in the sense that they looked the same.

"When you have two vintage absinthes, they *never* have the same color," he said. "They are darker or lighter, or more green or more brown. But these two, they were the *exact* same color."

The same color, despite supposedly coming from two different distilleries, in two different years. When I'd visited Grand in his distillery inside the church in Fleurier, he hadn't been able to— or hadn't wanted to—remember the details of the second bottle, which was by that point long gone, thrown out, given away, or who knows what; Grand wasn't the kind of guy to keep notes for things from the past. But as I'd seen that Grand still had one of the two fakes he'd received from Christian: the would-be Juillard & Babel pre-ban. He'd also showed me the messages Christian had sent, a few of which I'd photographed with Grand's permission. In them, Christian regularly asked if Grand would sell him several liters of absinthe on the sly, hinting that it should be kept secret as "a personal thing," even going so far as to say, "I won't tell anyone." In return, he was offering a bottle of what he claimed to be a Pernod Fils from the year 1900, holding it up in a grinning selfie when he made the offer. It sounded like that Pernod Fils and the Juillard & Babel were the two bottles Patrick was talking about.

Armed with a visual confirmation of Christian's fakes, Patrick and his collaborators moved forward with their collection of photographs of empty bottles from online auctions, creating a catalogue raisonné of bottles Christian listed for sale. Eventually, the empty bottles from the auctions and Christian's full bottles of would-be pre-bans matched up.

"You see, there are always little marks, bubbles in the glass or scratches that make every vintage bottle unique," Quentin said. "Every single one of them is different."

Many of those marks were visible in the photographs of bottles that had been sold empty, and then offered for sale as authentic pre-bans by Christian. A Pernod Fils with a particular pattern of cut-through wear on its foil wrapper—it almost resembled an absinthe spoon—and a dark red stain over the word "extrait" on the left side of its off-white label first showed up in a listing for a "rare, empty bottle" on eBay, before being offered for sale as an unopened pre-ban from Christian; both photos also showed a very particular chip at the eleven o'clock position on the bottle stamp. A Constant Pernot that had sold as an empty bottle on eBay in January had the exact same hairline crack above the P and four other clear identifying marks on the bottle stamp as the Contant Pernot that Christian had offered for sale to a collector in March. An empty bottle of the obscure Déchanet absinthe—whose unused vintage labels are still being listed on eBay today—was listed in an auction whose accompanying photographs showed several distinctive cracks: a double scratch through the D of Déchanet and a single scratch through the E and C, as well as a big missing section of the oval surrounding the seal at seven o'clock. The Déchanet that was offered for sale by Christian a short while later displayed the exact same scratches.

By that point, they were sure.

⋮

When I asked Patrick why he thought Christian did it, he said it must be money. He'd known pathological liars—he used the French word *mythomane*—and Christian was different.

"I've met pathological liars before," he said, shaking his head. "A pathological liar is not trying to make himself richer. He tells stories. But Christian, he was trying to make money."

But it seemed that he wanted to prove he was smarter than other people, I said, like the German scientist, Jan Hartmann.

Patrick agreed. "If you think of what he did, sending samples to Jan, that's really like you think Jan Hartmann is an idiot. It's crazy. Jan is someone I really like, because he's principled, absolutely. He wants the truth." In Patrick's eyes, that might have also inspired Christian. "It's like he's hoping to be able to say, 'Him, he's dumb—he wasn't able to figure it out. I'm better than him, and what I made was a good product.'"

But Patrick thought money was at the root.

"I mean, look, he made thousands and thousands that we know of. And there's definitely stuff that we don't know about. I'm sure that in the world of absinthe, there are many people who got tricked and never told anyone."

⋮

Both Patrick and Quentin seemed to understand the psychology behind the frauds quite well. That was part of what had made it hard to identify the forged bottles, Quentin thought, since, like Cary, many who bought counterfeit absinthes might not actually taste them.

"The problem with absinthe is that if someone buys a bottle for 2,000 euros or whatever, it's not guaranteed that they'll ever open it. They could buy it just for the beauty of the bottle, just to keep it in their collection, sealed. So just from the side of the taste, maybe no one would ever be able to see if it's authentic or not."

In addition, the collectors who purchased expensive bottles were generally not in the position to taste them objectively, he continued.

"For the person who does open an expensive bottle, it's a different story. If you put 2,000 euros down for a bottle, it's hard to say you've been had. Intellectually, it's almost impossible to say 'Someone tricked me.'"

Patrick nodded.

"You can't say it's not good. You *always* think it's good. You buy a historic bottle of absinthe for 2,000 euros. From the moment you put down 2,000 euros, you simply can't say it's not good. Psychologically, you just can't. You paid 2,000 euros, so you're no longer unbiased. You're going to find something good in it. *C'est obligatoire.*"

He'd come up against that same situation himself, including when he'd purchased the box of Berger absinthes. "When I found my cache of absinthe, it messcd me up, because when I tasted it, I found it exceptional," he said. "But I said to myself, 'That's because you paid for it.'" For an objective opinion, he asked for help from

Eric, as well as Quentin and others. "I said, 'Give me a review on this absinthe. I'm not telling you anything about it. Tell me what you think about it, because I'll tell you in advance, I'm the one who bought it.' Eric did his review, Quentin did his, and we have a friend Benoît who also did one, and everyone agreed. But the same thing can happen with an absinthe that is bad. When we've invested money, psychologically, we just can't say that it is not good."

Beyond that, he said, there was an element of goodwill on the part of the purchasers, some of whom were simply too trusting toward someone they considered a friend.

Part of that, he said, had to do with how well Christian had crafted his image in the absinthe world.

"When you trust someone, you trust someone, and he knew how to create trust. That's where he was very strong. He went around, he came to the Absinthiades in Pontarlier, he made friends, he participated in everything, the parties here and those, he bought antiques, he was very, very friendly. That's how he built his network. He had the same network as big collectors like me: he knew just about that many people. And when we talked about Christian, everyone said, 'Oh yeah, the Englishman, he's nice.' Well, yes. He was nice, yes. He was."

I asked if anyone else had said anything about Christian's motivation, and Patrick replied that he simply didn't care.

"The reasons why don't really matter to me. There's just one thing I can't stand: when someone betrays my confidence. In some ways, this was a person I trusted. It didn't cost me any money. I never bought any fake bottles, because maybe he realized that it would be a very bad idea to offer them to me. But regardless, he betrayed my trust."

⋮

Christian didn't just take people's money: his fakes had pretty much ruined the market for pre-ban absinthe bottles, which I guessed might be good news for collectors like Patrick who knew what they were doing. That said, counterfeits from would-be scammers were still bouncing around. Just a couple of months earlier, Patrick had been offered a forged pre-ban during a trip to Switzerland.

"Even when I looked at it, I could see it probably wasn't a real pre-ban. But when I'm not sure, I have a kit, a syringe with a long needle, so I can check the taste. I went through the cork and took my sample. It turned out to be a Swiss clandestine that was maybe thirty or forty years old, quite good, but just a simple absinthe from the old Swiss underground. Someone had put in in a pretty bottle with a nice label. The price was supposed to be 3,000 Swiss francs."

He got out a stack of old labels and set them before me. None of them had brand names, just the word "absinthe" printed in artistic, nineteenth-century lettering. In the Belle Époque, he said, absinthe was sometimes sold in bulk and bottled by restaurants, bars, or retailers, who used generic labels, echoing what I'd heard about the Palazzo Cache.

"For historic absinthe labels, there are dozens and dozens and dozens without specific brands, like this. You can easily find this kind of label for one or two euros at a flea market. You can find an old bottle on eBay for ten euros. Take a label like that, stick it on a bottle and that's an old bottle of absinthe. Your base cost is less than fifteen euros. Then make a decent blend, add in some kind of old cork, a small piece of wax and sell it at a cut-rate price, like 700 or 800 euros, instead of 2,000 or 3,000. It's easy."

A few people had lost a few hundred or a few thousand euros, he said. Others had lost much more, having paid $20,000 or more for Christian's fakes, he said. For most of the victims, there had been no recourse. By chance or by cunning, Christian had managed to commit his crimes *dans la vide* between countries, Quentin said, in the void between nations, where no courts had jurisdiction.

"You couldn't bring a case against him, because he bought empty bottles from France or Italy on the internet. He bought absinthe like a Tarragona from Spain. He bought a bunch of Grand No. 5 in Switzerland. He made his blends in England, and then he sold them to an American. It's impossible."

There was just one collector who had managed to get his money back: a former British policeman who lived in France. He'd kept a residence in his home country, which meant he could file charges there. Instead of filing suit, the former cop had accepted some kind of deal with Christian, getting compensation that kept Christian out of jail. It seemed like a missed opportunity for justice, but it also looked like a new line of research for me, and I made a note to track the former cop down.

We finished up the afternoon by raising a glass together, starting with le Père François from François Bezençon, the distiller and antiques collector I'd met in the Val-de-Travers. Patrick expressed the greatest respect for Swiss distillers, whose absinthes he found generally well balanced and round, without a single element or aroma that stood out, while he thought many French absinthes were much more herbal, with a much stronger focus on wormwood.

"Every country, every population has its own expectations in terms of taste," he said. "But honestly, we both prefer Swiss absinthes."

He was not so fond of most American versions, and although he declined to name any names, he did say that some Americans seemed to think they'd invented absinthe. Though he clearly loved the Swiss products from his favorite maker Claude-Alain Bugnon, he did not care for the Butterfly absinthe Bugnon made for the U.S. market—supposedly following a historic recipe that originally came from Boston—due to its "American" flavor profile. He saved his strongest words for Czech absinthe, which he described as "a catastrophe," other than the spirits from Martin Žufánek and the younger maker Petr Šlechta, the only two Czech producers he considered "correct."

We moved on to Grand Absinthe Blanche. It had a very different taste when compared to le Père François, still refreshing and delicious, but with something like a cinnamon or star-anise note in the mid-palate, I thought. When he sipped his glass, Patrick seemed to be reconnecting to an old friend.

"A little bit less round, slightly less balance, with more grand wormwood in the finish," he said. "*Oui. C'est très bon.*"

Even after what had happened with the fake bottles, he still loved absinthe, he said. It was a small but tightly interconnected world of collectors, a demimonde of close colleagues who truly cared about the drink and its rich history. Absinthe had given Patrick friends all over the world, he said, even one from a country that was not traditionally well loved by the French.

"Absinthe has meant that I have friends in Switzerland, in Japan, in the U.S., all over the place. I even used to say, 'I have a friend who is an Englishman, who is really, really nice," he said. He shook his head. "That was Christian."

I made a mental note to solve the question of Christian's nationality, whether he was English or from somewhere else. Before I left,
I asked Patrick what he thought had been the cause of Christian's
downfall. Was it greed? Arrogance? A secret desire to get caught?

He shrugged.

"He wasn't very good, because he messed up the details."

FORGERS
OF ALCOHOL

Most people in the absinthe community had no suspicions: Christian was widely viewed as an expert, a hyper-
knowledgeable collector whose opinion on pre-ban bottles
and antiques was authoritative. But as collectors like Anthony Sacco
started to wonder if everything was on the level, their minds turned
to a well-known fraudster from the world of wine: Rudy Kurniawan,
whose story had been the subject of an amazing documentary, *Sour
Grapes,* just a couple of years earlier.

Born and raised in Indonesia, Kurniawan apparently came to
the United States to study at Cal State Northridge in 1998, entering
on a student visa which he subsequently simply overstayed, despite

being told to leave by U.S. Immigration after his visa expired. By 2003 he was buying and selling absolutely huge amounts of top-shelf Burgundy, especially bottles from Domaine de la Romanée-Conti, which soon earned Kurniawan the nickname "Dr. Conti."

Known in wine circles for his impeccable tasting palate and wealth of knowledge, Kurniawan was vague about his origins and the funding behind his business. Wealthy collectors didn't seem to care. Nor did journalists, with the *Los Angeles Times* running a glowing profile in 2006 under an eye-catching headline: "$75,000 a Case? He's Buying." That year, Kurniawan sold wines worth $35 million in two auctions held by the New York wine dealers Acker, Merrall & Condit, now known as Acker Wines, setting a single-auction sales record of $24.7 million in the second. Eight of the bottles from Kurniawan's 2006 auctions were especially precious: magnums—double-size bottles containing 1.5 liters—of 1947 Château Lafleur. Later, experts would point out that only five double-size magnums had been produced at that winery in 1947, as lawyers representing the billionaire Bill Koch noted in the fraud suit they filed against Kurniawan in 2009.

It was a remarkable story of a rocket-like rise and an equally precipitous fall, with Kurniawan going from an immigrant college freshman to a recognized fraudster in just over a decade. His 2006 *L.A. Times* profile had claimed that Kurniawan spent a million dollars a month on wine, and he was famous for driving both a Bentley and a Ferrari. That must have been a pretty sweet life, especially compared to what followed Koch's civil suit: after defaulting on a $10 million loan from the auction house, Kurniawan was arrested by the FBI on the morning of March 8, 2012, and charged with five felonies, including wire fraud and mail fraud. The U.S. Attorney for his case was Preet Bharara, now a podcast host and media impresario, whose statement at the time read: "As alleged, Rudy Kurniawan held himself out to be a wine aficionado with a nose for a counterfeit bottle, but he was the counterfeit, pawning off prodigious quantities of fraudulent wine himself to unsuspecting auction houses and collectors." At his home in Southern California, FBI agents found what they called "a sophisticated counterfeiting operation," though the images I saw in the documentary made it seem homey and simple, like a school science project a B-student teenager might come up with down in the cellar. There were inexpensive older Burgundies and modern Napa Valley bottles on a table, ready for blending, with handwritten notes on their amounts in certain blends, as well as the recognizable tools of a counterfeiter: corks, corkers, rubber stamps bearing the names of celebrated producers, and thousands of labels.

Researching Kurniawan's story, I spotted familiar details, though I had never heard that he had been presenting himself as an expert who could detect counterfeits, or that he had ever accused anyone else of counterfeiting wines. Other parts of the story were very different from anything accused Christian of doing—no one I knew remembered Christian driving a Ferrari or a Bentley, and he certainly wasn't spending a million dollars a month on pre-bans. That said, there were similarities, including that both men were known to have remarkable palates and were seen as authorities in their worlds. Kurniawan had famously held bucket-list wine tastings in chic restaurants, which, in retrospect, offered a hint as to what he might be doing, as an article about the documentary on the entertainment-industry website *Deadline* pointed out: Kurniawan asked for the restaurants to return the empty bottles to him after tastings, which meant he was probably refilling them with his own blends.

I wondered if anyone remembered what had happened to the empty pre-ban bottles that Christian had opened at absinthe festivals and private soirées: as collectibles, they were worth at least a bit of money, so it wouldn't have seemed terribly strange to keep one you'd brought to the party and shared with your friends; Scott had even mentioned keeping a pre-ban bottle as a "gratuity" for having organized a bottle share. Nor would it have been terribly weird, I imagined, to ask if you could keep a friend's empty pre-ban bottle as a souvenir of a wonderful, shared experience. But if you were a forger, that would have given you another vessel to fill with your fake blend and then sell on to the next sucker.

There was an early foreshadowing in Kurniawan's case that had no analogue in Christian's story, at least not that I knew of. In April 2008, more than seventeen months before Koch accused Kurniawan of fraud, an auction of some of his wines by Acker, Merrall & Condit was paused for an important announcement: one of that day's biggest attractions—ninety-seven bottles from the cult Burgundy producer Domaine Ponsot, to be sold in twenty-two lots—was being withdrawn. Laurent Ponsot, the fourth-generation winemaker at the family domaine, had voiced concerns about the Ponsot wines that were about to be auctioned before the event, but Acker, Merrall & Condit hadn't known that the man would show up in person in the hope that he could stop their sale. With the Ponsot scion in the house, the prized lots being offered by Kurniawan were pulled halfway through the auction.

The *Wine Spectator* journalist Peter Hellman covered the scandal of the aborted sale in an article the next week. The canceled lots were supposed to contain thirty-eight bottles of Domaine Ponsot from the Clos Saint-Denis Grand Cru appellation dating from the years 1945 through 1971, but the winemaker explained that Domaine Ponsot hadn't produced that wine until 1982. Four bottles with Domaine Ponsot labels, supposedly from 1929, would have been made by Laurent's grandfather, Hippolyte, but the elder Ponsot did not begin bottling his wines with those labels until 1934. Other discrepancies included even more basic errors, like neck labels on a slew of 1962 wines that claimed that they'd been produced for the Nicolas chain of retail shops, though Nicolas had never stocked Ponsot wines, Laurent said. Other bottles were sealed with red wax, which he said Domaine had never used.

Kurniawan was in attendance at the stopped auction, and Hellman managed to get a quote from him: "We try our best to get it right, but it's Burgundy, and sometimes shit happens." (Burgundians must have wondered, "What the hell does that mean?") Later, he commented that he'd be working with Laurent Ponsot to figure out who'd created the frauds, effectively saying that he was now going to find the real killers. For his part, Ponsot declared that he was not a rich man, but that he would be happy to spend his money to look for those responsible.

It was hard to imagine a great counterfeiter being so careless with basic details about his forgeries, though I remembered that some of those echoed the points that Patrick Roussel had mentioned. It was also hard to imagine why Kurniawan had been allowed to continue selling wines after that sale, even after the Koch lawsuit against him the next year: Kurniawan apparently snuck some wines into a London auction the month before he was arrested. But if there's one constant in the world of wine, it is that fraud is always with us. In fact, counterfeits are common in all types of alcohol, and have been for nearly as long as we've been drinking it.

⋮

I knew a bit about fakes from my work on Czech beer, which sounds weird when you consider that a Czech beer—a bottle, a can, or on draft—might cost a few dollars, while you can find a single recent bottle of Romanée-Conti selling for $20,000. There's simply a lot more margin in wine, fake or real, compared to lagers and ales. But I'd done historical research for the Pilsner Urquell brewery, and I had seen papers in their archives detailing the brewery's own lawsuit over beer that was being falsely sold as the original Pilsner by a pub owner in Bratislava as early as the 1930s. There was also a well-known story in Czech beer circles that the Communist authorities had sometimes passed off beer from the Krušovice brewery as the much more sought-after Pilsner Urquell, back in the days when Czechoslovakia's lager exports brought in much-needed hard currency. Now owned by Heineken, a decent but not stellar beer like Krušovice might sound like a dubious substitute for the beloved original from the city of Pilsen, but the story was told by old-school Czech brewers as a way of illustrating just how much more bitter and charismatic Krušovice beer was back in the day. And of course, I'd heard several times that a few pubs in Germany had claimed that the Czech dark lager they were selling was the great Flekovské pivo from Prague's U Fleků, a brewery restaurant dating from the year 1499 that, somewhat famously, did not export its beer. What was on sale in those German outlets was probably a dark lager from the Kozel brewery not far from Prague, currently part of the Pilsner

Urquell group under the larger Asahi umbrella. Kozel is okay, but
it's not even close to Flekovské pivo when you actually drink it. But
if those German pub-goers didn't know the taste of the original,
how could they even tell?

⋮

That was a big part of the problem with fake pre-bans, I realized: the
world had lost its culture of drinking absinthe, so much so that most
people didn't even know how to serve it, and connoisseurs themselves struggled to grasp how to use equipment like the balancier at
the start of the drink's renaissance, as Cary had recounted. Forget
the labels, corks, or other visual aspects of counterfeit bottles, and
just go on the sensory analysis of the drink's flavors and aromas. If
you tasted an absinthe that was supposed to have been made a century or more ago, would you even know what to look for?

Despite the lack of a ban on its production, century-plus wines
had the very same problem, as an earlier wine fraudster, Hardy
Rodenstock, had shown when he opened a would-be 1784 Château
d'Yquem and many other well-aged bottles at a celebrated event
for connoisseurs and collectors in Munich in 1998. That week-long
tasting included two Yquem bottles that were said to date from the
eighteenth century, as well as forty that were said to come from the
nineteenth century, plus samples of all the Yquem vintages that had
been released in the twentieth. Although it sounds incredible, it has
never been proven that any of the bottles at that tasting were fakes.

Others from Rodenstock, however, almost certainly were
fakes, including several that had been bought by Bill Koch, who
sued Rodenstock for fraud in 2006, just three years before his suit
against Kurniawan. At issue were bottles of Bordeaux that had been

discovered behind the wall of an old house in Paris, Rodenstock said, which he had bought from the finder and then passed on to the dealers who later sold them to Koch, among others. They were believed to come from what had been Thomas Jefferson's cellar when he lived in Paris, and they included would-be 1784 and 1787 bottles of Château Lafite and Branne-Mouton, the precursor of Mouton-Rothschild. Those bottles were said to have been authenticated, for whatever that was worth, by Michael Broadbent, one the world's leading experts on old wines. Later, a retired FBI agent and an industry consultant hired by Koch argued that the initials "Th. J." had been scratched into the bottle glass with a power tool and were thus unlikely to have been so marked in the eighteenth century, while experts at the Thomas Jefferson Foundation in Monticello, Virginia, said they did not believe that the bottles had ever been owned by Jefferson. Rodenstock refused to participate in Koch's suit, noting that a U.S. court did not have jurisdiction over a German citizen living in Germany, making it another case of an alcohol-related fraud case that had apparently taken place in the no-man's-land between two countries. The story was turned into the 2008 book *The Billionaire's Vinegar* by the writer Benjamin Wallace, after which Broadbent sued the book's publisher, Random House, for libel and defamation in the U.K. The publisher settled for an undisclosed amount, apologized, and stopped selling the title in the U.K., though no changes were made to the edition that Random House kept on sale in the U.S. and other countries.

Rodenstock's story offered a bunch of parallels with the absinthe world. I'd heard several stories about pre-bans being found behind or inside the walls of old houses, like the cache of Premier Fils pre-bans that Eric had found in France, and the Legler-Pernod White Absinthe that Adrian Mørk had scored out of Massachusetts. Just like Christian with his pre-bans, Rodenstock had never revealed the location where he'd found his "Th. J." bottles (though that reluctance to reveal the whole story also held for many trusted absinthe dealers, including people like Patrick Roussel). More surprisingly, several wine connoisseurs had been taken in by Rodenstock, or at least embroiled in his world. Tasting a magnum of a supposed 1921 Pétrus from Rodenstock, Robert Parker wrote, "This huge, unbelievably concentrated wine could have been mistaken for the 1950 or 1947," a verdict which now reads quite differently than how Parker probably meant it at the time. Similarly, at the 1998 Yquem tasting, a writer for *Wine Spectator* noted that the would-be wines from the late eighteenth century tasted "decades younger."

While it was the small group of absinthe connoisseurs who ended up tracking and exposing Christian's frauds to the world, some authorities on the drink had apparently been fooled, too, including people who ran absinthe groups and who sold the spirit professionally. It's impossible to be on your guard constantly, of course, especially when you're dealing with someone who has the status of a connoisseur in your world. But much like Rodenstock and Kurniawan, Christian clearly didn't just trick small-timers or novices.

Other parts of the fraud stories simply didn't line up. Although a German court had found in 1992 that Rodenstock had "knowingly offered adulterated wine" to buyers, he appeared to have largely escaped legal troubles before passing away in 2018. Kurniawan, however, was found guilty in his Federal trial in Manhattan in 2013 and subsequently sentenced to ten years in the Reeves County Detention Center in Pecos, Texas. After his release in late 2020, he was deported to Indonesia the next spring. As far as I could tell, Christian's story seemed to have been more like Rodenstock's.

As for Acker Wines, the New York City boutique was accused of selling a different kind of counterfeit booze in 2021, when *Inside Edition* reported that "America's Oldest Wine Shop" was selling fake bottles of Colonel E. H. Taylor Four Grain bourbon for $1,000 each, more than ten times the suggested retail price; a bottle that was bought from the shop was tested at the distillery and confirmed to be fraudulent. Two years later, Acker Wines agreed to pay the New York State Liquor Authority the maximum fine of $100,000 to settle that case.

I could see a final set of echoes between the absinthe forger and the other alcohol counterfeiters, and while those might have also been less than perfect matchups, I thought they might indicate something deeper I hadn't considered about Christian's psyche. Like Kurniawan and Rodenstock, Christian had always played fast and loose with his background, his friends said, hinting that he came from wealth, but never really explaining how he'd acquired the funds to pay for his finds.

Another small part of Christian's story reminded me of the two famous wine forgers. Although everyone in the wine world knew him as Rudy Kurniawan, the birth name of the swindler also called "Dr. Conti" appears to have been Zhen Wang Huang: the story goes that he'd been given a local name by his Chinese father to help him fit in, in the country of his birth. Similarly, few people knew that the infamous Hardy Rodenstock had the legal name Meinhard Görke.

In this and in other ways, Christian wasn't quite at the same level: it looked like he had merely appended a British-sounding surname to his foreign-sounding last name. Virtually everyone in absinthe knew him by those three names, however. As with his nationality, I found myself wondering if that was his legal name, or if the added part was an affectation, or something even less authentic.

J'ACCUSE!

Absinthe is to many, as to me, the chief necessity of life.
Because, however uncertain in its other phases it may
prove, it can be absolutely relied upon to kill Conscience!
—MARIE CORELLI

In light of Christian's status in the absinthe world at the time,
the note that appeared on April 2, 2019, sounded preposter-
ous, and many absinthe fans initially thought it was just a
delayed and not terribly funny April Fool's joke. It was posted as
coming from Cary René Bonnecaze, but it went up simultaneously
in various Facebook groups and online forums, including at the
Wormwood Society, where it had since disappeared, probably because of a lawsuit, I imagined, though I managed to track down a
cached version of that post at Archive.org. It read as follows:

Many of us in the absinthe community know, or are familiar with, Christian from London, England. Throughout the years he has been well liked, thought of as knowledgeable in the field of absinthe and a trusted friend to many of us. But until recently, what none of us knew, is that Christian is also a fraud.

Christian has been selling to many of us fake pre-ban (before 1915) samples and bottles of absinthe for years. He buys empty pre-ban bottles, often on eBay, fills them with something other than its original contents, redresses them as originals and sells them as authentic pre-ban absinthe bottles. And in the case of samples, blends a combination of modern and Tarragona-era Pernod Fils, then adds certain essences that can change its flavor so the taste mimics that of an antique absinthe.

For those of you who are not aware, a sample of pre-ban absinthe can cost hundreds of euros per 50ml, while a vintage bottle can easily reach into the thousands of euros.

Many of us who have purchased from Christian never had a reason to doubt the authenticity of his absinthes. He sold himself well.

With the help of well-known and respected absinthe collectors, sellers and makers from France and the U.S., over time we have compiled overwhelming evidences of his intentional deception. We recently confronted him, and he was given a number of days to respond with a solution—to right his wrong, by repaying victims of his scams, or this private matter would go public. He chose not to respond and to delete his Facebook account.

Christian took advantage of friendships and did so while committing fraud.

While what Christian has done is unforgivable and illegal, please do not hold others in our community in the same light. We have truly reputable and professional sellers, which should never be confused with likes of Christian. We all are here out of our fondness and love of absinthe. This is why we come to these groups and forums, to share and to learn, as friends. Hopefully we can use this moving forward as a way to bring us all closer together. Santé!

Attached are examples of Christian's handiwork as proof, and we have much more.

A complete translation into French followed the English text, backed up by twenty-one photographs that showed empty bottles on online sales pages, with details of their unique marks—various cracks, bubbles, stains, and other specific scars from over a century of age—as well as Christian's photos offering those same bottles, full, as authentic pre-bans for sale. Although it might have sounded like a gag, the visual evidence was incontrovertible, and readers who first thought of it as a bad joke quickly found themselves sampling their way through a long buffet table of human emotions—shock, anger, disappointment, and regret, as well as other feelings they couldn't quite name.

⋮

Although Cary hadn't been a member of the group that had tracked the forgeries, they'd told him of their results before the announcements went public and asked him to be the one to share their news with the world. It was a nice touch, since Cary had probably lost the most money on Christian's scams. That brought a bit of justice to the situation: a former victim was allowed to strike a blow.

Admins of the various groups wasted no time kicking Christian out of their clubhouses, just as they would a racist or a troll. Since Christian wasn't an admin himself, there was nothing for him to do about that. His direct messages on Facebook were blowing up, however, so much so that he couldn't keep up with them. Distillers, collectors, and longtime friends were writing to ask if he'd really done this, or just jumping straight to the point and asking why. Former customers were demanding their money back. And I can imagine that at least a few people he didn't know—people who had never bought anything from him, ever—were writing to tell him he was a fraud, a liar, and a terrible person. As I'd seen from the messages that had been shared with me, he'd admitted to a few people that he'd made forgeries. He was sorry for those—he used the word "heartbroken" repeatedly. And then he simply started blocking people, and soon no one could find his Facebook account.

⋮

There are understatements, and then there's saying that April 2 was an important date in the absinthe underground. When you read through the reactions of group members after the fact, the tone takes on an apocalyptic air. And like any major event, it wasn't initially clear what had actually happened and who was involved. At first, Wolfgang Klotz was accused of fraud and kicked out of the groups as well, though Mira and others pointed out that the evidence for Christian's forgeries didn't extend to Wolfgang, and the early posts accusing Wolfgang were soon edited to say things like "Wolfgang appears to be clear." One user recalled that Christian had warned him not to buy any of the "Fake Dubied" samples from Wolfgang, to which another member said that Christian had said the very same thing to him, mirroring Preet Bharara's statement about Rudy Kurniawan ironically presenting himself as an aficionado who could help collectors identify and avoid counterfeit bottles. When Christian was still seen as an authority on absinthe, that warning would have been taken very seriously. Once it was clear that he was a fraud, his words sounded more like misdirection, or even a kind of confession.

Dozens of members posted about the sadness, shock, and disbelief they were feeling directly under the initial announcements. As the news settled in, group members started putting two and two together, recalling details about Christian's behavior that seemed to clash with his reputation. Scott shared that someone had received a chipped absinthe glass from Christian and asked other members if they'd had any similar experiences. The group had plenty to share.

One absintheur shared that he'd bought a glass and water dripper from Christian that had never shown up. When he'd written to ask what was going on, Christian claimed they had been returned because of a bad address, and that he would resend them. They never arrived. The buyer had just let it go.

Others recalled that he had been very rude when they'd tried to purchase from him, which had come as a surprise from someone who was supposed to be an important figure in the absinthe world. Because of his status, they'd never raised the matter publicly.

One absinthe collector from Italy recounted how he had tried to buy a 1920 Escat—another Spanish *absenta*—from Christian, but that package was never delivered, which he'd assumed had been the fault of the postal service in Italy. When the collector followed up, Christian offered to include a sample of a 1950 Tarragona to make up for the loss. The collector never received the second shipment, and although he'd requested a tracking number, Christian told him he couldn't remember it. The collector asked Christian to send it again, this time with a tracking number. When that package finally arrived, three months after the initial purchase, it only included the Escat sample, and not the promised Tarragona. "At the time I didn't think about fraud, I just assumed Christian was really unprofessional and decided never to buy anything else from him," the collector wrote.

Similar stories followed. One of the recurring themes was that Christian would only ever offer a partial refund, if there was to be any refund at all, even when the fault was clearly his own, a true chiseler's move.

Hindsight is easy, of course. But if you looked back, all the signs were there.

⋮

Christian might have gone to ground soon after the announcements were published on April 2, but it didn't look like he had moved on, at least not if he was the person who sent a weird email to Scott a few weeks later. It read like a variation on a common porn-themed blackmail message that had been floating around the internet for years, but with a couple of changes.

The last time you visited an absinthe website with old
   guys trying to be cool,
you downloaded and installed the vírus I developed.
My program has turned on your cam and recorded the act
of your louching.
My software also downloaded all your email contact lísts
and a list of your friends on Facebook.
I have the - Louching.mp4 - with you dropping water
onto spoons, as well as a file with all your contacts
on my computer.
If you want me to delete both files and keep the secret,
you must send me the Bitcoin payment.
I give you 72 hours only to send the funds.
If you don't know how to pay with Bitcoin,
visit Google and search - how to buy bitcoin.
Send 2,000 USD (0.386917 BTC)
to this Bitcoin address as soon as possible:
AbsinthefiendrXsBJkFxSU6BndhtyeoodjzxwDon'tpisso
   ffChristian
(copy and paste)
1BTC=5,230USD right now, so send exactly 0.386917BTC
to the address above.
Do not try to cheat me!
As soon as you open this Email I will know you opened it.
I am tracking all actions on your device..
This Bitcoin address is linked to you only,
so I will know when you send the correct amount.
When you pay in full, I will remove both files and deactivate

my program.

If you choose to not send the bitcoin . . .

I will send your Grande Absente vídeo to

ALL YOUR FRIENDS AND ASSOCIATES from your

contact lists that I hacked.

Here are the payment details again:

P

Send 2,000 USD (0.386917 BTC)

to this Bitcoin address

You can visit absinthe police but nobody can help you.

I know what I am doing.

I don't live in your country and I know how

to stay anonymous. I am a member of the Czech

    absinthe Mafia, BTW.

Don't try to deceive me - I will know it

immediately - my spy software is recording all the

Absinthe websites you visit and all your key presses.

If you do - I will send this víd of you drinking bad

    absinthe to everyone you know,

INCLUDING THE POPE, and all the guys from your

    absinthe trips to France and the VDT. Even to

    Hector and Clint.

Don't cheat me! Don't forget the shame and if you

    ignore

this message your absinthe will be ruined.

I am waiting for your Bitcoin payment.

You have 72 hours left.

Anonymous Hacker

I didn't get the reference to the Pope, but Hector and Clint were well-known members of the online groups, and of course many connoisseurs saw Grande Absente as a complete waste of time, with an overall rating of just 2.2 points out of a possible 5 by members of the Wormwood Society at the time. As for not pissing off Christian, it seemed like that was a little late, though I couldn't imagine what he might do.

⋮

As the weeks progressed, things started to seem a bit clearer, and more hints about Christian's psychology started to surface. Anthony remembered a weird comment Christian had made in response to a post from Scott about prices and what was worth spending money on in the absinthe world:

"End of the day, you pay for what you get. The only modern absinthe worth a crazy price tag in this category is Grand No. 5. And Scott MacDonald, you are wrong. People are intelligent. Worthy of making up their own mind. There's no worthiness to protect, other than the individual decision to do and pay whatever we all feel we need to in order to fulfill our own happiness and journey."

In hindsight, Anthony thought, that last line read like a justification for screwing people over.

⋮

Although the first reactions were of shock, sadness, and disbelief, doubt started to spread through the community. It wasn't just about Christian. Mistrust extended to the entirety of absinthe culture. Part of the problem was that no one knew how long the counterfeits had been circulating.

"These are just the fakes that you and your friends have identified," one collector posted. "Can anyone make an educated guess how many bottles he has faked over the years?"

One user requested that the group pin a list of reputable dealers, while others asked if it was true that Christian had been involved with those reputable dealers. "He was involved with everyone, he was a wolf in sheep's clothing!" an admin replied. One user mentioned that he'd often said that Christian was "in the process of cornering the market in pre-ban." A few commented that they'd always found it suspicious that he had shown himself opening so many expensive bottles of pre-ban. One collector said that he'd found himself wondering what Christian had done for a living to be able to afford his lifestyle. "Guess now I know!" he added.

Some younger members noted that their interactions with Christian had made them lose faith in the community. To say nothing of selling fraudulent absinthe, it was obvious that he'd treated many of the people who'd bought antiques from him quite badly, and no one had stood up to him at the time. One member noted that everything that they'd experienced just about every bad thing people were saying about Christian, and when they'd tried to talk to others about it, they'd been brushed off.

"Because I was relatively new in the community, only knew people as Facebook avatars and Christian was obviously a respected and knowledgeable persona, I didn't say anything for a while. After I met some folks in person I did actually mention the problems, but was received with shock because they had never heard of such complaints against Christian."

At the time of the announcement, group members were planning to purchase an entire bottle of 1910 Pernod Fils from Patrick

Roussel, after which they would split it up. Scott, the organizer of that group buy, announced that he was canceling the purchase a few days later: too many people had sent messages accusing him of trying to cash in on the situation, although he would have been paying an equal amount for his own share of the bottle. "So now I'm out," he wrote. He'd been an administrator of his own absinthe group, and a "top contributor" in other groups, but the mood had shifted. "I think I will just be involved more quietly in this community. It has become a minefield when someone trying to do something good gets kicked around. Some of you need to grow up, know what you're talking about, and realize your toxic energy affects people."

Christian had damaged the absinthe world in ways beyond mere fraud.

⋮

It didn't take long for many of the absinthe collectors to start asking about justice. Were charges ever going to be brought against this fraudulent being?

One collector suggested that they make a list of everything everyone had purchased from Christian, to figure out the amount of damages. "I think this is really useful for a clean legal and correct indictment in court," he said.

It was Adrian Payne, the former British police officer, who stepped forward with comments that explained how the U.K.'s legal system worked. As far as he could tell, there wasn't a lot of hope for a case. Once the bottles had been opened in private, it would be impossible to prove that the fake absinthes had come from Christian. And if there ever were a trial, he noted, most of Christian's buyers were overseas. Would they be willing to travel at their own expense to the U.K. to testify?

That was a common theme in the first few weeks after the allegations, Anthony said, but it eventually faded out.

"At the time, Christian was going to jail, but of course that never happened. But it was a nice thought."

At the Wormwood Society, the first comment under the announcement of Christian's fraud said the same thing.

"I would love to see this thief prosecuted."

But as far as I could tell, that didn't happen. And a lack of justice isn't good for the mood in any group.

⋮

Patrick Roussel had said that Adrian Payne had been the sole victim of Christian's fraud to have been made whole afterward, since most of the crimes appeared to have been committed in what they called a legal void. In addition to being a retired police officer, Adrian had an advantage the other victims didn't have. Although he had retired to France, he still held a British passport and frequently made trips back home.

I reached out to him and we found a time for a call one rainy afternoon after he'd walked his dogs through the Normandy countryside. In terms of making a criminal accusation, he said, it would have been very hard for police officers to understand what the victims were even talking about.

"I can imagine walking into the front desk of a police station and saying, 'Yeah, I've just been sold a bottle of 110-year-old absinthe, which I believe to be fake.' The first thing they would ask is, 'Well, how do you know it's fake?'"

The second problem for the police would lie in recording how the crime had happened.

"The issue there is: Where did the offense take place? Is it when he sent the bottle from the U.K.?" he said. "Or is it when he received the money? Or when the bottle lands in the U.S. and the buyer takes possession of it?"

Even if the police could get their heads around the allegations, he continued, most prosecutors simply wouldn't see the sale of relatively small amounts—this was generally concerning the sale of individual 1-liter bottles, and sometimes just 50-milliliter sample bottles, but certainly not cases or pallet-loads—of fake vintage absinthe as something in the public interest.

"That's the other thing: would CPS run it?" he asked. "The Crown Prosecution Service in the U.K., would they run it? It just wouldn't have been easy to get it to court."

When I asked how he'd gotten his cash back from Christian, it turned out that wasn't quite the case. Like Cary, Patrick Roussel, and many others, Adrian was much more into antiques than spirits, he said, although he did drink the stuff occasionally. He'd started out with historic glassware, examples of which I could see on the shelves of the home bar in the background behind him, and had moved on to artworks and promotional material from various distilleries. But a few months before the allegations had gone public, Christian had offered Adrian what was supposed to be a pre-ban Pernod Fils from a cache he claimed to have recently uncovered. The bottle was in decent shape, despite a particular tear through the word "extrait" on the label, and the price was low: just £1,200, or about $1,700 at the time. After agreeing to the sale, he'd met Christian to pick up the bottle in a Middle Eastern restaurant around the corner from where Christian worked. Adrian remembered that Christian had generously paid for dinner, because he'd done so with a company credit card from his employer.

Months later, just before the allegations were made public, Adrian had been given a heads-up that his bottle was a likely fake by Eric, who lived not far away from him in the north of France. There were numerous problems with the bottle that also caught Adrian's eye, once he looked at it more closely: the wax seal was too bright and shiny for something that was supposed to have been sitting in a cellar for over a century. The foil seal, as well, didn't appear to go over the cork, as it should. He didn't say anything to Christian until the accusations were made public.

"I basically threatened Christian," he said. "I said to him, 'As far as I'm concerned, the bottle's fake. You've been caught out.' I gave him a choice. I said, 'You either pay me back, or my next stop when I'm in the U.K. will be to the police station just round the corner from your office. And I'll also be dropping a little telephone call or email to your boss telling him what you're up to.'"

Christian never admitted that the Pernod Fils he'd sold was fake, Adrian recalled, insisting that it had come from the unnamed cache he'd uncovered, but he agreed to take it back anyway. Unfortunately, he didn't have enough cash on hand to return Adrian's payment. Adrian counter-offered. Christian had posted photos of some very nice pieces of antique glassware, and Adrian would accept £3,000 worth of antiques in exchange for the fake bottle of Pernod Fils, naming the various items he wanted from Christian's collection. The next time Adrian was back in London, they met at a bar between King's Cross and St. Pancras. It was a beautiful sunny day, so they sat outside while Adrian examined the glasses he'd agreed to accept. While he was looking them over, Christian mentioned that he'd lost his job and was on his way to a job interview, though Adrian didn't believe him. Obviously, that could have been a feint, since Adrian had threatened to tell Christian's boss what he'd done.

Even at that meeting, Christian insisted that he'd done nothing wrong, but Adrian was over it, accepting the antiques and moving on to his life back in France. He appeared to have pretty much forgotten about Christian until I reached out, though while we talked he recalled numerous details, including about Christian's wife, where his parents lived, and the firms where Christian had claimed to have worked. He didn't seem exactly suspicious of where I lived, but he took notice of it, mentioning that he thought Christian had also spent a lot of time in the Czech Republic, an angle on the story I hadn't heard yet. Christian was always flying around Europe for his work, he said, and he was always on social media, as well. The two didn't always match up.

"One of the things I remember was that he claimed to be somewhere in the U.K., but if you looked at his Facebook page it said he was on holiday in South America. He couldn't have been in two places at the same time. It was all bullshit, even then."

Similarly, Christian once told him that he owned a full bottle of pre-ban Terminus. Only three or four pre-ban Terminus bottles had ever been found, Adrian said, and all were empties. No one in the absinthe underground had ever tasted a drop of Terminus.

I started to ask if he thought Christian was a compulsive liar, and he answered "absolutely" before I could finish.

He thought silently for a minute and said that he remembered one more thing, something Christian had once said that he should have seen as a red flag at the time. In the restaurant where Christian had paid for their dinner with a credit card from his work, he'd gone on to describe his own status in wild terms.

"He was bigging himself up, all the pre-bans and his collection," he recalled. "And I remember exactly what he said: 'With what we have, we are gods within the absinthe community.' Those were his exact words. And I just thought, 'You arrogant shit.'"

⋮

Maybe the legal system couldn't do anything about that god of the absinthe community, but it didn't take long for Christian to become the butt of group jokes, which functioned as justice of a kind. Part of his last name was changed to "Fraud" by one commenter. A meme of a dorky goth kid with a foamy beer cup filled with bright green liquid—captioned "When you don't have absinthe, so you use green-apple dish soap for your photos"—was posted in one private group as a supposed shot with the headline "Christian in his younger days." Within a few months, however, he was only being referred to rarely, usually as someone who would not be named. And in the following years, the absinthe world moved on from Christian, though many of the members appeared to move on from absinthe as well.

⋮

Both Adrian and Anthony described the fall-off after the allegations as pretty steep. What had once been a vibrant community, both online and in real life, started to wilt and fade.

"The Christian episode really put doubt in people's minds," Adrian recalled. Since legitimate dealers of vintage spirits like Eric had been seen as close friends with Christian, many collectors ended up doubting the legitimacy of any vintage spirit. "People said, 'Well, hang on: If Christian was fooling all these people, how do we know that what they're selling—either innocently or not innocently—is the real stuff?'"

Like Adrian, Anthony had remained a member of the old groups and forums, though he told me that he didn't post often anymore. In his eyes, the quality of posts in the groups had gone down remarkably. They generally contained much less information than before. In the olden days, collectors would share the histories of vintage glassware they'd found, explaining the nuances of an early nineteenth-century glass with a lemon-squeezer foot, or telling the story of a particular model of absinthe spoon. They might post a detailed history of small but noteworthy distillery. Or they might explain how they personally use a simple kind of absinthe dripper, known as a *brouilleur*, posting a video that showed how to set one atop an individual glass so that it would slowly drip cold water below, creating an elegant louche as it troubled the spirit. An expert like Patrick Roussel might share the history of a vintage absinthe fountain or a promotional poster. There was a lot less of that, he said, and more posts that focused on banal elements, like tasting notes when someone received a new bottle, or simply saying *santé*, or cheers, around the holidays. What had been a bustling location for people to share their love of a drink and a lost culture started to lose its relevance, like a once-busy café that no longer had enough customers to maintain a decent atmosphere. The old days of the absinthe underground were gone.

Not all of that was because of Christian, of course. But what he'd done certainly didn't help.

THE SCIENCE
OF FRAUD

If Patrick Roussel had shown how he and his group of amateur absinthe detectives had identified Christian's fakes visually, and Scott MacDonald had explained how he'd spotted the fraudulent sample from Christian through a careful tasting, the scientific proof that came out after the public accusations of Christian's fraud was way more complicated, involving techniques and equipment that I knew nothing about. To learn how that worked, I sent an email to the German scientist and absinthe maker Jan Hartmann, asking if I could visit his laboratory.

It was high summer, the start of the tourist season, and every

single express train I had booked across Germany that Monday
was either late or canceled, belying Europe's commonly held belief in Teutonic efficiency. Eventually, my last regional train from
Cologne pulled into its temporary end station at the small town of
Düren, from which I transferred to a replacement bus service for
the final stretch, along with a huge crowd of frustrated, end-of-day
commuters. The bus ambled through flat, open farmland toward
the village of Langerwehe, close to the ancient city of Aachen, a former Roman Empire stronghold against the Gauls. As the landscape
spread out beyond the windows of the crowded bus, it looked more
like the neighboring Netherlands than the more mountainous parts
of Germany close to the Czech Republic. Standing with my bag at
my feet, with one hand holding the crossbar overhead while I was
locked in position by the crowd of packed commuters, I texted Jan
a note that I'd been delayed, to which he responded with an offer to
pick me up at the train station.

He was younger than I expected and he placed my bag into
the back of his recent-model Mercedes with considerable care and
deference; even the Linkin Park tracks on the car stereo were at a
responsible volume. A few minutes later, we pulled up at his work:
a flat, expressionless, one-story building that looked like an office
complex back in California, with the heavy air of an elementary
school that had been abandoned for the summer holidays. It was
still light out, about an hour after my normal supper time, though
I didn't feel at all hungry: after thirteen hours in transit, I mostly
just wanted a chance to use the toilet. When I asked, Jan nodded
thoughtfully, as if he was realizing that this was something that
should have been obvious to him, and that he should make a mental
note to remember this kind of thing in the future.

Although the office bathrooms were near to the room with the equipment he used, I couldn't help noticing that he waited for me outside, probably not so much out of the worry that I might steal something as out of a sense of duty and responsibility. If he was bringing me into his place of work after hours, I thought, he must have requested and received permission to do so in advance, almost certainly in writing.

The room was small and filled with equipment, with a rectangular workspace in the center that was roughly the size of a large family dinner table. Countertops with workstations framed it, facing the three walls that did not include the door, with just a strip of walking area around the central workspace island, in which it was possible, if not completely comfortable, for one person to pass another. It was roughly the size of a teenage boy's bedroom, though it looked like a science classroom. Somewhat fittingly, Jan was dressed in skateboard-style sneakers with fat tied laces, loosely tied, a gray polo shirt and long, loose-fitting jean shorts. He might have earned his PhD, but he almost looked like he could still be in high school.

When he spoke, however, he sounded like a university lecturer, maybe even one with tenure.

"This is equipment for gas and liquid chromatography," he said slowly, gesturing to a pair of metal boxes on the counter to the left of the room's entrance. "I am the head of the laboratory and the production department. This is the gas chromatography lab." He pointed to the box that was closest to him, caught his breath and relaxed visibly.

"Basically, this thing is an oven," he said. "A very programmable and precise oven."

They actually did look like microwave ovens, only without windows and set vertically instead of horizontally. At the top, tiny dials and buttons resembled those on hospital equipment. The two closest to me were labelled "GC3" and "GC4," both with big yellow warning stickers showing exclamation points inside black triangles. Another bright orange sticker recommended caution: "Warning of using hydrogen. Shut off hydrogen and cap unused column fittings to prevent accumulation of hydrogen in oven and possible explosion." Boxes filled with both crescent and monkey wrenches in dozens of sizes stood on the counter. Nearby was a sample bottle made of heavy, dark glass, like some of the house-produced tinctures and gargles sold by old-school pharmacies in Eastern Europe.

Jan hadn't learned how to use a gas chromatograph during his doctoral studies, he said, which had only included the briefest introduction to the devices. Instead, he had gotten into it on his own while first researching how to make his own absinthe, when he had purchased a broken gas chromatography machine from eBay and restored it to working order. That hobby-like repair job and the experience of having run his own gas chromatography research had led to the position he'd found here. From then on, his employer had allowed him to do analysis in his free time on the professional equipment at the office. That research included modern absinthe, historic absinthe, and the individual chemical compounds in its many ingredients.

He pulled up a folder on the computer and looked inside, confirming that he'd run some 300 gas chromatograph experiments to date. From where I stood I could see that one of his folders was labeled "Fake Absinthe." I asked what that was.

"Yes, there's quite a few samples I got from Christian," he said.

"We can get to that later. I have a very nice presentation. I can show you how I figured out what his fakes are, and that they definitely *are* fakes. Others figured it out from the bottles. But for the samples where you don't have a bottle, I can show that they are also fake, and I was able to show how he made those fakes."

In addition to his work on authentic absinthes and its ingredients, Jan had used the gas chromatography machines to test more than a dozen absinthes that Christian had sold.

"I got a whole lot of samples from different people who had bought from him and analyzed them," he said. "I didn't find one absinthe that was real."

⋮

That wasn't quite true, he corrected himself a minute later: there was at least one example from Christian that was authentic, though it was a real rarity in a couple of ways. But before he got into that, he needed to show me how a gas chromatography machine worked.

The company where he worked didn't make the machines themselves, but only produced the so-called "capillary columns" and other parts that they used. He held one up. It was about the size of a saucer, looking like a coil of looped copper wire.

"Basically, it's really fine glass." It was related to the fiberoptic cables that are used in high-speed communications, with one major difference: it was hollow. "For fiberglass optics, they use a solid glass rod, but in this case we use a glass tube."

It was so thin that it was hard to imagine how you could fit anything into it—the whole thing seemed to be about as thick as a strand of hair from a horse's tail. It was coated on the outside with a thermo-resistant plastic, he said, which helped to protect it from breaking, while its interior was coated with a material that helped separate the different chemical compounds in the sample as it was being analyzed.

He attached both ends of the column to one of the machines. One end had the inlet, where the sample would enter, while the other end lead out to the detector, which would register what was coming through the column.

That could be just about anything, he said: gas chromatographs could be used to measure environmental samples, air samples, food, medicines, and pesticides—just about anything that needed to be checked for toxins, the aromatic compounds known as PCBs, or almost anything else, including alcoholic spirits. For absinthe, that mostly meant the neurotoxin thujone, the amount of which was strictly limited by authorities in both the United States and the EU, as well as methanol and other regulated substances.

Once the wire-like coil of thin glass tubing was hooked up inside the chamber, he flipped a switch and a high-pitched, electric buzz like that of an old laser printer filled the room.

"So, basically, you have an injection port where you inject the sample," he said. "It's vaporized, and then it goes into the column by a carrier of gas. In this case, we use ultra-pure nitrogen gas, because it's inert, it's not too costly, and it works well for the separation."

With such a thin coil of tubing, the sample's volume was almost impossibly small: just five microliters, or about a one-thirtieth of a drop, which he would insert into the tube with a syringe. That tiny amount would be slowly pumped through the capillary glass coil by the nitrogen gas until it reached the detector on the other side, where it would create electrical signals.

"In this case, the detector is a flame ionization detector, which works by having a hydrogen flame. So you also need hydrogen and air, which you burn, and you measure the electrical resistance of this flame," he said. "Now, if there are no organic compounds in this flame, the electrical resistance is very high, because there are no ions. As soon as any carbon compound comes in there—basically, any compound that is present in absinthe except water—you get a lot of ions, you get lowered resistance, and you can see a signal."

The compounds themselves weren't visible with such a machine, he explained, but they could be clearly identified by the times when they separated from the main sample and revealed themselves to the detector at the end of the column. For that, the coating inside the narrow glass tube played an essential role.

"Different compounds interact differently with this coating, and exit the column at different times," he explained. He turned to a nearby computer and opened a file, pointing to a line graph on a yellow background, as if someone was tracking the daily price of gold or another precious metal on the commodities market. "This is a gas chromatogram of a pre-ban absinthe, and what you see is the signal intensity you get from the detector over time."

The chart was mostly flat along the bottom, with occasional sudden peaks, like the outlines of skyscrapers standing in a barren desert landscape, with a few shorter, fatter buildings a few miles away. He pointed at the biggest skyscraper on the chart, whose apex stood somewhere way up, far out of frame.

"Here you have a very large peak that is cut off at the top, because it's so huge. That is, of course, alcohol, because you have about 60 percent alcohol in this sample, whereas you have maybe fractions of a percent of the essential oils. But those are what actually interest you," he said. He pointed to a jump in the chart that, to me, looked a lot like the Burj Khalifa. "You have another compound here. That is actually quite a lot also. That is anethole, the main component of the essential oil of anise." The chemical compounds of the essential oils in absinthe would separate and get picked up by the detector at very specific points on the timeline, like fenchone, a chemical compound found in fennel. "This is fenchone, at 23 minutes. At 23.8 or so, you have alpha thujone. And this is beta-thujone," he said, pointing at another spot. "You have one peak, basically, for every compound that is present in an absinthe. It's really a kind of fingerprint."

The fifty-two-minute graph we were looking at came from the gas chromatograph of a pre-ban Premier Fils, my favorite pre-ban during my tasting with Wolfgang and a spirit, I remembered, that had earned a shout-out in one of Alfred Jarry's weird Ubu plays for marionettes. For comparison, Jan pulled up a chromatogram analysis of a pre-ban absinthe from an unknown maker in Belgium. The two charts had quite a few similar spikes, including the off-the-chart skyscraper peak of alcohol around the eight-minute mark, though there were also some small differences. An absinthe based on alcohol distilled from wine—effectively, an absinthe with a brandy base—created a different set of sub-skyscrapers than an absinthe that had been made from neutral alcohol, he said.

Unlike more complicated devices, the gas chromatography machines couldn't identify compounds by the times at which they appeared on the graph. But Jan had figured most of those out, through his work on his own absinthe, Aixsinthe, whose brand name neatly echoed Aix-la-Chapelle, the ancient French name for the city of Aachen, where he'd done his doctorate. He had done scores of single-ingredient distillations with the goal of creating what he called "a LEGO set of herbs for making absinthe"—various types of wormwood, as well as chamomile, cinnamon, coriander, black pepper, and dozens of other ingredients, which he had then analyzed via gas chromatography.

"For each of those botanicals, I have a chemical signature," he said.

He'd also analyzed other chemical compounds, like ethyl alcohol—the kind we drink—as well as isoamyl alcohol and other fusel alcohols, known as higher alcohols.

When it came to figuring out the authenticity of a would-be historic absinthe, there were two ways to check. First, the analysis could show the presence of compounds that a sample was not supposed to contain, peaks on the chart that would not show up in the gas chromatograph of a hundred-year-old spirit.

"There are quite a few compounds in absinthe that are not that stable," he explained. "Limonene, this lemony aroma that you get from lemon balm, is very oxidation prone, so typically in vintage absinthes you won't find it. That would be an indicator that someone had used a modern absinthe to approximate a pre-ban. If you find limonene in there, it's highly unlikely that it's actually authentic."

Then there was the flip side, whereby gas chromatography analysis could reveal the absence of chemical compounds that pre-bans normally contained. Jan said that he hadn't identified all of them yet. But he did know that they only showed up in historic spirits, and he did have their gas-chromatography fingerprints.

"You have certain compounds that are formed during the aging process, some oxidation products, some compounds that are only present in vintage absinthes, or sometimes also in absinthes that have been stored in wooden barrels for a long time, like Patrick Grand's No. 5," he said.

"That's kind of a famous one," I said.

He nodded.

"Yes, because it was also used by Christian for his fakes. It really has a vintage touch. But as you'll see, I have the chromatograms, and there you can still see a difference, very clearly."

⋮

Once Patrick Roussel and his gang of absinthe detectives announced the visual evidence of forged absinthes through eBay listings and identifying marks on bottles and labels, he said, absinthe collectors immediately started reaching out.

"My mailbox just exploded," he said. "Everyone was writing and asking, 'Have you tested this? Have you tested that?'"

Martin Žufánek and other absintheurs sent in samples they'd bought from Christian, giving Jan plenty of absinthes to study. Christian himself had inadvertently started that collection, by brazenly selling Jan four samples of his supposed pre-bans the previous year. Those turned out to be fakes, as did another ten that other collectors had bought from Christian.

"I got fifteen samples and ran them through the GC," he said. "All of them were fake, except for one sample from Christian."

That lone authentic sample was the pre-ban bottle of absinthe "essence," or concentrate, made by the Bush distillery in the U.K. sometime before 1890—the very same spirit I'd tasted with Wolfgang Klotz. After running it through gas chromatography, Jan was convinced it was authentic. But the fourteen others failed his tests.

The gas chromatography machine whirred through its analysis on the far counter as he opened a file labelled "Pernod Fils Christian 2019" on the computer.

"With Pernod Fils, they were distilled so cleanly they don't have the higher alcohols, the fusel alcohols," he said. Often considered to be off-flavors, those included compounds like isoamyl alcohol, a common by-product of alcohol production.

He went back to the file picker and opened another chart from his analysis of an authentic Pernod Fils pre-ban sample sent in by Patrick Roussel. He pointed at the chart, showing a very short bump, almost invisible, where the fusel alcohols stood. "On this one here, they are very, very low."

He switched to the chart from Christian's supposed Pernod Fils and pointed at a much higher peak on the graph.

"Look here, and here. This is isoamyl alcohol." He switched back to the authentic Pernod Fils from Patrick Roussel, then back to Christian's chart. The two graphs were very different. Where the chart for the authentic Pernod Fils was nearly flat, the counterfeit absinthe from Christian rose up to a high level from the baseline, almost up to the peak of its ethyl alcohol.

He went back to the folder and opened another would-be pre-ban, as well as the chart for Grand No. 5.

"This is an authenticity testing with another sample from Christian, supposedly E. Deniset Fils," he said. "Just looking at it and comparing it to the Grand No. 5, you can see that the chromatograms are very, very similar. For this one, you can really see that it was based on Grand No. 5."

The two graphs looked almost the same. However, there were few unusual peaks on Christian's sample he pointed out.

"Apart from those, you can see they're the same chromatogram. This fake E. Deniset Fils was made from Grand No. 5. And you can actually see what he added."

He pointed to a raised line on the graph. To my eyes, it looked like just a small bump in that day's gold price. To him, it showed the presence of the chemical compound menthol.

"So he added either menthol or mint oil or something, just to get the aroma and flavor a bit off," he said.

Another difference was that there were no higher alcohols in Patrick Grand's modern version. Like most Swiss distillers, he had made it with a neutral alcohol, which did not contain those higher alcohols.

"Whereas here in the fake, you have some amount of higher alcohols and also a little bit of ethyl acetate," he said. He opened the chart for Christian's sample again. "That's characteristic for a wine alcohol base. So he added a little bit of brandy and a little bit of mint oil to Grand No. 5 to make his fake E. Deniset Fils."

To Jan, the gas chromatography analysis of the samples from Christian left absolutely no doubt. Once he had completed his analysis, he was so sure of what he'd found that he had even reached out to the distiller in Switzerland.

"I contacted Patrick Grand with this and asked him, 'You know Christian is using your No. 5 to fake absinthes?'" he recalled. "And he said, 'Oh, yes? So that's why he wanted to buy a barrel of No. 5 from me.'"

⋮

I'd already heard that Christian had traded fake pre-bans for large volumes of Grand No. 5; Christian had even gone as far as to admit that he didn't need the bottles, just the absinthe inside them. But Jan said he had evidence that Christian had also used other bases to forge his counterfeit absinthes.

It was getting late, so we left the lab and Jan drove us to his home a few minutes away. His apartment was large and airy, with the open living room area running directly into the kitchen. He had the newest consoles from Xbox and PlayStation, neither of which I had yet seen in person, along with a suite of gaming DVDs lined up under the screen, which I presumed had to be in alphabetical order. The shelves on the living room wall displayed trinkets related to military planes, including a detailed F-16 model and a mounted reproduction of a fighter pilot's helmet on a stand, with a Chicago Bulls baseball cap on top of that. These were all mementos from his time as a child with his family in Virginia Beach, he said, and the jet noise locals there called "the sound of freedom." A deer's rack was mounted above the television, which paired with the slew of German hunting magazines laid out on the shelf under the top of the coffee table.

On a desk that stood where the living room ended and the kitchen began, Jan roused his computer from sleep, and opened a presentation on absinthe analysis that he'd given to a group of graduate students in chemistry. He clicked through the slides, reciting most of the presentation's text from memory, starting with a long quote about absinthe from Oscar Wilde. Afterward, he opened more gas chromatography charts.

Although Patrick Grand's celebrated No. 5 had been used elsewhere, he'd found at least two fraudulent samples from Christian, he said—a would-be Gempp Pernod and a supposed H. Deniset Jeune—that were both clearly based on a post-ban Pernod Fils from Tarragona in Spain. Because Jan didn't know which Tarragona Christian had used, he had less of an exact match than with the Grand No. 5: Pernod's post-ban Tarragonas had been produced over five decades, with many variations from batch to batch and from year to year, leaving an array of relatively easy-to-find bottles that were available to collectors or forgers. Although they were appreciated by absintheurs, they definitely sold at much lower prices than actual pre-bans.

He rotated through the three graphs: the Gempp Pernod and H. Deniset Jeune that two of his friends had bought from Christian, and a chart from a Pernod Tarragona. Despite the uncertainty over the year of the Tarragona base, the three looked remarkably similar.

"I got a sample that's as close as possible to the Pernod Fils Tarragona he used," he said. "Of course you have aging indicators in these, because it is a vintage absinthe—probably 1960s." He clicked from the graph of the real Spanish Pernod Fils to the fake pre-bans that Christian had claimed as dating from pre-1915 France. The three graphs repeated the same highs and lows, the same flatlands and skyscrapers, with just a couple of different peaks visible in the charts of the two samples from Christian.

He pointed at a peak in the chart.

"It's quite obvious that these chromatograms are related to the original Pernod Fils Tarragona, again with the difference being that you have menthol."

Beyond the addition of menthol, just about the only other aspect that differed from the Tarragona was the increased amount of higher alcohols. In his opinion, that meant that Christian had also repeated the way he'd added a touch of wine-like character to the absinthes he'd based on Patrick Grand's No. 5.

He tapped at the point on the graph.

"It's fairly certain that he also added some brandy here," he said. "So he didn't even change his recipe."

⋮

The restaurants in Langerwehe were all closed on Monday evenings, so Jan put together a late supper for us both while I scrawled a few notes about his research. As he cooked, he occasionally opened the cupboards over the stove. In them, I noticed a line of carefully labeled bottles that contained his own distillations of rosemary, wormwood, and other herbs.

He wasn't much of a cook, he apologized, but within a few minutes later he'd plated two beautiful salmon filets, both dressed with deep red andaliman—a lemony, peppery spice from Sumatra that I'd never heard of. Outside, the long, early-summer sunset cast its first shadows on the large wormwood plant on his balcony.

He'd grown close to a hundred wormwood plants from Switzerland at one point, he said, taking over a plot of land owned by the elderly neighbors of his parents as a wormwood farm for several years. He had used gas chromatography to analyze the plants when they first arrived from the Val-de-Travers, and then again a year later, after they had acclimatized to the much milder weather in his low-elevation corner of northwestern Germany. The plants seemed to prefer life in the Jura.

"What I saw is that the combination of essential oils remains the same, but the content of the essential oils dropped by half, just from growing here."

When we finished our meals, he got out a bottle of his Aixsinthe. It was stumpy and black, with the brand name broken into three-letter segments in an oversize, white Gothic script on the label. A smaller sticker noted that this was Aixsinthe Blanche Noire. It was made in the style of an uncolored Swiss bleue, he said, but with a twist.

When he poured it, a familiar, lemony, peppery scent filled the room. It was andaliman, he explained, the same spice he'd used for our supper. It felt like one of the modern bleues I'd tasted in the Val-de-Travers, but with a unique touch from the andaliman, which gave it a stronger citrus and pepper character.

A few minutes later, we moved on to a second bottle, Aixsinthe Vivide, a verte. He'd settled on the final formula for this one after 104 test distillations, combining several styles of absinthe from a storied recipe book by Pierre Duplais. The name came from a 1922 prose eulogy for absinthe by the writer Ernest Tisserand, in which he lamented the ban of 1915 and said that he knew of no other plants that were "more vivid or proud than those in absinthe." Jan seemed most proud of the wormwood he'd used in it, which came from the town of Boveresse in the Val-de-Travers. He quoted Tisserand from memory:

"And it is the wormwood, finally, the grande wormwood and the petite, chaste ornament of the mountains and seashores, daughter of the pure high winds, wheat of virgin spaces, emblem of untamed freedom."

Wormwood was probably the essential character of the spirit, though it was much more subtle and certainly less well known than the anise that gave the drink its louche. And of course, one of wormwood's major chemical components, thujone, was known to be a neurotoxin. But poets had a different understanding than scientists. When I asked Jan what wormwood brought to absinthe, he reached into his desk and handed over two small vials.

"This is anethole in pure form, and this is thujone in pure form. If you like, you can smell them."

The anethole was familiar: that sweet-smelling, licorice-like scent I knew from ouzo and pastis. But the thujone arrived as a curve ball that came in bright and sunny, like a shot of lemon peel mixed with pine needles. It was intoxicating, and maybe even literally, I joked. Jan offered a gentle correction: the toxicity of thujone was overrated. In chemistry, there was something called the NOAEL, or the "no observed adverse effects level." In laboratory rats, the NAOEL for thujone had been established as ten milligrams per kilogram of body weight for males, and half of that amount for females.

"Rats are typically less sensitive, but that's still a huge amount of thujone you'd have to ingest as a human being," he said. A man who weighed 80 kilograms, or 176 pounds, would have to consume at least 800 milligrams of thujone to pass the limit of NOAEL. In Europe, absinthe can contain a maximum of 35 milligrams of thujone per liter, meaning that the 700-milliliter bottles that are standard in Europe have, at most, 24.5 milligrams inside them. "And this is the amount that you'd still not observe any effects with. You'd have to take more. You'd have to drink liters and liters of absinthe even to reach this level."

Even if you could somehow drink that much absinthe, there was a cute little catch. Because of how it works on the body, alcohol functions as an antidote to thujone poisoning. Even Valentin Magnan, the doctor who was obsessed with "absinthism" and its role in the decline of French civilization, had noted that the convulsions in dogs were delayed when he gave them alcohol mixed with wormwood's essential oils, while a dog that was forced to ingest a small amount of alcohol before receiving an intravenous wormwood injection notably only had a single convulsion, with no further attacks. Magnan correctly attributed this difference to the alcohol, though he did not understand how that worked, and clearly missed many other important points.

It was extremely unrealistic to think that you could get thujone poisoning from a properly made absinthe, Jan repeated. It was also incorrect to believe that thujone levels had been higher in nineteenth-century absinthes than they were in the modern spirits, as Ted Breaux and others had already proven. It was just basic science. If the distillation process and the ingredients were mostly the same, the spirits would be mostly the same.

"Nothing has changed about the method, nothing has changed about wormwood," he said. "The content of thujone for modern absinthes and for pre-bans back in their time is identical."

Wormwood and the thujone in it certainly had a nice aroma, and it clearly made absinthe a compelling spirit. But it wasn't thujone that made people go crazy or hallucinate after drinking it.

"The psychological effect is due to alcohol," he said. "It's just alcohol."

⋮

I focused on tasting the absinthe Jan had made and its piney, resinous aromas from the Swiss wormwood. Just "above" that note, as I envisioned it, I found an aspect to the anise scent that reminded me of cinnamon.

"It's always funny to hear other people talking about it when you know the recipe," he said. Even distillers like Martin Žufánek had trouble identifying the herbs that were in it. "I was talking to Martin and he said, 'I love the chamomile,' and yet there's no chamomile in it."

The combination of ingredients in any recipe can make it seem like you used something else, I suggested.

"Yes, there's very interesting effects there," he said. "For example, if you combine a pear flavor with almond or marzipan, you get cherry. And for absinthe, many of the botanicals have similar ingredients. Anise and fennel are very similar, just different combinations of different amounts of the respective components. So depending on how you mix it, you can create impressions that there are other things in there which there really aren't."

It was kind of like jazz, I said, where individual players had a chance to remake standards in their own fashion, or like the mixology twists that Martin had mentioned. Jan nodded more excitedly than he had all day long.

"That's the one thing I love so much about absinthe: you don't have very strict rules, that it has to contain this and that, and it has to be produced exactly this way." In Germany, he noted, there were no legal requirements at all: you could sell peppermint tea as absinthe if you wanted to. The only real requirements were in Switzerland and France, but even those left a lot up to interpretation. "It just has to be made from anise, fennel, and wormwood. It has to be distilled. Anise, fennel, and wormwood have to be detectable in the taste and aroma, and it has to louche when you dilute it. That's it," he said. "You can add anything else you like as long as it's safe to use for food and you can play around so much with the proportions, with everything else you add. You have so much freedom to create something new."

In addition to using gas chromatography to analyze absinthes, he'd also used it to help reconstruct historic recipes, echoing the work of Ted Breaux. But sometimes a careful sensory analysis could work just as well. When David Zibell at Israel's Holy Spirit Distillery had asked Jan for help identifying the makeup of a nineteenth-century Absinthe Romans, his input had ended up being largely supplementary.

"All of the botanicals in there that I'd found by gas chromatography, he'd identified just by their taste," he said. Jan had made a small contribution to Zibell's research, however. By using liquid chromatography—a similar process to gas chromatography, in which a liquid carried the sample through the coil instead of gas—he had been able to show that Absinthe Romans had been colored with wormwood, an ingredient that most nineteenth-century distillers had eschewed in that stage of production.

"Normally you don't have *Artemisia absinthium* in the coloration, because it just gets too bitter," he said. "And I let him know that there was also licorice in there."

In addition to gas and liquid chromatography, Jan had recently started using mass spectrometry to analyze spirits and identify their chemical compounds. Soon, he said, he would have his own combination gas chromatography–mass spectrometry machine, known as a GC–MS, which sounded ridiculous when he explained that those machines normally cost 100,000 euros or more. A university in the area was going to sell off a slightly outdated GC–MS for a symbolic single euro, which Jan was planning to buy and restore to working order, much like he had with his original gas chromatograph. The

GS-MC would join another analytical device he'd just picked up to target counterfeit corks: an infrared spectrometer.

"Cork is actually a pretty ideal indicator," he explained. "If you have an old cork, it's hard and brittle, and you can't use it to reseal a bottle that you filled with a fake. It won't seal. It'll probably just break apart when you try to push it in. Whereas of course for all the fakes, new corks have been used that have been in some way made to look old—in most cases, by just charring them with a lighter to make them dark. But that is something that I am highly confident will be visible in the infrared spectra. If you look at the cork, you can say yes, this is actually an old cork, or no, this is just a new cork."

Ultimately, he wanted absinthe collectors to avoid the mistakes they'd made with Christian. He wanted buyers to know that they could request an analysis before—or even after—buying a bottle for $3,000 or more. And that, he hoped, might send out an important message.

"I want potential counterfeiters to think twice about faking something, because they could get caught."

It was late and I gathered my things to leave, fueled by the absinthe and a mind full of science. Before I set out, I asked if he really thought that vintage absinthe forgeries might continue to be a problem going forward. With every passing day, every hour, even every second, we were getting further and further away from the pre-ban era. At some point, it would have to be widely recognized that there simply couldn't be any pre-bans left, which might mean there would be no point to forging them.

He shook his head.

"I assume there will always be people trying to fake it," he said. "There's money to be made."

CHAPTER
16

À LONDRES

Car JE est un autre . . .
—ARTHUR RIMBAUD

I didn't know exactly what Christian had done to get out of the
spotlight he'd created for himself, but I learned that there are
several new tools to help you do that.

To start, Facebook has made it easy to deactivate an account
temporarily, or even delete it permanently. When I went to see
how that worked, the instructions made it sound like there was
no big difference between the two, at least not in terms of what
your contacts saw. One big downside for both: any messages you'd
sent were still available to whomever you'd written. Those would
simply never go away. However, most users wouldn't be able to

see your timeline, search for your name, or post on your wall. With your account temporarily deactivated, your biggest problem would be over.

⋮

After that, you'd have the problem of the online articles and blogs outside of Facebook that connected your name to forged absinthe. For example, there was the blog post from Habu, which even included Christian's photo, crudely photoshopped to show him behind bars. However, that post was in Czech, and thus nearly illegible. More seriously, there was a post at the blog of the absinthe museum in France, which fully identified him by his first name and double-barreled last name, which called him "un fraudeur" in the headline, followed by three exclamation points. That was worse, because many people could read some French, or at least guess what "fraudeur" might mean. And then there were the blog posts in English, like the one at the Wormwood Society, that called him a forger, a fraud, or a counterfeiter. Those would have taken a bit more work, perhaps even the threat of a lawsuit.

In the early days online, I remembered, bad search results seemed to stay around forever, but the internet had grown up a bit, with new protections, like Google's Personal Data Removal Request Form, which were primarily meant to help people who had been treated unfairly. As part of a decision by the Court of Justice of the European Union concerning "the right to be forgotten," the company had made it easy for Europeans—which, at the time, still included U.K. residents—to memory-hole any URL from the search results that were connected to their names. You could simply search for your own name and something like "absinthe," "forgery," "counterfeit," or "fraud," copy the URL of the resulting website or blog, and then paste it into the form with a request that it be excluded from whatever showed up in Google when someone searched for you.

In addition, LinkedIn had changed things for its users, following a scandal that involved a victim of sexual assault who had been subsequently stalked on that platform by her abuser. On that platform, you could now change your public profile's visibility and make it disappear temporarily or even make it invisible to search engines.

⋮

After that, it probably got easier. If you wanted to stand out early on in your career, having a name like Christian paired with a very common last name wasn't ideal: you could be any one of a few hundred, perhaps even a couple of thousand people with that combination. Adding a British last name and doubling them up worked wonders: it suddenly sounded very established and proper, the name of a single individual on this planet, with lovely echoes of public-school ties and old money. But if you later wanted to disappear, you could just drop that added-on British last name and suddenly become anonymous again.

What had once been a disadvantage would now be a plus, a former hindrance that now provided you with helpful camouflage. You were now just one of many Christians with that last name, and it was hard to say which one. The person who had forged counterfeit absinthes was someone else, a man with a double-barreled last name. And as far as anyone online could tell, that man was now dead.

⋮

Unfortunately, I had no idea how I could learn anything about Christian's background or contact him—I could still access the messages from our previous conversations on Facebook, but it told me I couldn't write to him and that he would no longer see any messages sent from me. He appeared to have deleted his LinkedIn account, or perhaps merely geo-blocked it, either for people in my country, or for everyone outside of his. But in a bit of uncharacter-istic foresight on my part, I had copied-and-pasted notes from his work and education history when I still had access to his LinkedIn profile, and I started trying to figure out what I could figure out from those pieces.

What I knew was that he had worked at a number of high-profile media agencies in London, though apparently not straight through. When I looked at the entries, I realized I didn't know if Christian had gaps in his résumé, or if I had accidentally left some in my notes.

As I pondered that, I remembered that several of the people I'd interviewed had used the phrase "pathological liar" to describe Christian or agreed that it probably applied to him. For them, he was someone who simply couldn't tell the truth. On top of that, I knew, there were the normal exaggerations and simplifications that most of us allow ourselves when describing our work histories. For a few minutes, I contemplated just deleting my notes, since they were prob-ably valueless. But they were all I had, so I decided to try them out.

⋮

Most of the job titles Christian claimed were unfamiliar to me, which made me feel out of my depth, though after a second I real-ized that this could also turn out to be an advantage.

Not really knowing how to use LinkedIn meant I had a lot to learn. While I had enjoyed Facebook and Twitter for a few years, I had always found LinkedIn to be kind of pointless, intended for the sort of corporate-world careerism that I had always found nauseating, and which isn't really part of freelance writing, which depends much more upon clips of your recent articles, in the form of links. A few of my friends used LinkedIn, I knew, but I was always more interested in seeing what they were up to than posting my own news there. I had turned off notifications for the site years earlier, having found that most of the people who contacted me sounded like spammers, offering invitations to events or publications miles from my location or fields of interest. When I first logged in to start trying to find out more about Christian, I found a LinkedIn invitation to connect with someone whose name was shown as "Selfie Stick." It was literally just a spam ad trying to sell the product in question.

When I started clicking on the links for the employers Christian had mentioned, I didn't see much that we had in common. However, at a house party in Prague several years earlier, I'd met a British guy who showed up as someone who knew people who worked at a giant agency Christian had listed. When I wrote to him, he answered immediately, offering a high-level contact at the company's Amsterdam office.

I started combining searches for Christian's preferred job title with the names of his previous employers. Sometimes I found a contact with the same job, but at the U.S. or European branch of the same agency. I wrote a half-dozen LinkedIn messages one afternoon. A few days later, I checked back.

Unsurprisingly, there were no responses. Why would there be? As far as those people were concerned, I was the selfie stick.

:

There were other websites, of course, with different results that came up when I searched for Christian's full name. Through a random search I ended up on a British government website, Companies House, which had a listing for some kind of creative agency under Christian's double-barreled last name, including a street address. The business had been dissolved in 2020, it said, with just one officer—listed as Christian, but without the double-barreled name—whose year and month of birth would make him a little more than seven years younger than me. So much for the speculation of the international absinthe community: Christian's nationality, the site clarified, was not British.

I could probably also say goodbye to a claim Christian had made to me back in 2018 about pre-ban bottles: "I've been collecting them for twenty-seven years now." Twenty-seven years earlier at that point would have meant January 1991, a point at which Christian was eleven years old.

When I punched his address into Google Maps, I got a street view of a modest, two-story attached house, painted bright white. Between the door and the sidewalk, a black compact car was parked. The yard on the left had a few bushes, shrubs, and flowerpots, as well as a privacy wall next to the sidewalk, while Christian's side was completely covered with a pad of asphalt.

I looked back and forth through the frames of the street view, but nothing meaningful came into focus. Other searches brought up nothing. Eventually, however, I stumbled across an old About.me page, which I copied and pasted into my notes. It stated that Christian had graduated with a fine arts degree, after which he had joined a large agency, where he spent years learning "all about" photography. His work had won many awards, it said, though he was currently working as a freelancer. It added that he was also a keen absinthe antiques collector, gardener, and guitar player.

I was definitely learning more, but I wasn't there yet. At the same time, I couldn't help but wonder what kind of evidence from my own life I had left all over the internet. Learning where Christian lived and where he'd worked in an afternoon made me question having ever put anything online.

The big difference, I realized, was that none of my friends were accusing me of fraud.

⋮

I'd never been a big connector or networker, and I only have a modest number of people I'd consider friends or acquaintances. But by chance, two of them had grown up in the very town where Christian had gone to university. I put out feelers for information about the art department at Christian's university through the writer Matthew Curtis. And during a story meeting, I bounced a few questions about the city off my editor at VinePair, Tim McKirdy. It started to become a normal train of thought and conversation: does this person maybe know Christian, or possibly know someone who knows him? Can this person tell me something about the kind of training a university art student might receive? Do I know anyone who can explain what someone with his job title does? How can I contact Christian's old coworkers without him finding out?

Unfortunately, I was falling behind: I just didn't have enough information. The information I'd copied from his CV ended with a job he'd left several years earlier, and I had no idea what he'd done since then: after he'd supposedly deleted his Facebook account, he seemed to have dropped off the planet. It seemed crazy for a person who worked in an industry that, unlike freelance writing, seemed to love LinkedIn: even the language of Christian's About.me page struck me as sadly careerist and job-focused. But if all I had was Christian's questionable description of his earlier years, I'd have to use it as best I could. I'd had no luck contacting Christian's previous employers. But one thing I hadn't tried was reaching out to random people who had graduated from his university, especially those who had also studied art.

I found myself grimacing and shaking my head whenever I thought about doing that: I didn't want to spook Christian, or have it get back to him that I was asking about him, though I didn't really know why. He'd already deleted his online life, as far as I could tell, so it wasn't like he could remove all traces of his existence: there were basically none left at that point. It just seemed rude to ask people about someone without letting that person know that I was asking. Somewhere at the back of my brain, deep down in the dark spaces closest to my spinal column, I was hiding a pale hope that Christian would agree to talk to me—that he would tell me to my face why he'd done what he'd done, and that he would be willing to explain why someone would cheat his own friends out of a small fortune. At one level, I was thinking that Christian might be willing to talk—we'd met in person, after all, and had once been Facebook friends, whatever that was worth. And in another way, I simply wanted to be honest about the work I was doing, both to Christian and to myself. I didn't want to be a coward, or a liar.

So one morning in late spring I opened my word processor, wrote a letter to Christian and printed it on a piece of plain white paper, since I didn't have his email address. I explained that I was writing a book about the absinthe forgeries and that the book would come out in the next year. I pointed out that really the only way for him to have any influence over what went into my book, if he was interested in that, would be by talking to me. I said that I'd already talked to many people from the absinthe demimonde, and that I thought I had a good idea of what had happened, but that I was curious about "motivation"—I did not ask about "your" motivation, but just motivation in general, as if it existed outside of the person who had made the forgeries. I never accused him of anything, only asking if he'd be willing to be interviewed about his background, his interests in collecting historic absinthe and the absinthe forgeries. I noted I would be in London later in the year, and that I'd be willing to meet for an in-person interview, or we could talk over Zoom or some other kind of video call.

Perhaps that wasn't the right way to do it, I don't know. But at least it felt like I was being honest with him, and—more importantly—with myself. And then I dropped the letter off at the local post office and returned to my research.

⋮

I felt better knowing I was no longer operating sub rosa, so relieved that I immediately got back on LinkedIn and began contacting as many former students from Christian's year at the university as I could find. I reached out to a likely candidate: a front-end developer who had received his BA in graphic design in 2001. I introduced myself as a journalist and mentioned that I was working on a book and trying to find out more about someone who had gone to the same university. I was looking for people who knew him or who could point me to instructors from those days, I added.

"Hi," he replied. "Who are you referring to?"

Cards on the table, honesty is the best policy, and all that. I typed Christian's name but skipped the hyphenated British surname it looked like he'd added to it, and asked if that rang any bells.

"Yes," he wrote.

I can tell you now that this was clearly the wrong approach. While I felt more comfortable being open and honest, I can see now that I should have not started by mentioning that there was a "person" I was trying to investigate. What I should have done was say that I was trying to find out about a general but related subject, like what it was like in the arts program at the university at the end of the millennium. If he'd agreed to an interview on that subject, I could have established trust and possibly built up to asking about a particular fellow student, if the signs indicated that might be an acceptable thing to ask. But starting with the idea of trying to find out about a specific person was pretty dumb, especially via text. Direct messaging doesn't have nuance the way your voice does, and it doesn't give your correspondent a lot of clues that might indicate that you're a good person yourself, and not a scammer or a selfie-stick spammer. What I should have done was to think of it more like a con man or a trickster. But I guess that's not in my nature.

I said "Oh great!" and asked if he remembered Christian well. It took a few minutes for him to reply.

"I do remember him well, yes," he wrote. "What's the context you're asking in and also does he know you're researching him?"

And before I could answer, I got a notification that I'd just received an email from Christian.

⋮

His email read:

> Dear Evan,
>
> I hope this finds you well.
>
> It's come to my attention that you've been asking vari-
> ous people within my circle about me for the purposes
> of writing about me.
>
> Please can I ask that you stop this as my friends don't
> appreciate it and nor do I.
>
> I am a private individual and you have no right to
> publish articles about me in your professional capacity
> without my prior consent. Which I do not grant.
>
> Kindest,
>
> Christian

It was quite polite, I had to admit, and I could certainly appreciate not wanting people to contact your friends and ask them
if you'd been a particularly good student in your fraud courses
in college or if they knew anyone else you'd stolen from. I was
shocked, however, that it had happened so quickly: my very first
shot at one of Christian's fellow university students had spooked
my target. Then again, I remembered that I'd called myself a journalist, which might sound different to someone who had grown
up in the U.K.'s culture of stolen voicemails and trash tabloids.

Fortunately, I could tell Christian that I'd just written to him via
post. I copied and pasted the letter I'd sent requesting an interview.
I added a TL;DR that clarified that it wasn't about an article, but
a book. I reiterated that I was very interested in hearing his side of
what had happened and asked him to think it over for a few days.

It took him twelve minutes to write back.

> Hi Evan,
> That seems fair and there is a big side to my story that
> has been green walled so to speak, thanks to many indi-
> viduals, who have a lot to hide and by pushing me out of
> the social media groups I had no defence to the rumours
> and talk as I couldn't see or hear any of it. So if I'm not
> named in your book, then yes I would consider giving
> you an interview.
>
> > Best wishes,
> > Christian

It felt bad even to consider giving Christian anonymity, but that was
all I had in exchange for an interview with the main character. Writing
is a series of compromises, and if it helped me get the story and understand why Christian had done what he had done, I guessed it wouldn't
be so bad to call him by a different name in my book. It wasn't the
truth, but it was still pretty close. I just wished I didn't have to do it.

⋮

When I read back through our emails, I have trouble believing what
I'm seeing. Writing it sounds ridiculous, as if I'm making this up
without a thought to verisimilitude or credibility, but it's all completely true. Christian agreed to an interview with me and then canceled or skipped our appointment, always with a different excuse,
seven times through the summer of 2023.

He started out by saying he was very busy until the end of the month, which I said was fine by me. However, roughly a week before the end of that month, some ten days later, he wrote to say that he was free to do an interview via Zoom the next day. I asked what time he'd prefer, to which he didn't respond. When I checked in again in the next day, he apologized and said his work had been manic, and that we could catch up and reschedule the next week.

Five days later, he wrote to me to suggest another meeting the next week. He was very curious, he said, to hear what people were accusing him of, since he'd been blocked from the absinthe groups and hadn't seen anything that anyone had written about him. "Apart from a false article by that little shit Anthony Sacco, which is all made up. He was an irritant for some years. Very jealous chap. Don't trust anything he says," he wrote.

I suggested that we leave aside the accusations and even the subject of the forgeries at first, and instead just talk about absinthe in general and maybe his own background. I was mostly wary of doing too much talking myself, and possibly ending up with an audio recording that was mostly my own words. I explained that I wanted him to trust me and understand where I was coming from, so maybe it would be best to leave the heavy stuff aside for our first chat. He said fine and suggested 11:00 a.m. the next day. When I asked if Zoom was okay, he said he'd send me a Google Meet invite instead.

In my experience it's never an ideal situation for an interview subject to control the interview in any way—even just in terms of how it feels, it works best if the journalist chooses the format and sends the invite: the journalist is driving the car, and you're just along for the ride. But I desperately wanted Christian to talk to me, or even just to get to know me, so that we could work up to him telling me why—and maybe even clarify how—he'd done it. I knew most of the details, but I hadn't figured out everything. And in his defense, he did actually send me a Google Meet invite for noon the next day, which I took as a good sign.

But just twenty minutes before the start, I saw that he'd changed the time of our meeting to the end of the day without explanation. When I wrote to confirm that new time via email, he sent his apologies, claiming that he now had a work meeting at noon. A couple of hours later, he canceled the rescheduled meeting, because of too much work, he said, adding, "I do want to have the call with you," as if he knew it seemed like the opposite. He suggested we talk either the next day or in two days. "I'll be home both days, so a long video call would be a much more relaxed affair." A short while later he sent a new invite for the following day at 5:00 p.m.

There was no one else there when I tried to join the meeting that day, and I got no response to my email asking if he was going to show up. A half an hour later I wrote again, noting that it looked like this wasn't going to happen, and informing him that I was moving on.

I wanted him to think that I might be done with trying to talk to him. And I probably should have moved on, if only to save my time and sanity. But a day later, I received the following message.

"Hello from hospital. Got hit by a car yesterday. I'll message you when I'm home again."

⋮

It's difficult to know how to approach a person repeatedly described by others as a pathological liar. Do you have to assume that absolutely everything is a lie? Personally, I don't want to live a life ruled by that type of pathology, or any other: I'd rather go through the world focusing on trust and hope than set suspicion and doubt as my default, if that is my own choice to make. At the time, the phrase "trust but verify" bounced into my head, as did "the benefit of the doubt." I didn't know that Christian *wasn't* hit by a car. I can tell you that it didn't make any news reports that I could find online. London is a big city, and maybe "Media Freelancer Hit by Taxi" isn't the sexiest headline.

The only way I could respond, as far as I could see, was to express my best wishes for a full recovery and gratitude that he was still alive. And none of that was a lie from my side: if it was true that he had been hit by a car, I really was glad he wasn't dead, and certainly wished for him to get well. I just didn't think any of that was very likely.

⋮

A few days later I wrote to ask about his recovery and offer to send a care package. He replied that he was still not out of the hospital, recovering from a concussion and a few broken ribs. A car had hit him from behind, he said, when it had jumped the curb while speeding away from the police.

I tried again a couple of weeks later, at which point he said that he was available, though he had a bit of a bad head due to previous night out in a pub. That seemed like something you might try to avoid a couple of weeks after a concussion, but what did I know?

He promised to send some open time slots in his calendar, but those never arrived. The next time I followed up, I tried a new approach of including a list of softball topics I initially wanted to ask him about: his time at the university, his work, his memories of first trying absinthe. I described the topics as "basic stuff, nothing hard." He replied by saying we could talk the next day. When I asked for a time, he never answered.

A few weeks later, I tried a different approach, writing to tell him that I was researching an aspect of historic absinthe and I wanted to get his insight. He wasn't available, he said, but he could definitely talk on Monday at 11:00 a.m.

I sent a Zoom link. On Monday, a half hour before the meeting was due to begin, he canceled.

I felt like I was casting to a very spooky fish. In terms of the warmth of his responses, I seemed to get closer when I was offering to share something with Christian, rather than when I was asking for something from him. He'd mentioned that he wanted to know what his friends in the absinthe groups had said about him, right? I wrote again, telling him I needed to share some notes with him, so that he's on the page and not in the dark. Just fifteen minutes of talking, I wrote. Nothing heavy. Got a slot for me?

Friday at 11:00 a.m. looked good, he wrote.

That's great, I said, but if this meeting didn't work out, I'd have to assume he was just stringing me along. I included a Zoom link.

"Not stringing you along, Evan. I'm literally too busy to give it the time it deserves with a clear head. Friday I'm yours, I promise."

He didn't show, and after a half hour's wait I sent a message saying I was done. A few hours later, he wrote to say he was sorry:

he'd been at a very important awards show the previous night and had only just woken up, but he was free to chat that afternoon.

I didn't write back. I didn't really mind, because I already had a plane ticket to London.

And in a weird shift, a recent internet search had turned up a functioning LinkedIn page for Christian, showing all the work he claimed to have done over the previous four years. A number of jobs had only lasted a couple of months, I noticed.

⋮

Technically I was supposed to go to Norwich, not London, to serve on the jury at the World Beer Awards, but I could base my travel around the capital. I had no time to try to find out anything about Christian on my way to the event, since my flight from Prague to London was delayed, getting me in quite late. That was followed by an early train to Norwich and three days tasting and evaluating the beers that had been entered in the competition, which somewhat implausibly took place in a large, windowless boardroom deep within Norwich City Football Club. When the competition finished, I hopped another train back down to London, where I finally had a day and a half to look around.

In a previous era, a journalist could walk into a company's offices and simply explain who they were and ask if they could talk to someone. In some countries, things still do work like that, and I generally do have pretty good luck when I try to bluff my way in. Hypothetically, this can even work if you don't know who you wanted to speak to—"Could I speak to someone from the marketing department?"—though that was iffier: it worked much better if you knew your target's name and asked, for example, if Kate Stevens was available. Unfortunately, those days seem to be long gone, at least in post-pandemic London. I'd learned my lesson when I'd contacted Christian's old university classmate, and I was hoping to start out by simply asking if someone could just explain what his job title does, before adding that I was trying to find out more about a particular person with that job title who used to work there. But when I tried a couple of the largest companies where Christian claimed to have worked, the combination of an international corporation's front-desk security, the popularity of working from home and an upcoming holiday weekend meant that I had no luck. Almost no one was in the office that day, I was told at one firm. I'd have to come back when I had an appointment, I was told at another.

Although Christian's CV had added a bunch of names, I was more curious about the big gaps in it. Had he been fired? Was he just not very good at his job? Nothing was listed between October of one year and March of the next, when he said that he had taken a job as a freelance producer at a company for three months. Then it looked like he had no company listed, just "freelance" for another couple of months, before he had taken a job as lead producer at a big agency. In his bio, he claimed to have worked with some truly big names, including Helmut Newton and Patrick Lichfield, though he spelled the latter's name incorrectly. When I looked them up, I saw that those legends of photography had died in 2004 and 2005, respectively. Christian was talking about a time when he was either twenty-four or twenty-five years old, and of course no one could ask them now if they remembered working with him. Neither of them could tell me what Christian was like, or why he'd done what he'd done to the people who called him a friend.

That was probably the least important thing I could ask him. There wasn't much else I could do, and my flight back to Prague was approaching. So I grabbed my bag, got into the Tube and headed out into London's suburban sprawl.

⋮

Travel has changed incredibly in recent years, and the differences in the Big Smoke are impressive. In earlier visits I'd often wasted time trying to buy or fill up an Oyster card for the London Underground, which made the switch to using my phone quite welcome: no card, no topping-up, just bonk the phone next to the reader and pay as you go. To get to where I thought Christian might live, I had to take one of the Underground lines almost out to its terminus, a journey of about forty-five minutes from my hotel in Bloomsbury. Once I'd made my connection, I settled in to the ride and counted the stations as I tried to think about what I was doing. It made little sense to confront him directly, and for that matter, I imagined Christian wouldn't take kindly to getting doorstepped by someone who was writing about the crimes he'd been accused of. He'd never admitted any wrongdoing to me, though I had seen messages to Martin Žufánek and Patrick Grand where he admitted to having made forgeries. I couldn't imagine he would deny having made them, but I didn't want to force him to admit it, either. I really just wanted to understand why he'd robbed his friends.

It was approaching but not yet the end of the workday, and the fatigued commuters around me looked at their phones, read paperbacks, and sighed heavily as they gradually emptied from the train over the course of the next quarter hour. The old commuter station closest to the address I had for Christian was built with cast-iron girders painted deep green, with white wooden overhangs that edged up to the tracks, limning the open space of the no-man's-land between them; unlike the literally underground stations of the city center, this one stood at surface level, a semi-dilapidated construction of discolored red brick made brighter by the timeless, Roman-numeral faces of the antique station clocks. Christian had to look at these every day, I imagined. This construction, this weird assemblage had to make sense to him, as the kind of thing he looked at so often he no longer saw it clearly. To me, the station's various parts reeked of their original construction in 1856 and renovation in 1892, along with cruft from the twentieth and twenty-first centuries. It seemed strange, a real relic from the era when it would have been cutting-edge, but which now seemed run-down and outdated, not nicely kept enough to count as a valuable antique, and thus more like a simple piece of junk. It was something from the nineteenth century that had been carried into the twenty-first with only partial success, bringing with it a sense that things didn't have to be this way anymore, that we now had better ways and means, and yet we were stuck with this, like wearing pocket watches or shaving each morning with a straight razor.

It was raining and I wasn't keen on hiking out to Christian's street in the soaking wet, but the early commute meant that waiting taxis were lined up just outside the station. I climbed into the first and gave the taxi driver the address that was next door to Christian's place. I was writing a book, I told him, about a famous artist, and I needed to see where the artist had once lived. The ride would be £8, he said, and he'd bring me back to the station afterward.

I didn't know what I was expecting, but what I got was a fairly sad suburb, especially on a gray, rainy afternoon, the kind of place you'd probably find deadly boring as a teenager dreaming of anywhere but there. There were high shrubs that needed trimming in front of many of the houses, just like the overgrown greenery around the station, and the sidewalks were patched and cracked; bare yards in front of some of the multi-apartment buildings were fenced in but clearly unused for either gardening or recreation. When we turned left onto Christian's street, those three-story build-ings disappeared, and we started passing a row of attached homes, all mirror-image duplexes with one driveway and one entrance on either side of the central wall that joined them. Several were painted in slightly different colors—gray on one half, cream on the other— as if the owners wanted to make the split between them more obvi-ous. That was what I saw through the rain when we approached the address of Christian's next-door neighbor, who owned the yellowy beige half on the left, which clashed sharply against Christian's stark white house on the right.

There was a small overhang making what could optimistically be called a porch, which was framed by tall plants on the left and a small flower box on the right. Christian's black car was parked on the drive, though I imagined he probably wouldn't be home yet. Next to it was something covered in a gray tarpaulin.

It was short and squat with only the bottoms of the tires and an inch of its wheels visible. It looked like a classic Jaguar or some other highly collectible car from the 1960s or '70s. The bumper was probably too low for it to be a Jaguar E-Type, and there was a sharp line at the rear wheel well that didn't fit my memory of that model's curves, but it didn't matter. It was simply a fancy car, the kind of thing you'd need a big pile of money to purchase.

I didn't know exactly how Christian had done what he'd done, but I realized that I didn't need to. I understood why he had betrayed his friends. I could imagine why he had offered to sell bottles of would-be hundred-year-old absinthes that he had mocked up himself, mixing various bits of younger Swiss, Czech, or Spanish spirits with some brandy to approximate the taste of a pre-ban that had been distilled from wine, before adding a touch of mint oil for freshness. It was probably standing right there under the cover that protected it from the rain: a vintage automobile worth fifty or a hundred grand or more. I couldn't identify the car, but even covered up, I knew that it was beautiful. And for this guy, at least, that particular beauty was worth betraying his friends and taking their money.

Oh, sure: he might have enjoyed feeling like he had tricked all the so-called experts. He had probably loved what it felt like to sell distillers blends of their own spirits back to them, inside old bottles he'd bought for just a few euros. He'd laughed at the collectors, the connoisseurs, and the science types. He'd rubbed all their noses in it. He'd flown plenty close to the flame, and it was all good and funny. But when he had told Patrick Grand and Martin Žufánek he had sold his counterfeits because he had needed money, he probably wasn't lying. He just committed his frauds for money, because he simply wanted it, even if he already had enough. He needed it for that car.

I'll confess that I didn't ring the doorbell. I didn't even look under the tarp. I took a couple of pictures and video clips, after which I told the driver to take me back to the Underground station. And then I flew back home, finally feeling that I understood the absinthe forger well enough to forget all about him.

CHAPTER
17

EPILOGUE

Aux yeux de ces amateurs d'inquiétude et de perfection,
un ouvrage n'est jamais achevé,—mot qui pour eux n'a
aucun sens,—mais abandonné.

—PAUL VALÉRY

There's more to it, of course, there always is—writing is a series of compromises, after all, and when you read a book, you can sometimes see that not everything has been included. It simply couldn't be. For readers, the story has to include enough to make sense. For a writer, it's just as important to consider what to leave out of your writing as it is to measure carefully the elements that you want to keep.

I didn't reach out to Christian again after that, though we did have an interesting exchange when he wrote to ask for an email address for "the publisher of your publication" to pass on to what he called his legal counsel, apparently still operating under the impression that I was writing an article, although I'd clearly told him I was working on a book. When I looked up the firm he claimed was representing him, I saw that its first area of specialization was branding and trademarks, which seemed to be related to his work. That impression wasn't helped by the fact that he didn't give me his attorney's full name, only stating that he was being represented by "James." I forwarded him the first and last name along with the email address for my publisher's legal counsel in New York, and I would be lying if I said I didn't laugh out loud when I hit send.

Although most forged pre-ban absinthe disappeared after Christian was publicly named as a forger in 2019, a few fakes still showed up every now and then. There's not much point in trying to make a business out of fake pre-ban absinthe, however: the market never returned to what it was before the scandal. Many people stopped buying altogether, and the only people who are still buying pre-bans are getting them from legit sellers like Patrick Roussel.

Although he had been one of the main members of the team that exposed Christian, the dealer Eric pretty much dropped out of the absinthe world afterward, seemingly turned off by the betrayal of a close friend, as well as the reluctance on the part of many collectors to buy a lot of vintage absinthe in the aftermath. Many of the websites which used to sell small samples of pre-ban Absinthe Romans, full bottles of Pernod Fils, and the like are offline. Having been burned by the early accusations that tied him to Christian, Wolfgang Klotz only sells absinthe and other vintage spirits to people he knows well. The last time I checked in on him, he was getting ready to release the first products from his own spirits brand.

The bankruptcy and closure of the modern spirits retailer Absinthes.com, formerly known as Rue Verte, came as another blow to the culture in mid-2021. After that site disappeared, it became a lot harder for fans in the United States to source bottles from small European producers. For better or worse, American makers have tried to fill that gap, although as a European resident I haven't been able to taste most of their products. Patrick Roussel certainly seemed unconvinced.

Although many of the Facebook groups kept going, there was a pronounced slowdown over the years, accompanying the social network's general loss of popularity. Scott MacDonald closed his group on Facebook and stopped allowing new posts, though he left all the old posts up in the hope that they would serve as evidence of Christian's misdeeds, and to testify to all the fun the group had had before the scandals broke. With a year or so, he sold off most of his collection of absinthe antiques. Sometime later, someone scammed their way into being named a new administrator of his Facebook group and subsequently locked it, making it impossible to read the old posts. Surprisingly, that person was not Christian. Instead, the new admin appeared to be a Leeds-based hypnotherapist who was later given a twenty-nine-month prison term for telling a patient under hypnotism that she was putting on sunscreen and needed to take off her clothes, as well as for the possession of indecent images of children, according to a BBC News story that another Facebook user pinned to the new admin's wall.

The Wormwood Society's website went down for a while, then reemerged without access to its forums, but it turned out that was only due to a botched server migration, and there was never any legal threat from Christian, despite the post on the site that named him as a forger. The Society continued, posting regularly on Instagram and Facebook. As Facebook's traffic began to slow, the r/absinthe group on Reddit emerged as one of the more active sources for absinthe reviews and news.

⋮

Cary René Bonnecaze did end up speaking to the FBI about what he could do to recover his money; though he was told that his case likely qualified for wire fraud, he had few legal options, due to Christian's residence in the U.K. As far as I can tell, Christian never faced any legal issues there. Over the next few years, Christian did show up on eBay every once in a while, selling off his absinthe antiques under various names as earlier ones got reported or were given bad reviews by members of the absinthe underground. Many absintheurs continued to keep tabs on him, following closely when he switched to selling stuff on Etsy, for example, where he eventually listed the same Pernod Fils bottle with the particular tear through the word "extrait" on the label—now devoid of any liquid, authentic or fake—that Adrian Payne had originally purchased for £1,200 as a full bottle of pre-ban absinthe. Described by Christian on Etsy as an empty antique absinthe bottle, it sold for just over 116 euros, or about $127, not too long ago. Many absintheurs believed that Christian wasn't just selling off his absinthe stuff, however. At one point, Habu sent me a link to a report about a sketchy guitar on eBay, which he attributed to Christian.

As for the fraud, I ended up thinking that it was probably much larger than anyone recognized. After I got back from London, I heard back from Christophe Racine, who'd gone through his correspondence with Jean-Jacques Charrère, the former clandestine distiller, then legit producer, who'd used DuVallon as his nom de guerre. In a couple of screenshots, DuVallon asked if Racine had seen the initial announcement about the forgeries, followed by a link to the post that identified Christian as "un fraudeur" on the blog of the Musée d'Absinthe in France. "That guy was my client," DuVallon wrote. In particular, Christian was a big fan of two of his absinthes, Lait du Jura and Nocif, he said. "I sent those to London without knowing that they would end up inside Pernod bottles." He included a screenshot of an email from the same Gmail address that Christian used with me, in which Christian told DuVallon that he was writing from Budapest and that he would send payment the next day.

That location seemed to mean something to DuVallon, though it was news to me. The directors of the Maison de l'Absinthe in Môtiers might want to re-evaluate the authenticity of the Dubied bottle in the museum's collection, DuVallon wrote, since that one had also come from "an eastern country," something I hadn't yet heard. I wondered if that was why people sometimes looked at me a certain way when I said that I lived in the Czech Republic. There was an additional question as to how much DuVallon had helped Christian. The way Racine read their messages, DuVallon indicated that he was the one who had told Christian how to make a new cork look old: by burying it in the garden and leaving it there over the winter. But when I read through their exchanges, it looked like DuVallon was simply explaining what he thought Christian had done, not that he had told him how to do it. That was everything that he could find, Racine said, adding that most of their communication had been in person at his distillery, which meant that his memory was the only remaining record. It would be hard to know how many people Christian had cheated without knowing how much absinthe he had purchased, and DuVallon's messages didn't indicate the amounts.

⋮

In the years since the forgeries were announced, Christian had apparently done some work to clean up his reputation, but others seemed to have let things go. I can no longer find the blog post that called Christian "un fraudeur" by his full name on the site of the Musée de l'Absinthe, but I can find the 2017 blog post in which the beloved grande dame of absinthe writing, museum founder Marie-Claude Delahaye, identified him a "recognized specialist." In it, Christian and Eric offered their tasting notes on a rare pre-ban; most of the photos, the post noted, were Christian's. The truth, it seemed, had disappeared from the museum's website, while something closer to a lie—a "specialist" is not how most people would describe a man who admitted that he'd made fakes—was still around.

Similarly, I saw that Martin Žufánek still had the tasting notes from Christian on the web page for one of his absinthes. It's not like Martin needed an excuse, like having been robbed of several thousand euros, to justify taking it down, as Christian's prose description of the product was pretty purple, if not UV: "Roasted almonds dancing with divine A.a. upon a carpet of mountain herbs . . . Magically flying with Captain Anethole and his co-pilot Fenchone supporting him all the way to the landing strip."

At some point, all of this will go away, the remaining claims washed down the river of memory until they don't exist in any way that matters. But for now, I find it strange that almost all the articles and posts that identify Christian's crimes have gone away, due to the constant impermanence of the web, while the writing that testifies to his expertise somehow lives on.

⋮

In the very last screenshot Racine sent to me, DuVallon shared a picture of another Dubied bottle that he said had never been published, saying it another obvious fake. After I saw it, I found myself wondering if any of the half-dozen nineteenth-century Dubied bottles I'd seen over the last year were actually real. I certainly wanted to believe they were.

And maybe that was the whole point of the forgeries—that people wanted to believe that something magical from the past could enter and influence our world today. In that regard, it was sad that the pre-ban craze was over: people need things to believe in. But it was stupid, too, since there's clearly something magical about the absinthe of today. After tasting one pre-ban at Distillerie Guy and several more with Wolfgang Klotz, no one could convince me that absinthe was wildly better in the Belle Époque, and that the Swiss bleues that you can buy for a fair price right now are somehow lesser products. A lot of it is what you bring to it, of course, either as a drinker or a reader, which leads you to something like a reader-response theory of drinking.

In that school of thought, it's up to you to find your own meaning in the glass. You don't need to open a bottle that has languished for over a century in the cellar of a noble home somewhere in the south of France to be inspired, or at least I don't. Absinthe in the Belle Époque was an element of modern life at the time, not a quest to track down the rarest of hundred-year-old bottles. Even as I type this now, absinthe is growing in new and exciting ways, gaining new life, presenting new characters, and developing new storylines that go far beyond the tales and figures from its past.

For me, that is the true inspiration that absinthe offers, not a mysterious cellar filled with dusty bottles from a century ago—not even the ones that just might be real.

THE END

AUTHOR'S NOTE

This is a work of nonfiction reportage. Everything written here concerning the absinthe forger is as close to what I understand actually happened as I can describe it. For the sake of narrative structure, some of my travel, conversations, thoughts, and experiences have been shifted slightly in the timeline, though those events themselves are true and accurate as presented. In addition, some members of the absinthe community requested to be referred to by a pseudonym, rather than by their real names. Out of respect for their privacy, this wish was granted. All of the quotes in this book are true and accurate, backed up by audio recordings. All translations from the French, German, or Czech languages are my own, and any errors or discrepancies in them are mine. Other than the imagined passages about the absinthe forger at the start of the book and in Chapter 16, all of the events in these pages happened in the way they are reported.

Evan Rail
Prague
January 2024

ACKNOWLEDGMENTS

This book would not have been possible without the hard work of Max Sinsheimer at Sinsheimer Literary: a writer couldn't ask for a better or more understanding agent. Thanks also to Carl Bromley and the team at Melville House, a publisher I have long admired, as a reader of Dennis Loy Johnson's old MobyLives blog, since before it even existed. Don't think about it too much; time isn't real.

I'd particularly like to thank my wife, Nina, who believed in this project and helped me find the time and space to finish the manuscript, as well as listen to more stories about absinthe, toxic herbs, travel disasters, and alcohol forgeries than she ever wanted. Thanks also to our children, who let their father leave town in midwinter to write in full-on Overlook Hotel mode in a remote location in South Bohemia for several weeks, after a year of him frequently disappearing on trans-European journeys. A book is made of words, kids.

To my dear father-in-law Václav Valvoda and my milá tchýně Jarka Valvodová, srdečně děkuji za místo na psaní a za všechnu pomoc. Jste nejlepší.

Thanks to my mom, Tori Rail; my brother, Jordan; and my sisters, Cori and Sarah, for their love and support.

A big *santé* goes out to the global absinthe community, with toasts to Štefan Habulinec, Scott MacDonald, Mira Müller, Anthony Sacco, Martin Žufánek, Patrick Roussel, Quentin Roussel, Cary René Bonnecaze, Jan Hartmann, Adrian Payne, and Wolfgang Klotz. I will never remember many of the wonderful experiences we had together.

Thanks to everyone in the Val-de-Travers, a very particular part of a very particular country. Merci à vous, Christophe Racine, Patrick Grand, Odile Churchward-Gogniat, Yann Klauser, Claude-Alain Bugnon, François Bezençon, Jonas Vouga, et Shinsuke Matsushita. Merci vielmals auch an die Familie Mürset-Baumgartner in Brugg AG.

For her infectious enthusiasm and kind encouragement, I hereby acknowledge that I owe Carrie Napolitano at least one well-made cocktail, at Tales in New Orleans or wherever else she'd care to claim it.

Shout-outs to a bunch of great writers for inspiration, friendship and shared dirt: Emma Jansen, Beth Demmon, David Farley, Dave Infante, Katie Parla, Camper English, Emily Saladino, Cat Wolinski, Joshua Bernstein, Will Hawkes, Joe Stange, Lars Marius Garshol, Adrian Tierney-Jones, Pete Brown, Matt Curtis, David Nilsen, Zach Johnston, Andreas Krennmair, Ray Newman, Anthony Gladman, Jamaal Lemon, Michael Stein, Courtney Iseman, Katie Mather, David Wheatley, Alistair Noon, and many others I'm not actually forgetting, I'm just a little messed up on Swiss bleue right now.

To my Prague pals Justin Quinn, Rob Sawkins, Paul Grabec, David Hoffmann, Joshua Mensch, Mike Winfrey, and David Surowiecki, thanks in advance for buying the next round.

Sending a "hey doode!" to Matěj Novák, a χαῖρε to Jason Aftosmis, and cheers to Michael Kloster.

The ink-stained wretches from *The Prague Post*, including but not limited to James Pitkin, Mindy Kay Bricker, Jennifer Sokolowsky, Jen Hamm Mir, Michael Mainville, Heather Faulkner, Louisa Di Girolamo, Jakub Svěrák, Kryštof Hilský, František Bouc, Fiona Gaze Houlihan, Sam Beckwith, Kate Swoger, Steffen Silvis,

Theo Schwinke, Jan Macuch, Vladimír Weiss, Mark Nessmith, and David Anesta, all deserve a beer.

Muchas gracias to Howard Junker for getting me started, and for publishing my first Baudelaire translation.

Hat over my heart to Clay Risen, a raised Stella to Dave McAninch, and the high sign to Warren Bobrow. Thank you, sirs.

Kind appreciation to the editorial team at Good Beer Hunting, especially Bryan Roth, who gave me the support to get this out the door when crunch time crunched. Thanks to Kate Bernot, Ren LaForme, Emma Jansen (hi again!), Claire Bullen, and Michael Kiser.

Big ups to everyone at VinePair, especially Tim McKirdy, Joanna Sciarrino, Danielle Grinberg, Adam Teeter, and Zach Geballe. Thanks to Suzanne MacNeille for sending me to write a cover story about the emerging absinthe trail for *The New York Times* travel section in 2013, and for giving me an assignment ten years later to eat a week's worth of meals on trains, some of which were actually pretty good.

My sincere thanks go out to you, for reading this book.

NOTES

CHAPTER 1

Much of what I know about the rebirth of absinthe in the 1990s came through firsthand experience. The detailed "Absinthe Revival" page on the website of La Fée Absinthe explains how EU legal loopholes were used, initially to import Hill's Absinth from the Czech Republic to the U.K., then to produce absinthe in France as an export product, followed by domestic sales as a spirit "aux plantes d'absinthe," before it could eventually be sold there under its real name. Additional information about the U.K.'s absinthe revival can be found at Simon Difford's excellent online drinks resource, Difford's Guide, under the heading "U.K. Absinthe Craze." Aspects of how the absinthe forgeries were put together came from my interviews with Patrick Roussel, Quentin Roussel, and Jan Hartmann.

CHAPTER 2

Although Christian blocked me on Facebook once I asked him if he would talk to me about the forgeries, his messages to me are still accessible.

CHAPTER 3

In addition to personal experience and my own research for articles about absinthe, this chapter was informed by a several pieces of scientific writing, including Dirk Lachenmeier's 2009 letter to the editor of *The Journal of the Royal College of Physicians of*

Edinburgh, "The Concentration of Thujone in Absinthe from Valentin Magnan's Time," and the earlier paper to which it responds, "Absinthe, Epileptic Seizures and Valentin Magnan" by M. J. Eadie from the same publication. Additional sources include "Thujone, a Widely Debated Volatile Compound: What Do We Know About It?" by Éva Zámboriné Németh and Huong Thi Nguyen in *Phytochemistry Reviews*.

The history of distillation in Europe can be found in many sources, including *Alcohol: A History* by Rod Phillips. For the early history of absinthe, I relied on two books by Jacques Kaeslin and Michel Kreis from their L'absinthe au Val-de-Travers series: *La vie des pionniers entre 1750 et 1830* and *Les origines et les inconnu(e)s*.

CHAPTER 4

I owe much to my professors of French literature, especially Gérard Gengembre and Michèle Praeger. Additional information came from various academic papers, including "Absinthism: A Ficticious 19th Century Syndrome with Present Impact" by Stephan A. Padosch, Dirk W. Lachenmeier and Lars U. Kröner from *Substance Abuse Treatment, Prevention, and Policy*, *The Animal Rights Struggle: An Essay in Historical Sociology* by Christophe Traïni; and Théodore Challand's 1871 work on Magnan's studies, *Étude expérimentale et clinique sur l'absinthisme et l'alcoolisme*. Other sources included the online Musée Virtuel de l'Absinthe and *La route de l'absinthe*, a promotional guide jointly published by the Val-de-Travers and the city of Pontarlier. For the Lanfray murders, I relied on contemporary newspaper articles and Maurice Zolotow's excellent feature "Absinthe," from the June 1971 issue of *Playboy*. Marni Davis covers racism and the prohibitionist movement in *Jews and Booze*.

CHAPTER 13

There are almost too many great articles about Rudy Kurniawan's spectacular wine frauds, including Benjamin Wallace's "Château Sucker" from *New York Magazine*, Peter Hellman's "FBI Arrests Wine Collector Rudy Kurniawan" in *Wine Spectator,* and "A Vintage Crime" by Michael Steinberger in *Vanity Fair,* as well as Mike Fleming's piece on the documentary film in *Deadline.* Patrick Radden Keefe covered the Hardy Rodenstock and Bill Koch saga in detail in "The Jefferson Bottles" at *The New Yorker.*

CHAPTER 15

This chapter was aided by "Absinthe, Epileptic Seizures and Valentin Magnan" by M. J. Eadie from *The Journal of the Royal College of Physicians of Edinburgh.*